The God Of Truth

Autograph Page

Roger Dale Wallace

Published by

The Village Carpenter Publishing House

TheVillageCarpenter.info

The God Of Truth

Copyright © 2007 Roger Dale Wallace.

All rights reserved. No part of this book may be reproduced in any form without permission in writing from the publisher, except in the case of brief quotations embodied in critical articles or reviews.

Scripture taken from The Holy Bible, The Authorized King James Version (KJV) which is in the public domain in the United States; you may copy and quote from it without restriction.

All books are available in Braille, Giant Print, Kindle… Auto-delivered wirelessly and for corporate training, premiums, or special promotions.

For details contact Charles Lee Emerson, Proprietary Markets, The Village Carpenter Publishing House, PO Box 133, Lakeview, Ohio 43331 USA or call 740-777-1525.

TheVillageCarpenter.info.

ISBN 978-1-60585-521-9

Printed in the United States of America.

The God Of Truth

January 22, 2009

JESUS IS LORD

This is the testimony of:

Roger Dale Wallace

TheVillageCarpenter.info

The Village Carpenter
Publishing House
PO Box 133
Lakeview, Ohio 43331 USA

Acknowledgements

To my Heavenly Father and His Holy Spirit, and to my Lord and Savior, Jesus Christ. For unto them: I Am found as a Christian, who is found in Jesus Christ, forever faithful, AMEN.

And, it is, that I wish to also acknowledge my thanks to my friends and family, particularly: Bridget and Mitzy, who has stood beside me faithfully, as I have written these things for our God. And as our God has said, His Word shall be fulfilled, for in Isaiah 55:11, it says: So shall my word be that goeth forth out of my mouth: it shall not return unto me void, but it shall accomplish that which I please, and it shall prosper in the thing whereto I sent it.

I, Roger do know our true God, and His Son Jesus Christ, shall surely, come quickly and will judge this earth, in righteous true judgment, that true judgment, it shall be given of God Himself, forever. SELAH.

Ji hong Deng Spurlock, Chinese Interpreter.

Juan Manuel Chavez, Spanish Interpreter.

Dedication & Preface

This book is more than just simple reading. It is a book, that is written through Godly, sincere, true inspiration in Jesus Christ.

This book is now written. I give my mother great credit, in always being about our Father's business, when it came for me, to begin my learning and understanding about God The Father and Jesus Christ, His Son.

Throughout all time, since Christ's birth, many in Jesus Christ have looked to the day, that this written enclosed true testimony, would occur from our true God and from Jesus Christ His Son, and now: It has been written eternally forever. It is now written through Godly true inspiration, as being eternally forever seen. And is felt from God The True Father, in Jesus Christ, as forever true. AMEN.

Roger Dale Wallace

The God Of Truth

Short version

I Am truth and I Am the life, called man forever. And I will grant unto the righteous of myself, who are found in Christ Jesus, forever:

That their name, should always be recorded in the book of eternal true remembrance, that is called God forever.

For I Am God forever, and I Am forever true, and I Am that I Am, forever true. And I Am the life and breath;

That is called eternity forever true, saith thy eternal true maker, who is seen and called: "Life forever."

....
...

In this the day and hour… I do call unto Israel… to rise up in myself… that is called Christ forever.

....

ROGER DALE WALLACE

Why this book exists.

This book exists because of the present true fulfillment of Revelation 11:19. And this true book, it shall testify, as to that true eternal, ever lasting, true fulfillment, and that is now occurring, as we speak. And this book, it is a great seen true knowledge:

As it is concerning forever, our time of days, as it is concerning the true fulfillment of Bible prophecy. And, by reading this book. One shall go into once hidden Biblical true mysteries of scriptures that had once been sealed of our true God, in our everyday King James Bible. And those things, they are now, unhidden by our true and kind God, forever.

Therefore, let us go on inside, into these once hidden true mysteries of scriptures. For Christ the Son of the living true God has loosened the true seals in The Book of Revelation. In our generation. And which, has in turn, placed the open unsealed Holy Book,

That is God's Holy True Word, into the angel's true hand. To be prophesied again, as unto them that dwell in the fallen true earth, forever. And that is found forever, as it is found in this true day and true hour, forever. And that is found, through a spirit of true utterance. As it is seen, as being "Thus saith the Lord of heaven and earth," forever.

And, most surely, that is found through spiritual true interpretation of scripture, as being eternally forever true. And that is concerning The Book of The Revelation of Jesus Christ, forever.

And this, prophetic, true book, with all of its spiritual true interpretations. Those interpretations. They are all and each, as all considered, forever. As being, seen and felt, from God, forever. As being, released unto the earth, now and forever. And this is seen, as being:

Thus Saith The Lord Of Heaven and Earth, forever.

The inspired writer of this book.

Roger Dale Wallace

Table Of Contents

Chapter		Page
1	Thus saith the Lord	14
2	Godly recompense	20
3	True recompense damnation	27
4	Unrepentfulness	31
5	I Am found of Israel	39
6	Christly Israel	47
7	Eternal life	51
8	Christ Jesus	59
9	Pure love	68
10	End time Judgment	76
11	Unending day	84
12	I Am the life	92
13	That glory	100
14	The beast	107
15	Unrepentiful sin	115
16	Beastly people	128
17	Recompense called God	136
18	O Israel	148
19	Beastliness	158
20	Damnation against God	173
21	Blackness of darkness	184
22	Living forever true death	190
23	The beastly image of death	203
24	Repentance	211
25	Antichrist damning sins	220
26	I Am	234
27	Truth	239
28	Unholy nations of death	250
29	That image	258

Table Of Contents, cont.

Chapter   Page

Chapter	Title	Page
30	Perditious sins	268
31	Recompense	288
32	Unending Holy light	299
33	Eternal death	310
34	The darkened beast	319
35	Antichrist nations	328
36	Great White Throne	342
37	Heavenly true salvation	353
38	Heavenly salvation	363
39	Living death	378
40	My most Holy, True name	395
41	God's oath with Israel	405
42	The judgment of the nations	422
Part 1	All nations	429
Part 2	Pleading with the heathen	450
Part 3	My hand	471
Part 4	They that worship the beast	497
Part 5	Israel's messiah, forever	525
Part 6	The dome of the rock	562
Part 7	The mount of God	581
Part 8	Thy first love	599
Part 9	Prophet Judge	610

Introduction

W / 21 verses

1 In these days, is this written, that Israel may obtain, all that is promised by me (God), unto Israel, eternally forever.

2 And I (God) Am a Father unto Israel forever, and I (God) Am God forever. And in me (God), Israel shall obtain, all that is promised, as eternal Biblical true promise, that is promised unto Israel, eternally forever true.

3 And I (God) shall grant, at this time of the earth, forever. That Israel, may and go and obtain, all land, that Is seen, as Israel Biblically forever,

4 And I (God) will destroy her (the word her, is Israel) enemies forever, and I will destroy and punish, all that shall come against Israel, eternally forever.

5 And, in these days, O Israel, I (God) shall and will, plant thee firmly and forever, in all thy Biblical, true land, forever.

6 And in thy nationalizing, all Biblical true land, that is already granted, unto thee, forever. Then thou shalt be seen, fully in the earth, forever. As Israel, fully in her land, truly forever.

7   And when, thou art found fully within thy land, that is called Biblical true Israel. Then I (God), shall cause all war, to stop unto thee forever and unto the world forever---and is stopped, when thou doest fully pursue me (God), in Christ Jesus, forever sure.

8   And unto thee, is the peace granted in the earth forever, and the world shall learn war no more,

9   For at the valley of decision, I shall teach all nations to never seek war again, least they die unto me (God) forever.

10 And thy savior, who is called Christ Jesus. He is spiritually sent unto thee forever, with the gift of eternal salvation, that is me (God). And that salvation, it is, called God forever.

11 And, as thou seeketh me (God), in Christ Jesus. I (God) shall bless thee, as my (God) wife forever, and I (God) shall put the rings and wedding garments, back on thee, forever, even as found in Christ Jesus forever,

12 And we (God and Israeli people), shall never depart, from each other, again and forever. For I (God) Am thy husband, that is seen, and heard, as being Jesus Christ, as forever true.

13 And I (God) shall grant, eternal, true life, unto thee forever. That life, it is found, as Christ Jesus, forever.

14 And through, Christ Jesus, soon returning to the earth, in like matter, as he was caught up me and caught up to heaven. Then thou shalt, enjoy heaven, on earth, as being forever true,

15 And I (God) will never destroy the earth again, and forever. And the earth, truly shall remain, as long, as time, shall be called God forever.

16 For I (God) do create unto the thee and unto the repentful in Christ Jesus, a new heaven and a new earth, that is this earth, changed through Christ Jesus, eternally forever,

17 And the old ways of sin, as found, as this old as a garment, true earth. It Is being burned up, by me (God), through Jesus Christ, forever. And hell, is granted unto the unrepentiful true ones, as being forever seen.

18 And they, who are found and seen, in the fallen true earth, as forever true. As being seen, as being unrepentiful, unto me, forever true and forever more.

19 They most surely, do choose death, rather than me (God), as I (God) Am found, in Jesus Christ, forever true.

20 And, as thou calleth upon me (God), forever. I (God) shall be, and I Am found, of Israel, forever, saith thy eternal God, as being eternally forever and ever true, and, forever seen.

21 And I truly shall bless Israel, in all that is given of me, unto Israel, as it is seen, as being, Jesus Christ, as being forever seen, and, forever true.

The God of Truth

1 Chapters 1-42
2 w / 3,862 verses
3 Chapter 1 w/ 37 verses   Thus saith the Lord

4 This prophetic book, that is called: "The God Of Truth," It is given unto me, from our righteous, Holy God. And it is found, through Jesus Christ. And this Christ, who is our true savior, and, who is forever seen of God,

5 He (Jesus Christ) has given this book, unto me, Roger Dale Wallace, to give unto the nation of Israel, forever. And, it is given of God forever, through Christ Jesus, forever,

6 And, it is given, that Israel, may truly come into the evening light of God, that is called Jesus Christ, forever, And, in these eternal, true days, forever. I (God) Am considerate of Israel, and I (God) will help, Israel, forever.

7   For, Thus saith the Lord of heaven and earth (August 3, 2006). I do see the current turmoil that has been placed upon my people of the nation of Israel.

8   And thou O Israel, thou art my chosen, holy people. And this, current, evil terrorism that has came thy way (the current war Israel is in). Shall soon have an expected, eternal, living true end, forever, and will be found in most heavenly true righteousness, that is called God, forever.

9   And, as a result. Israel shall come into the direction for obtaining all Biblical true land, that I (God) have given to Israel, under the sworn oath, that is found of me (God), that has been recorded by me, through out the days of old.

10   And I (God) shall fight thy enemies, O Israel. For my mighty, ever lasting, great eternal true name. It is, most surely, found in Israel, in these days of this transgressing, unrepentiful, fallen, beastly, Antichrist, true earth, forever.

11   Yet with all certainty, thou O Israel. Thou shalt most surely, see upon, all of thy enemies, forever. My (God) eternal, living, forever and ever, true hand, that is called recompense unto all that hate thee unjustly forever. And my hand, is mighty in both, judgment and most eternal, living forever, true power.

12 And my (God) given, righteous, Holy, just judgments. They shall always be upon all of the nations, that chose to be thy everlasting true enemies, unjustly forever.

13 And they are found, forever true. In this fallen, unrepentiful, transgressing, beastly imaged in most sin, old as a garment, true earth.

14 And unto those ungodly true nations, that hate thee unjustly , O Israel. They (ungodly nations) shall be clean dissolved by me (God) in Christ Jesus forever.

15 And those fallen, unrepentiful, ungodly, beastly true nations. They shall reel to fro, under my, great, eternal, living forever, Godly True righteous, forever and ever, true name.

16 And again, these ungodly true nations, that are unjustly against thee, forever, O Israel (Israel). They shall, most surely, be removed, as a cottage, forever.

17 Therefore, all ungodly nations, that are of the entire true earth, that do within themselves, hate thee unjustly, forever. They are all-unjust, and are, unrepentiful true nations.

18 And those nations, they are also considered by me, as being unholy and unjust, forever true nations. And they are seen forever true, by me, as

being unrepentiful and ungodly, unrighteous true nations, forever.

19 They are, most certainly, unrepentiful, ungodly true nations. And are by their own personal choices, without Christ forever and ever true in themselves, forever.

20 And they are seen by me (God), in their fallen, unrepentiful, ungodly true shape, forever. And they are seen, by me, forever true. As concerning the unrepentiful true sinfulness, that is found eternally forever true, within themselves, as being forever true and forever more.

21 And I (God) shall, and I do forever, see those ungodly true nations, that will not ever accept thee, O Israel, forever, and they are many,

22 And those many, non-Christian, ungodly, true nations. They are without Christ. And they are called by me (God), as unholy true nations, forever. And they are most certainly, found forever true, by me (God), forever,

23 And they are found, by me, as being forever seen, as being ungodly true nations. As they are seen, as being, true beasts of the earth, that are called: unrepentiful true men, forever.

24 And they are unrighteous true nations, that are found and seen, as being, without the heavenly true salvation, forever,

25 That salvation, it is called: "Christ In The Earth, Forever And Ever True Of Me (God), as I Am eternally forever and ever true," in the fallen true earth, forever certain, and, forever more.

26 These non-Christian, ungodly, true nations. They are not like Christian nations, who have the heavenly true salvation, that is called: "Christ within Them", forever.

27 Christian nations, they are a branch of my planting, in the earth, as being forever sure, and, as being forever seen. And that, is true, that the earth, may bring forth, Godly True fruit, that is called repentance unto me, forever.

28 And through my planting, of Christian nations. I shall see forever true. That through my planting, in the earth forever. That I (God) may walk, with man, for all of true eternity, and that is forever and ever true, saith thy God, eternally forever and ever true.

29 Christian nations, they are all, found in my, eternally, living forever, true forgiveness. And that forgiveness, it is found in the remission of one's seen sins.

30 And my forgiveness, it is found in them, forever, who do accept, Jesus Christ, forever, and that is, eternally forever and ever true, of themselves (Christians forever), in the earth, as being forever seen, by me, as I Am God, as I Am forever true.

31 Therefore, let it be known that all sins are against me (God). No matter how small they may appear to be. For all sins are against me (God), forever true. And I Am, the creator of, most forever and ever, heavenly forever, true life.

32 And my, eternal, true forgiveness, for sin. It is found, in my (God) true righteousness, that is found in the heavenly true salvation, that is salvation of me (God). For I dwelleth, in the most high heaven of heavens, eternally forever.

33 Eternal living, forever forgiveness, it is of me (God), in Christ. And is found of me (God), eternally unto them, who dwell in the earth, as being forever true.

34 All ungodly nations, are without the Christly true salvation. That is my salvation, that is of my (God) own, eternal, forever and ever, holy true presents. As being forever seen by me, as being, forever true.

35 And, those ungodly true nations, they are death unto me forever. And they shall most surely, receive of me (God), Godly true

recompense. That is found, given of me (God), unto this fallen true world, forever, saith thy Lord, of both, heaven and earth, eternally forever and ever true, and, forever seen.

36 And I (God), The Lord. I Am "Most Holy, Seeing Forever, Heavenly Eternal, Unending Forever, Heavenly True Life," And I (God) shall repay, these ungodly, non-Christian nations, to their face, forever.

37 And they are repaid of me (God), as according to their desired true deeds, that these ungodly true nations, do perform against me (God). That they do desire, unrighteously forever true, and, as being forever seen of themselves, as death, forever.

Chapter 2   w/ 41 verses   Godly recompense

1 Therefore, in the days to come. Israel shall see my (God) great Godly true recompense, that is and shall be, upon all of thine troublesome enemies, forever and ever true.

2 And I shall, even send the angels, as they were sent by me, in the days of old, upon all of thy enemies, to fight for thee, saith me (God), the God of heaven, and of this fallen, transgressing, true world, forever.

3 And all, ungodly, unrepentiful true nations, they are seen by me, forever true. As desiring to

never ask for Christ, for Christ Jesus, to be their seen Savior, forever.

4 And, they are seen, as being unrepentfully fallen true nations. And they are seen, without Christ, in them true nations. And these, beastly, eternal true nations. They are without Christ, by their own personal, true choices, forever.

5 And, they, are seen, as beastly eternal true nations, that are without me (God). And my presents, it is called: "Life eternally forever true," and, forever more.

6 Therefore, these fallen, ungodly true nations. They are most certainly, considered of me (God), as: "Being utterly beastly," by human, fallen, sinful true nature, forever.

7 And these beastly true nation's, they are rebels against me (God). And, these same rebels, they are most surely, ungodly without the Son called "Christ," in them nations.

8 Therefore, those sinful without Christ beastly true nations. They are each considered of me (God), as "Unholy and Ungodly Corrupt." And those, same brute beasts (unrepentiful true nations), they are seen, as being, enemies of me (God), forever true, saith God.

9 And I (God), do say. That these unrepentiful true nations. They shall most certainly, perish in

their worldly, true corruption, that is seen and called: "Damningly true corruption," that is called "The Creature Without God, And Is, Without Christ, Forever And Ever True."

10 Moreover, these ungodly, willful without God in them nations. They are willfully without Christ, in themselves, forever.

11 And, that is seen, by their own personal true choices. And they are considered of me, as being quite beastly by fallen human true nature, forever. And they are certainly, considered of me (God), as being ungodly, sinful, beastly, unjust, and unholy true nations, forever.

12 Those unholy true nations, they are fallen beastie nations. And they are most certainly, found by me, as forever true. As being without Christ, as Christ Jesus, being their seen Savior, as being forever and ever true.

13 And they, are without Christ Jesus, by their own, personal true choices. As being eternally forever and ever seen, and, true forever.

14 For if they chose not Christ, then they have become, unholy true nations, forever.

15 And they are found, by me, forever. As found in ever most, beastly forever, heavenly true corruption, that is a forever true corruption, that is called, eternal dead death, forever.

16 And that, corruption, to be death forever. It is seen, as being forever true. As being, beastly heavenly forever and ever, true corruption.

17 And, that is not, a hid true corruption. But it is seen, as beastly eternal, ungodly true corruption. And it is forever seen, as a eternal, forever, truly seen, true corruption,

18 That I do see, through my heavenly true presents, for my presents, it is seen forever true and forever seen, as a seen presents, that is me as forever seen, as being eternal, never ending, heavenly true life, that is eternally forever true, in and of me (God), forever.

19 Yet, these, unrepentiful true nations, They are seen by me forever. As being without Christ, by their own personal true choices, as found in not desiring to receive Christ, as Christ Jesus, being their personal, true Savior, forever.

20 Therefore, these, corrupt, ungodly true nations. They are, most surely, without Christ. And are considered of me, forever. As them, being found, as eternally forever corrupt.

21 And they (ungodly, true corrupt nations), are, ungodly true nations, that are the fallen, beastly, imaged earth, forever.

22 That image, it is, unrepentfully against me (God), as being forever and ever true. And, it is,

against my (God) forever and ever, heavenly true righteousness, forever.

23 These same, corrupted, earthly true nations. They are without me (God), and they are without Christ. And they are seen by me. As I Am found in Christ, forever true.

24 And those, same, true, corrupted true nations. They are seen by me forever true, as being fallen against me (God), as trespassing nations, who are truly found in the fallen true earth, forever,

25 And, those nations, they are seen, by me, forever. As being in their desired, forever and ever, unrepentiful true sinfulness, forever. And that true sinfulness, it is eternally forever true, in being against me (God), as being forever and ever true.

26 And those nations, they do, most certainly, perish in their own, unrepentiful, true sins, forever.

27 And those, seen sins, they shall, and do cause me (God), through Christ: To clean dissolve, those unrepentiful, ungodly, true nations. That are found in the ungodly true nature, that is called: "Against God sins," forever.

28 Nevertheless, that ungodly forever and ever true nature, does cause me to remove that sin, from the entire true earth, forever.

29 And that, is found, through my (God) righteous and holy, given of me (God), just recompense. That recompense, it is found, in the most eternal, living forever, holy true judgment, called God.

30 These unrepentiful, against God nations. They shall, most certainly, shall cause to create from me (God). Their own, holy of God, true recompense. That is me unto them, in judgment, forever.

31 That creating, it shall, most certainly, cause clean dissolving of those nations, because of their desired by them, true iniquity.

32 And with all assurance, that true iniquity, it shall cause from me (God), given true recompense. That recompense, it is seen, in the earth, as being forever true,

33 As a seen, recompense, as being holy and righteous, forever, as a true recompense, from me, forever true. And, it is a granted true recompense, for the desired unrepentiful true evils,

34 That these ungodly true nations, do create back unto themselves, in eternal forever and ever, true damnation, as given recompense by me, forever, unto them, forever.

35 And that living forever and ever, true damnation. It is found, as a clean dissolving eternal true damnation, that the unrepentiful do create back unto themselves, as eternal recompense, from me, forever.

36 That true damnation, it is, a ungodly, eternal, living forever and ever, true damnation. That is created by them, as sin unto me forever, and as a result of that created sinful true damnation,

37 God shall then grant that true damnation from them, as true death, back from me, back unto themselves, as a holy recompense, forever.

38 And I (God) shall most certainly, give them true death, forever. Unless they repent in Christ Jesus, forever certain of themselves, forever.

39 And, if they repent not, then recompense, called true death, it is granted from me (God), unto them, most surely forever, as eternally forever true, of myself, forever.

40 I (God) Am, the God of forever and ever, eternal true truth. And my (God) truth, it is found, in Christ, the Son, eternally forever and ever true.

41 And I Am, true forever, saith thy eternal, loving, and kind God, forever.

Chapter 3 w/ 26 verses   True recompense damnation

1 Holy recompense damnation, is a living forever and ever, eternal, true damnation. That damnation, is a given, true damnation. That is from me (God), eternally forever and ever true.

2 And is granted by me, unto all ungodly nations, who are forever seen by me, as being eternally forever true. As being unrepentfully, truly lost, unto me, eternally forever.

3 And, they are, ungodly and unrighteous, true nations. That are found in this, fallen, unrepentiful, true earth, as being heavenly forever and ever true.

4 Nevertheless, these forever, eternally lost, unholy true nations. They are, eternally forever, without any natural repentant true desire, for, both me (God), and for all, that I (God) truly do stand for, forever.

5 And is most surely seen, and is most certainly, seen as a lack of eternal true desire, for me and for Christ Jesus,

6 And it is demonstrated, in and by themselves, towards me and towards Christ, as being eternally forever true, of themselves, towards me, as I Am God, as I Am forever true.

7   And, as they are forever seen, by me, as being against receiving my (God) eternal, living forever and ever, true righteousness. Then, they shall die, most surely, forever.

8   And my true righteousness, it is called: Christ Jesus, eternally forever and ever true.

9   Damningly forever, heavenly true life, it is called: sinfulness. And it is not my (God) heavenly true life, that is my (God) life forever. And they, that enjoy, their sinful true heaven, on earth,

10 Then I (God) shall create unto them, forever, eternal true fire, that is called judgment, as given from me forever, as given unto them, forever. As a created, eternal, holy and just, true recompense.

11 That recompense, it shall cause to create, true holiness, in the most forever and ever, true: clean dissolving of the ungodly true nations, as eternally forever and ever true.

12 And that true dissolving, it is concerning their personal, living forever, unrepentfulness that is seen by me, as they do chose to not ever chose to accept Christ, as Christ Jesus being their personal true savior, forever.

13 And that true desire, for one's chosen, unrepentiful true seen sins. That eternal true

choice, shall damn them, as being forever true. If they shall not repent, in Christ Jesus, forever.

14 That eternal, true rejection, to not to know Christ and to not know me, "The Father." That eternal true rejection, shall result, in holy, and just, true recompense, as being, seen and felt, as being eternally forever and ever true,

15 That true recompense, it is called death. And is seen as being eternally forever and ever true, and, it is from me, as reasonable forever and ever, true recompense.

16 That true recompense, it is most surely, eternally forever, granted from me, as being forever sure, and, forever more.

17 And, that true recompense, it is, a holy and just, true recompense. And, it is found of me (God), as being eternally forever and ever true, of me, through Christ Jesus, the Son, forever.

18 That granted of me, true recompense, it is found through my eternal, living forever, true Son. Who is called "Christ our righteousness," forever.

19 Holy clean dissolving, it is given of me (God), as being eternally forever and ever true. And that true recompense, it is found, given of me (God), as being faithfully forever and ever true.

20 And it is found, given by me, as given truly forever true of me, as being forever true. And it is true, in being, given by me, faithfully forever true, and, it is, truly faithful unto them, that hate me, forever.

21 And holy clean dissolving, it is found, in holy and uttermost, true truth, forever. And is a righteous, eternal, true judgment. And that true judgment,

22 It is, a true, holy true judgment. And it is given by me, forever certain, as a eternal, true, Godly true judgment. And is eternally from me (God), forever and ever true, through Christ Jesus, forever.

23 And, moreover, it is, most surely, a righteous, and holy, just recompense. And it is granted, unto the unrepentiful, forever true,

24 And it is granted, for one being found, in willful and desired, eternal, true unrepentiful true sinfulness, forever.

25 And that true unrepentfulness, it is seen, in the fallen. As being against me (God), as being forever true. And it is, eternally forever and ever true, of the damned, forever.

26 And that true unrepentfulness, it is forever certain, in the fallen of the true earth, forever.

Chapter 4 w 53 / verses   Unrepentfulness

1   Unrepentfulness, it is seen. As being, found in willful, desired, true unrepentiful desired true sinfulness. That true sinfulness, it is forever true, in being against me (God), as being forever certain, and, forever true.

2   And that true eternal, and most true, unrepentfulness, that is found in the damned forever. It is, found, in being, against all, that I (God) Am, and it is against, all, that I (God) truly do, stand for, forever.

3   And that true unrepentfulness, it is found, most surely, in being eternally against, all that I (God) Am, forever, as I (God) Am God, forever true. And it is, against,

4   All that is seen and known, that is of myself (God), as I (God) Am eternally forever and ever true, in Christ the Son, as I (God) Am forever seen.

5   And, moreover, righteous true recompense. It is given of me (God), for one being found, in eternal, unrepentiful, true sinfulness, forever.

6   And that true sinfulness, it is found, in the ungodly and unrighteous, true nations. Who are unrepentiful true nations,

7   That are found by me (God), in the earth, as being forever true. As being unrepentiful forever certain, and, forever more.

8   And those same nations, they are seen, as being unrepentiful true nations, eternally forever. And those nations, they do not ever desire,

9   To ever accept Christ Jesus. As this eternal true Christ, being their personal, living forever, true savior, forever.

10   And, all unrepentiful true sinfulness, it is seen, as to not ever to desire to accept Christ, as Christ being, one's personal, living forever, true savior.

11   That true desire, that is found within the damned. That is found as their desire, to remain unrepentiful towards both me (God) and towards Christ Jesus, forever.

12   It is seen, by my (God) eternal, living forever, true presents. And this unrepentiful true sinfulness, it shall be as fuel to the fire,

13   And that true fire, it is given of me (God). As a fiery, clean, dissolving, holy and true, recompense judgment. That is given by me (God), through Christ Jesus, unto the damned, forever.

14 And that true recompense, it is given by me (God), as being forever true, and, forever more. And it is, a granted, true recompense, that is given from me (God), as being eternally forever and ever true, from me (God), forever.

15 And it is granted true recompense, granted from me (God), forever. And is given, unto all, forever true. Who are found by me (God), as being, unrepentiful, ungodly, true nations, forever.

16 And, it is, most surely, given by me (God), forever true. And it is given by me (God), as being a forever and ever, clean dissolving, eternal, true judgment, forever certain.

17 And it is given, by me (God), faithfully forever true. As it is written of me (God), in Isaiah 24:19, as being forever true.

18 Clean dissolving, it is for the removal of sin. And clean dissolving, it is found from me (God) forever true, unto the ungodly non-Christian nations, forever.

19 And that clean dissolving true judgment, it is seen, in the earth. And is given heavenly of me (God), at this time of the earth, forever and ever true.

20 And it is eternally forever and ever true, unto the fallen, who are found, by me (God), forever,

in being against me (God), as being forever true, of themselves, in death, forever.

21 Clean dissolving, it is from me (God). And it is holy true recompense. And it is, given by me (God), unto the damned forever, because of their desired, unrepentiful, true sins, forever.

22 And those same sins, they are found, by me (God), forever. And they are found, as being against me (God), eternally forever and ever true. And clean dissolving, it is, and shall always be considered, by me (God), as being: "Just Holy, True Recompense,"

23 That true recompense, it is, a holy forever true, recompense, forever. And it is seen, as being a granted true recompense, from me (God), forever.

24 That true recompense, it is given by me (God), through Christ Jesus, forever and ever certain, unto the damned ones, forever,

25 And it is a granted, true recompense, for clean dissolving, judgment. And it is, to forever, to judgingly remove all, unrepentiful, damningly true sins, away from me (God), forever.

26 And that just judgment, it is, to remove, those sins, away from my (God) holy, eternal, righteous, living forever, true presents. And that judgment,

27 It is, to be eternally forever and ever found, as given true judgment, from me (God), forever sure.

28 And most assuredly, those ungodly true nations, who refuse Christ eternally forever. They are without Christ forever true. And they are without me (God), the Father of most eternal, living forever, true life.

29 And these fallen, forever, true nations. That are against receiving my (God) heavenly true salvation. They are considered by me (God), as corrupt, unholy true nations. And they are eternally forever and ever seen, before me (God), forever true.

30 And they are seen by me (God), as being desirethsome to never repent ever in my (God) Son, who is called Christ. Therefore, they shall be forever destroyed by me (God), forever.

31 And those nations and their peoples, and their tongues, and their kindred's. They are being destroyed by me (God), forever. And they shall be destroyed by me (God), forever,

32 And this is because of their seen sins, that they do in my (God) seeing presents, that is my (God) seeing presents of most given, forever, true life.

33 Many of those, ungodly, true nations. They shall never fully accept Christ, my (God) Son, forever. And this Christ, he (Jesus Christ) is, of my (God) very own, true essence, forever. And this Christ, he is, of all, that is of me (God), forever true.

34 Those nations, that do refuse, Christ Jesus, forever. They are unto me (God), forever, as reprobate nations. And they are seen, unto me (God) forever, as being unholy true nations. And, they shall never,

35 Fully accept the heavenly true Son, who is called "Christ," And those same, unrepentiful true nations. They are considered by me (God), forever, as being, truly, slow bellies in not believing all, that is written of me (God), forever.

36 And those same, unrepentiful, sinful true nations. They are forever, against me (God), true nations. And they do reject me (God) and do reject Christ Jesus, forever,

37 And they do reject, forever, all and complete true knowledge, that is given by me (God). As concerning myself (God), forever. And they do reject that knowledge, that is given of me (God), unto the earth, forever.

38 That rejection, that is seen and found, as being found in being against receiving Christly

eternal true truth, forever. That rejection, it shall damn them, as being forever seen.

39 Therefore, they do reject me (God) and do reject Christ Jesus, forever.

40 And I (God) have and do, give them complete and total knowledge. That is called Christ Jesus, forever. And that true knowledge, it is given of me (God),

41 Through my (God) eternal, living forever, most holy Son, who is called, Christ, who is seen, as being, forever and ever true.

42 And those, beastly nations. They shall never, fully, come unto me (God). In desiring me (God), to accept their repentance. As me (God) giving them, and allowing them, forgiveness from me (God),

43 That is found, through my (God) eternal, living forever, true Son, who is called Christ Jesus. As this Christ Jesus, being their, true savior, forever true.

44 And this true Christ Jesus, he seen and felt. As my (God) eternal, living forever, true Son, who is with, eternal life, forever true. And that life, it is, called me (God), forever.

45 Clean dissolving, it is granted, by me (God), forever. And it is found, through me (God),

forever true. And, it is found, through me (God), as Christ Jesus unto the damned forever,

46 And dissolving true judgment, it is called God. And it is truly found, written by me (God), and, it is me (God), as I (God) Am found written as judgment in Isaiah 24:19.

47 And that great dissolving, true judgment. It is in order, with my (God) eternal true plan. That plan, it is, heavenly, Godly forever, true salvation.

48 And, as it is written, also in the New Testament: "The meek shall inherit the earth," This inheriting, it shall be forever and ever true, of me (God), forever.

49 Again, all, unrepentiful true sins. They are found unto me (God) forever. In the unrepentiful, beastly, eternal true nations. Those nations, they are: "Beastly, eternal, damningly true nations,"

50 And, they are, seen, by me (God), forever true. As being, of, eternal true death, forever true and forever more.

51 And those, appalling true nations. They are seen by me (God) forever. As being, most certainly, forever true. As being against me (God), forever more,

52 In desiring to not have Christ Jesus. As this Christ Jesus, being their personal true savior, forever. And, they are, seen most surely, by me (God), eternally forever true,

53 And my true presents, it is my (God) holy true presents. That is me (God), as I (God) Am found, in Christ Jesus, forever.

Chapter 5 w/ 53 verses   I Am found of Israel forever

1 In these days, I (God) Am found of Israel, forever. And I (God) Am Israel. And I (God) and thou, O Israel. We are righteously forever found together,

2   Through my (God) holy, living forever, eternal true Son, who is, called Christ, forever, and I (God) shall love thee forever, and, without true end, forever.

3   And, all unrepentiful, ungodly true nations, that do hate thee unjustly. They are considered of (the of means the word by) me (God),
forever,

4   As being, wicked, unrepentiful true nations, that do surely hate my (God) great name, that is found in thee, O Israel,

5   And my (God) great, eternal true name. It is found in Israel, in these last days, that are of this

utterly fallen, transgressing, beastly, unrepentiful, old, hardened against me (God), true earth, forever.

6 And, unto all nations, and unto, all peoples, who hate my (God) great name, that is called Israel. I (God) shall not meet them as a man, but I (God) shall meet them, as their creator,

7 And I (God) shall meet them forever true, in holy, given of me (God), righteous eternal, living forever, just judgments. That are just, true judgments,

8 That are granted unto the unrepentiful true nations, that are found by me (God), in the fallen true earth, forever.

9 And, my (God) holy and righteous, true judgments. They are of me (God), and they are given by me (God). And those just, holy righteous true judgments,

10 They are, most surely found, given faithfully by me (God), unto all nations, that are found by me forever, as being ungodly true nations, that do afflict thee, unjustly forever, O Israel.

11 And those just judgments, they are, end time, Godly, just true judgments, that are given by me (God), through Christ Jesus, upon the head of all of the wicked true nations. Who do, unjustly afflict thee, forever, O Israel.

12 And thou, O Israel, thou art, O Israel, that is my (God) eternal, living forever, heavenly true Son, who is called Christ, forever. For Christ Jesus, doth live in thee, forever, and thou in him, forever.

13 And those nations and peoples, who do, unjustly afflict thee. They are, shameful, unrepentiful true nations, that are without Christ, in them, nations.

14 And, they are, living eternal, true nations. That are already, damned by me (God), forever. And they are seen, unto me (God) forever,

15 As being unholy true nations, that shall most certainly, find unto themselves, forever, true death, forever.

16 And, those, nations. They are seen, in living forever, true shame, that do, hate thee (Israel), unjustly, forever, O Israel.

17 And thou, O Great Nation (Israel), thou art called Christ Jesus. And thou art called O Israel, and thou hast been recreated, by me (God), again, and forever, and this is, starting in and from, 1948 AD, and forever.

18 And I, most surely, do love thee forever true, O Israel. And thou art, most surely, called by my (God) eternal, living forever, most holy, eternal, true name. That great name, it is, of ever lasting,

true Godliness, forever. That great name, that is called Israel. It is with most forever and ever, true holiness. That holiness, it is and is of me (God), as being forever true.

19 And that eternal, true name, that is, called Israel. It is, and shall always be, eternally forever and ever true, of me (God), forever seen.

20 And, that eternal, living forever, true name. It is a wonderful and exceeding, righteous true name. For that true name, it is my (God) own, true name, forever true.

21 And that name, it is of my own eternal, true greatness, as I Am God forever true. And I Am eternally forever and ever, true unto them, who are of the fallen true earth, forever.

22 That name, it is of myself (God), and it is called Israel. And it is a most beautiful and most Godly, true name, that is found of me (God), unto the fallen Sons of men, forever.

23 And that name, is called Israel, and it is given of me (God), forever. And the name, that is called Israel. It is seen, as being said, also as being, the name, that is called, Jesus Christ,

24 And that great name, it is, most surely, given unto them, that dwell in the fallen true earth, as being forever seen.

25 And, through that great name, that is Called: Jesus Christ. That name, it is given by me (God), forever. And is given by me (God), as life forever. And, it is, that through, that great name,

26 That is called Jesus Christ. It is, that all true men and all true women, may repent and receive Jesus Christ, as this Christ Jesus, being their personal true savior, forever true.

27 And that great eternal true name, that is called Christ Jesus. It is a everlasting holy true name, that is forever true of me, forever. And it is, forever found, unto the earth, as being forever found,

28 And it is, a found, holy true name, that is found given by me, forever seen. And that true name, it is found given and sent of me (God), forever true. And it is sent,

29 Into the earth, forever. As a sent, uttermost, eternal, living forever, true name. That true name, it is, a seen, true name. That is called: "Godly righteous, true life," as being forever seen, and true forever.

30 Therefore, the name, Jesus Christ. It is seen, as a kindly, forever, true name. And it is found, given of me (God), as being forever sure. And that true name,

31 It is seen, as being a true, and pure, true faith. That is me (God), as I (God) Am forever true, and I (God) Am truly forever.

32 And this true Christ, he (Jesus Christ) is seen, of me (God), forever. As being, seen, of ever most, gracefulness. That eternal, and most true gracefulness,

33 It is found, given of me (God), as being forever true. And it is given, in and of me (God), as being forever true. And I Am true forever, and I Am without true end, as being eternally forever and ever true.

34 And I (God) Am true forever, as: "THE GOD OF TRUTH." And I (God) Am forever true and faithful unto them, that do love me (God), through Christ Jesus,

35 As being forever certain. And that is a faithful and true saying, that is called God. And I Am forever seen, and I Am God, and I Am eternally forever.

36 Now, arise and shake off thy true sins, unto me (God), forever. By calling upon me (God), as I (God) Am found, as I Am Jesus Christ, forever,

37 That thou mayest, truly be forgiven of thy true, seen sins. That are, truly seen, unto me, forever. And in doing so, that thou mayest, be truly forgiven,

38 Of thy seen sins, forever, and I will never remember thy true sins, forever. And thou shalt be, with me (God), forever.

39 My (God) true name, as it is seen, as being Jesus Christ, my (God) Son. It is forever. And it is, truly, a great and wonderful, redeeming true name, that is seen and felt,

40 As God forever. For I Am God, who is found, in Christ Jesus, as being eternally forever and ever true, and, forever seen.

41 And that seen true name, that is called Jesus Christ, it is even called Israel, forever. And that great and eternal true name (Jesus Christ), that is given of myself (God),

42 It is given of me (God) forever. As I (God) Am God forever true and forever more. And it is (the name Jesus Christ), most certainly,

43 Eternally forever true, as eternal true righteousness. That is called God, as being forever true and forever more and ever lastingly, forever.

44 And that great name, that is called Jesus Christ, that dwelleth in me (God), forever. It shall, and shall always be, a Godly true name,

45 That is given, of myself (God), as I (God) Am God, as being forever true and forever more.

46 Even that great name (Jesus Christ), it is, seen. And is even seen, as being called Israel, as being forever true. And (the name that is seen and called: Jesus Christ), that name,

47 It is for all of given true eternity. And it (the name Jesus Christ) is seen forever more, and is righteously forever true, in and of me, forever.

48 And that true name, that is called Jesus Christ. It is even found, as being forever seen and felt. As I Am seen and felt, as I Am God, as I Am eternally forever and ever true.

49 And, moreover, that eternal, great name, that is called Israel. It is, most certainly, of me, as given by me, forever. And is gloriously given of me, as Jesus Christ, as being forever true.

50 And, it is, a glorious, heavenly, eternal true name, that is called God forever. And it is, Jesus Christ, as being eternally forever and ever true, and it is, forever more, as heavenly given of and by me, as being forever true.

51 The true name of Christ Jesus, it is the name of Israel, forever. And it is, given, by me, forever true and forever more. And it is given by me, as I Am God, as I Am eternally forever and ever true.

52 Therefore, Israel is Christ and Christ is Israel. And this is, just as sure, as Christ is forever

found, in me (God), forever. And this Christ Jesus,

53 He (Jesus Christ) is found, in me forever, as being found faithful unto me forever. And this Christ, he is in and of me (God), as I (God) Am called Christ Jesus, forever.

Chapter 6 w / 25 verses   Christly Israel

1 In the plan, that is, heavenly forever, true life. Christ and I, (God) are one together, in all that I (God) Am, as I Am forever true.

2 And, we (Christ and me [God]) are, the same, together. For all of true eternity and forever seen.

3 And that is seen, as being eternally forever true. And this shall be Christly forever true, in all, Godly, and righteous, true eternity,

4 And that is, forever true, saith the lord of hosts, as being eternally forever true, and, forever seen. And that is seen, as I (God) Am faithful,

5 And I (God) Am, eternally forever true, and, forever kind. And I (God) Am God, as being forever true, and I (God), do live, forever sure.

6 Again, that great name of Christly Israel, it is found of me (God), even in the ever and ever, ever after. For that eternal, Christly true name. It

is, most surely, seen. As being, called Israel, forever.

7   And that true name, that is called Israel. It is seen, as being a lovely, forever true, eternal true name. That true name, it is a true name, of living forever and ever, true life. That true life, it is, me, (God) forever.

8   And my (God) Son, who is called Christ Jesus, he is found, in me (God), the eternal, true Father, forever. And that true name, that is seen and called, Christ,

9   It is, a most pure, and true, holy forever and ever, eternal true truth. That truth, it is, called God, as being forever true. For that holy, true name,

10 That is seen and called Christ. It is, my (God) eternal, true name, that is called: "God our righteousness, Forever."

11 And that Christly eternal true name, that is called Israel. It is forever true, and it is seen, in me (God), forever. And it is me (God), as I Am forever true, saith thy God, eternally forever,

12 And that Christly true name, it doth live, in me (God), forever. And that name, it is even found, as being eternally forever true, in me (God), as being forever seen,

13 For that true name, it is found, eternally forever and ever true, of me (God). And it is found, of me, as being eternally forever and ever seen.

14 And that, seen true name, that is called Christ. It is most certainly, Godly forever true. And is found, of me, forever, with heavenly true manifestation, that is seen and felt, in and of me (God), as being eternally forever true.

15 And that true manifestation, it is forever found, in eternal true love. That true love, it is of me (God), as being eternally forever and ever true, of me, for I Am the true Father, and I Am forever seen.

16 And it is truly manifested, as it is given by me, forever. And it is seen and felt, as I Am God forever true. And it is most eternal, as a living forever and ever, true love. That is called life, forever,

17 And, I Am Christly true life, for I Am Christly true love, and that love, it is forever seen and felt, as being forever true. And I Am, forever seen, as I Am (God) love, forever,

18 And Christly eternal true life, it is my (God) name, that is seen, as being Jesus Christ, forever. And this same Jesus, he is seen, and, is called Israel, as being forever true and forever more.

19 And Israel, is the light of eternal true men, forever. And that light, it is found, as being Christ Jesus, as being eternally forever and ever true.

20 And this heavenly forever and ever, eternal living, forever true, eternal light, that is called Jesus Christ,

21 It is, seen and felt, of me, forever. As being, Jesus Christ, as being eternally forever and ever true. And it is, most surely, seen and felt,

22 As my Christly true light, that is called Israel, forever. And it is found, as being Jesus Christ, eternally forever and ever true.

23 Christ Jesus, he is, the eternal, true light, of men, as being forever true. And this Christ, he is found forever and ever true, in me (God), as being forever sure and forever more.

24 Christ Jesus, is, seen and felt, as God forever true. And this same Christ Jesus, he seen of me, as found eternally forever true. In all, that is seen and felt, as ever lasting, true love, that is me (God) forever.

25 And this Christ, he is eternal, forever. For this Christ, he shall, always be found, in the heavenly, forever and ever, true after, that is me (God), forever, saith thy God, eternally forever and ever true.

Chapter 7 w / 52 verses   Eternal life

1   Christly love, it is a Godly, pure, eternal, true love. That is found, given of myself (God), forever true. And it is given, through, Christ Jesus,

2   As eternally forever and ever true, eternal life. That life, it is given of me, unto the Sons of men. That, they may, eternally forever true, repent unto me, as being forever sure, and, forever more.

3   And, my eternal, true forgiveness, for sin forever. It is given, by me forever. When one doth desire my forgiveness through Christ Jesus forever, as they seek that forgiveness, through their desired, true repentance.

4   That accepted unto me, true repentance. As it is found unto me forever, as concerning the repentful forever true, when they ask for Jesus Christ, to be their seen savior, forever.

5   That eternal true forgiveness, it is found, as a accepted true repentance from the sinner forever. When they have most surely, repented unto me forever, by accepting this Christ Jesus, as their accepted true savior, forever,

6   That accepted true repentance, unto me, forever. It is given by the Godly eternal true

repentful, who love me forever. And, they are found, unto me forever,

7 As they truly are found, in that they truly do, demonstrate eternally forever true, their desired and true repentance, unto me, forever and ever sure, of themselves,

8 As they truly do demonstrate that true and precious true desire, lovingly toward all, that is and is of me, forever. And that is certainly,

9 Forever true, of them, as they be found, unto me forever, in Christ Jesus, forever. And I shall accept and love them, forever.

10 And my gift of forgiveness. It is a gift, of true forgiveness. That is found, from me (God), as being forever true. And is given, unto them, of the fallen true earth, forever certain,

11 For these repentful, they truly do desire me (God), as being forever true, of themselves, toward me (God). As I (God) Am seen and as I (God) Am, known as the God of truth, as being forever sure and certainly forever more, and forever true.

12 And my (God) true forgiveness, it is eternal life, that is called God, as it is found given of me, through Jesus Christ, as it is found from me (God), forever true.

13 And that eternal life, that is called God. It is most surely, me, forever. And it is discovered from me, through Jesus Christ, forever,

14 And that eternal life, it is Christly true life, that is called God in Christ Jesus, forever. And it is a most precious, eternal true gift, from me,

15 As it is most surely found, in Jesus Christ, forever. And it is found, as it given of me, as being eternal life, that is seen, as being forever true,

16 And it is true, eternal life. Unto all, who will accept me, eternally forever. As I Am seen, in Jesus Christ, forever.

17 And that true gift, of eternal life. That is seen and called God. It is me, as being, forever seen, in Christ Jesus, as being eternally forever true.

18 And it is seen, of me, forever. With all, heavenly, Christly true, true righteousness. That true righteousness, it is, me, forever. And it is called God forever, for I Am God, eternally forever and ever true.

19 And that eternal life, it is called Christ Jesus, in me, forever. And it is seen, as a Christly true Godliness, that is me, as being forever true,

20   And it is found, in me, forever. And it doth come, from me (God), the God of most eternal, ever lasting, and ever lasting, forever,

21   Living, Godly, eternal true life, as I Am forever seen. And I Am forever seen, for I Am truth forever, And I live as truth eternally forever. And I Am the forever, saith thy God, eternally forever.

22   That eternal, true gift, it is most certainly seen, as Christ unto the earth, and, it is a Holy forever true, true gift. That is called God forever true,

23   And it is a seen eternal true life, that is called God forever, And it is seen, as being eternal true life, called God, forever,

24   And, it is, eternal life, as it found, given by me, as a great gift, from me, as being, forever true. And that great gift, it is most surely,

25   Called God, for I Am God, and I Am found, in Christ Jesus, forever. And that true gift, it is of me and from me, forever. And it shall never cease, from Among, repentful true men, forever.

26   And in that great day of days, that gift, it is found with eternal true life, forever. And that Christly true gift, of eternal true life, forever,

27 It shall be found, only unto them, in Christ Jesus. Who are found by me, through Christ Jesus. As being found unto me, forever,

28 As being, found truly unto me, in that great day, of eternal true days, as being Christ like, as being forever true.

29 And the name of Christ Jesus, is a name of most heavenly, and rewarding, forever true, eternal life, forever.

30 And that is a great eternal true name, found as being Christ Jesus, in me, the true Father. That great name, it is most surely, eternal. In all that I Am, as I Am God forever, and it is called Christ Jesus, the Son, forever,

31 That name, it shall truly, never depart from me (God), forever. For I Am truly true, as I Am eternally forever and ever seen, as being the eternal life, that is called God forever.

32 That eternal, lifely name, of Christ in me, forever. It is a holy forever, true eternal life name. As it is a given eternal life from me, as being forever true.

33 And that great, and eternal, true name. It is seen and felt, as Jesus Christ, as I Am eternally forever and ever, true eternal life.

34 And my eternal life, it is seen and felt, as even most eternal, as forever, truly holy, eternal life. And eternal life, is faithfully given of me and by me, forever,

35 And it is eternal Christly true life, that is most surely and certainly, as being forever true. And that is a true eternal life, that is even called God forever,

36 For I (God) Am forever, and I (God) shall love them, that love me (God) faithfully forever, as they be found in Christ Jesus, the Son, forever,

37 And eternal cleansed eternal life. It is seen, as being seen, as being, granted by me (God), forever. And that cleansed true life, it is found forever true, as them that do accept me (God) forever, as their savior called Jesus Christ, forever.

38 O Israel, thy name is Christ. And that great name, it is my (God) eternal, living forever, true name. And is a most holy of all names. For that ever lasting, true name.

39 It is, my (God) eternal, true name, forever. And it is, eternal life, that is called Christ Jesus. For Christ Jesus, he liveth forever true, in me (God), as being forever seen. As God, forever true.

40   And, in Christ Jesus, forever. I (God) Am seen and felt, forever true. As the God of uttermost, heavenly forever, eternal true truth, forever true.

41   And, that name, that is called Israel. It is called "Israel in Christ." And it is seen, as found in my (God), most holy, true blood, forever.

42   And that blood, it is seen and felt, forever true, in the earth and in heaven, forever more.

43   And that true name, called Israel, it is called Christ forever true. And that Christly Israeli true blood, of Christ Jesus. It is seen and felt forever,

44   As my (God) eternal living forever and ever precious true blood. And that blood, it is called "Israel in Christ" and is given and found of me (God), forever true. In all, that I (God) Am, forever true, saith thy eternal true God, forever true.

45   This Christ Jesus, he liveth in me (God), forever. And I (God) shall live in that great name, that is, of my (God) own, holy, true presents, forever true. And that great name, it is, called Christ, forever true forever more.

46   And this Christ, he shall always, eternally, live within, my most holy, forever, true presents. That presents, it is called life forever true and forever seen. That presents, it is me (God),

forever and ever true, as eternal, forever sure and forever seen.

47 This Christ, he is of me (God). And is found, forever true. Therefore, as I live, saith the lord, of both, heaven and earth. Thou, O Israel.

48 Thou shalt, most surely, see eternally forever true. That Christ Jesus, doth live within me, forever true. And that this Christ Jesus,

49 He shall live in me, forever and ever true. Even as seen, living in, my great, eternal, true name, forever true and forever more. And this, same, Christ Jesus. He is, called God, forever true and ever lasting forever.

50 Therefore, this same Christ Jesus. He is, a living forever, heavenly forever, true presents. That is seen and felt, from me, eternally forever true.

51 And that Christ, he is my Christ Jesus, forever true and truly eternal. And he is called "Eternal, Christly, true Life," forever true and forever more.

52 And Christ (Jesus Christ, the Son of God forever), he is seen, of me. As heavenly forever true and without true end, in all that I Am, as I (God) Am God forever.

Chapter 8 w / 60 verses   Christ Jesus

1   Christ Jesus, he is my (God) faithful, true Son, forever. And this Christ, the Son called Jesus. He is anointed by me (God), forever true and forever more.

2   And this same Christ Jesus, he is faithfully unto me (God), eternally forever true. As faithful unto me (God), forever. In all, that I (God) Am, as I (God) Am, God, forever true.

3   And he, is faithfully found by me (God), as the Son called Jesus Christ. And this Christ Jesus, he is faithful unto me. In all, that is me, as I Am eternal of myself, and I Am heavenly forever and ever true.

4   This Christ Jesus, he is most certainly, eternal of and in me, forever. And he is even seen, as the breath and light, that is called God, as being forever true.

5   And he is, even seen, as my given true life, forever. For he doth, proceed unto the earth forever true, as God forever certain and forever more.

6   For I (God) Am the life, that is called Christ Jesus, forever, saith thy God, as eternal of myself, forever true. Even as heavenly forever and ever true, of me, forever. And this Christ Jesus, he is without true end, in me, forever.

7   Christ Jesus, he is, very faithful unto me, as the eternal true Son of myself, who is given by me, with all, eternal true power, forever.

8   And Christ Jesus, he is even seen, as my eternal, true Son. Who is seen and felt, as I (God) Am God, as I (God) Am heavenly forever and ever true. Even as, forever sure, and, forever more.

9   And Christ Jesus, he is, that eternal, living forever, heavenly, true, Christly true presents. That is called: Christ Jesus, forever true.

10   And this eternal Christ Jesus, he is found and given by me (God), as my (God) eternal true Son, forever. And this eternal, true Christ. He is most holy, in me, forever.

11   And this Christ Jesus, he is even seen, as my, "eternal, true, anointed true cherubim," eternally forever true,

12   And thou, O Israel, thou shalt be found, always in my (God), most eternal, forever true, true holiness, forever. That true holiness, it is, of me (God). As eternal of myself, as heavenly forever and ever true.

13   And that true holiness, it is found forever true, of me (God). In most eternal, living forever, true Godliness. And that true Godliness, it shall be found, as being, forever true,

14 As found, in me, through Christ Jesus, as being true, in all, heavenly forever, true righteousness, that is given of me, forever.

15 And that eternal, most true righteousness, it is called God forever. For I Am God forever. And I Am found, as heavenly forever sure and true forever. For I Am the forever, and I Am without true end, as being forever true.

16 And my true righteousness, it is found, given of me, forever true. As being found, as being, my dearest true love. And that dear, true love. It is, of me (God) and is me, forever true.

17 And that true love, it shall be found, given of me, forever true. As given, by me, forever. As eternally forever found love, as found in and in all, that is of me, and is in me, as being forever true.

18 And I Am, unending forever, true love. That true love, it is, most eternal, and is, seen and felt, as being forever true. And it is seen, as being, Godly true love, as being heavenly forever and ever true, true love.

19 And that true love, is Godly eternal, true love. And it is seen, as being, Christly, true, Godly true love. And it is found of me (God), forever and ever true.

20 For I Am, the breath, that is found as being, of loving true kindness. That doth sustain the earth, as being forever true.

21 And I Am the breath of the earth, called life forever. And that life of the earth, it is found, given from me, forever true.

22 And I (God) Am, a living, forever true breath, that shall never die. And I (God) Am, a living, holy righteous, true breath. That breath, it is me, forever true. As I (God) Am, God forever true.

23 That breath, it is a living forever, true breath. That doth live, as a living forever, true breath, that is called God forever.

24 And it, is seen, as being, my very own, true breath, forever. And it, doth live, eternally forever, in me and is in me, forever. And I Am eternally forever. And I Am that breath, that is called, God forever.

25 And I Am, most surely, seen, as being ever lasting, forever true. And that true breath, that is, me forever. And it is found, in my own, eternal true Son, forever.

26 And that breath, it is most holy and it shall live forever and ever without true end, forever. For I live forever, saith thy eternal, kind God. For

I Am eternal and I live forever, and I Am truth, forever.

27 Christ Jesus, he is, most surely, found, of me, forever certain. In all that is me, forever, as I Am love forever, even as the very essence that is me, forever,

28 And I (God) Am found, as a great spirit of royal and kind, thoughtful true love, as being eternally and ever lastingly true forever, and that is forever and ever and ever true.

29 Forever true love, it is found, eternal from me, as being eternally forever true. And it is seen, as Christ Jesus, as being forever sure and certain, as it is found in me, as I Am the forever and the life, that is called God, forever.

30 And my breath, it is called God, and it is me forever. And it is most holy and pure, as pure true breath, forever.

31 And it, is even seen, as being eternally forever and ever true, in me and of me, as forever seen breath, that is even seen as the breath that is called, "The holy Son called Jesus Christ."

32 And it is found, most surely, as my breath that is given fully of myself, as found through Christ Jesus, as being eternally forever given, from me, as being forever true.

33 And that true breath of myself (God), that is seen, as being, and is: JESUS CHRIST. It is seen, as being found given by me, faithfully forever seen,

34 Unto the repentful, as they be found unto me forever true, in Jesus Christ, the Son of myself, forever.

35 Therefore, that breath, that is called life, it is from me, as found given of me, through Christ Jesus forever.

36 And it is found, in the hands, of eternal, repentful true men, as being forever true breath that is called God forever,

37 Even, as found, eternal true life, that is found in and of me. For I Am the true Father, forever. And they, who are found through Christ Jesus, with this eternal true life, that is called God,

38 Then, they are found given unto me forever, as my true Sons, called   God forever. For I Am God in them forever. And they are found, given unto me, forever,

39 And they are seen, of and by me, unto all of true creation, and that true creation, it is called God forever. As they be found unto me, in the Son, who is called, Jesus Christ, forever,

40 And they shall never die in sin, again and forever. But they, the repentful in Christ Jesus. They shall live unto me, as being forever true, and, forever seen.

41 And these repentful true ones, in Jesus Christ. They shall live forever. And they are found unto me, through Jesus Christ, the Son, as being eternally forever true and forever more.

42 And, they shall live, in Christ Jesus, forever. And shall they shall live, in me, forever. As being, in my, loving forever, true presents.

43 That true presents, it is forever and ever true, and is, forever more. And that true presents. It is, most surely, called life, eternally forever true and forever more.

44 And my loving true breath, it is even found, in some ways, as being found, in some ways, without words, to hardly even to begin, to describe, who I Am (God), as I Am thy God, forever.

45 And I Am thy God forever, and I love thee forever. And there shall be no end, forever and ever true, in and of me (God), forever,

46 For I Am the God of most eternal, living, forever, true breath. For that breath, it is me (God), eternally forever and ever true.

47 And that true breath, it is truly eternal, and it is called life, for I Am the life, that is called creation forever. And creation, it is, seen and felt,

48 As eternal in me, and is me forever, and it is found from me forever, given unto the Sons of me, as Godly salvation called Jesus Christ, forever,

49 And that salvation, it is called God, and it is given by me through Jesus Christ, unto the faithful who accept Jesus Christ, as this Jesus, being their seen savior, forever.

50 And that is forever and ever more, and, as being eternally forever true, for I Am true forever, and without true end, eternally forever, as saith,

51 Thy eternal--and kind--and great. Loving kind, eternal true God--who desirest thee, forever, o earth, and as thou to be found in Jesus Christ, my Son, forever.

52 Most surely, I love with thee with all mine true heart, forever. And without true end, eternally forever, O creation, that is called God.

53 Therefore, return thou unto me, in Jesus Christ. Who is thy first love, who is called God, O creation. For this same Jesus Christ, and I, we are one and the same, forever.

54 And, we are, together, as we (THE FATHER and Jesus Christ) are seen as me forever. And so it is, even as thou and me, are found together unto me through Jesus Christ, forever.

55 Ye are, then, truly, Christly true Sons of God forever, without true spot and without true blemish. For without Christ being thy eternal seen savior, forever.

56 Then thy sinful true spots and thy sinful true blemishes, they would have been found truly in thee, forever.

57 As thou wast at one time, then found unto me, as being forever seen, as being a eternal true sinner. As thou, being a sinner, wast in Satan's true likeness, that is called death, forever.

58 And, most surely, if thou hadn't chose this Christ Jesus, as this Christ Jesus, being thy seen, eternal, true savior, forever.

59 Then thou, wouldest most surely, had died in the second death, unto me, forever, and thou wouldest been in hell, forever.

60 And thou wouldest truly have been damned, by me, most surely, eternally forever and ever seen. For in Satan, thou art dead, unto me, already, as saith, thy eternal, kind God, forever.

Chapter 9 w 54 / verses   Pure love

1   My gracious, pure love, it is seen and felt, eternally forever and ever true, unto them. That are seen and known, by me (God), to be found unto me forever, through Christ the Son, as being forever true.

2   And they, in Christ Jesus, forever. They are seen, as seen and felt, forever true. As being, in me, through Christ, the Son, forever true.

3   And, as they are found, in Christ Jesus. Who is Christ Jesus, that is found, in my eternal, true love, forever.

4   These, they also, do know, the love and joy, that is me. As I Am found, as the oil of gladness and as great joy, forever true. And that pureness,

5   It is, seen in and of me, through Christ Jesus, as being eternally forever and ever seen. And that pureness, it is eternally forever true, for I Am that eternal, true pureness, that is seen purely forever.

6   My love, it is found, eternally through Christ Jesus, unto all men and unto all women, forever. And, I Am demonstrated through Christ Jesus, forever,

7   Even as, demonstrated unto the repentful forever. As heavenly pure love, found, through

Christ Jesus, in me, forever. And it is found, unto all, who are repentful unto me, as being forever true, in Christ Jesus, forever.

8 And I Am love, that is demonstrated, through themselves, as themselves, in Christ Jesus, forever. And it is demonstrated, when they, the repentful,

9 Do receive me in Christ Jesus, as this Christ Jesus, being their personal, seen true savior, as being forever true, and, forever more.

10 That pure love, that is, called Christ Jesus, who is found, in and through me, forever true. It is found, given of myself, forever true,

11 Unto the redeemed of the earth, forever. And that great love, that is me in Christ forever. It shall never depart, from Christ Jesus, eternally forever and ever true.

12 That true love, that is me forever, in Christ Jesus. It is most pure. And it is seen and felt, forever true. As found, given by me, through Christ Jesus, the Son, forever.

13 That love, is a living and undying, holy love. And that true love, it is a gracious, living forever, true life.

14 That true life, it is, called God and is, found demonstrated by me, through Christ Jesus, as being forever true.

15 And that true life, it is demonstrated, as God on earth, forever. And, without this forever eternal, living forever, true love, that is called God,

16 Then, ungodly, true sorrows, of just recompenses. They are surely given of me (God), eternally forever true, unto the unrepentiful, forever true.

17 And those just recompenses. They are given by me, through Christ Jesus, forever true. In Godly, unending, true recompense. That recompense, it is called death, as being forever true.

18 Therefore, as the unrepentiful, shall and do, reject me, as their personal true savior, who is called Christ Jesus, forever.

19 Then I shall burn, my great, wrathful and true judgments, back unto them, in punishment, that is called death and great destruction, forever.

20 And that eternal just judgment, it is given unto them, that do desire, unrepentiful true sin, forever. And that punishment, it is from me: "The God of truth," forever.

21 And, it is given, by me, through Christ Jesus, forever. And is given by me, forever. Unto all, who claim the name and mark, that is given of Satan, forever.

22 For they, are found, unto me, forever true. As being, Satan like, eternally forever and ever true, in themselves, forever.

23 Holy recompense is in great unending, forever eternal, living forever holy damnation.

24 When, these, the damned, are found unto me, in the beastly eternal true image. That is, called death, forever. These shall never know my love,

25 That is called Christ Jesus, forever. That is, if they shall never repent, unto me, forever and ever true of themselves. For without Christ Jesus, as Christ Jesus, being their, personal, chosen true savior, forever.

26 Then, they are seen unto me, forever. As being found unto me forever true, as being found in eternal true death, eternally forever true and forever more.

27 And, if they shall willingly, remain forever true, unto Satanism forever. Then, I shall give, utter true damnation, unto the unrepentiful, eternally forever.

28 And that true damnation, it is, called dead death, forever true. And it shall remain, faithful of me, forever true. Upon the head of the wicked, forever more.

29 That working true damnation, that is called death. It shall be, for all, true eternity, and forever. And it is forever true, unto them, that do desire, unrepentfully forever, to be as dead as Satan is dead unto me, forever.

30 For these, the damned, they desire not, the heavenly true salvation. That is found, in my eternal true Son, forever. And, who is called "Christ, the Son of the living God," forever.

31 Therefore, end time, righteous, holy just judgments. They are given of me (God), in holy, true recompense, forever. And these, eternal, just judgments, that are called life and death, forever.

32 They do, and shall, carry sorrow of heart and vexation. As found, given from me, through Christ Jesus, forever. And that, end time, righteous, holy just judgment,

33 It is given by me, faithfully forever true. Unto one's unrepentiful true spirit, as being eternally forever and ever true, from me, forever.

34 And, that is, a forever, Godly and true, just judgment. And that is, a granted just judgment,

found of me, forever. And is found of me, eternally forever,

35 And is found, as being, a true death, as being forever true. And, it is seen, as end time, just judgment. And those just judgments,

36 They do manifest them selves, forever true. And, they are seen, before me, (God). As my eternal, living forever, true presents.

37 As my (God) presents, is seen, in uttermost, most eternal, forever true, heavenly true judgment.

38 And that true judgment, it is concerning, life and death, as being forever true, saith thy eternal true maker, who is thy eternal true God, as being eternally forever true, and, forever more.

39 And, therefore, these, great, end time, last days, true judgments. They shall bring, all ungodly true nations, who desireth not Christ, unto end time judgment, forever.

40 And, in these, judged and being judged, eternal true nations. Repentance shall come forth, unto me, as being forever true, and, forever more.

41 That repentance, it is seen, as Godly forever and ever, true repentance. As found given unto me, forever. As found unto me, through accepting,

42 My eternal, living forever, true Son. Who is called Christ Jesus, as being forever true, and, forever more.

43 And this Christ Jesus, he is given of me (God), unto the earth, as being forever true. And this Christ Jesus, he is given by me, forever faithful, of me, forever true.

44 And Christ Jesus, he is given by me, forever true. As given true life, unto the redeemed forever. As heavenly true salvation. That salvation, it is found, in uttermost, heavenly true places, forever true.

45 Christ Jesus, he is given unto the repentful forever true. So that the repentful, may repent, of his or her, own true sins, forever true, and, forever more.

46 And seen sins, they are found, in eternal, living forever, true damnation. That true damnation, it is desired, by them, that perish, in eternal true death, forever.

47 And all, unrepentiful, desired true death. That is desired faithfully forever true, by the damned forever. It is found without Christ, forever true and forever more.

48 And, it is, most certainly, found. As being found, against my (God) eternal, living forever, great nature. As found, by me, forever true.

49 And it is, found and being found, by me, forever true and forever more. And it is, most surely, found by me, forever true. As concerning the damned, of the fallen true earth, as being forever true and forever seen.

50 And, through my living, eternal, true Son, who is called Christ Jesus, forever. End time Judgments, they are found, in the earth, as being forever true.

51 And those, end time, true judgments. They are, called life and death, forever. And those, eternal, just judgments,

52 They are given by me (God), O Israel, through this eternal one, who is called, Christ Jesus, as being faithfully, eternally forever and ever true.

53 And those, just judgments, they are given by me, faithfully forever true. Unto all, of thy, unrighteous and unholy, true enemies,

54 Who are thy ever lasting, true enemies, unjustly forever true. And that, do desire, thy ever lasting true destruction, forever true, O Israel.

Chapter 10 w/ 58 verses   End time judgments

1   End time judgments, they are called: "The Wrath Of The Eternal, Living Forever, True Son," And that true Son, he is called: "The Lamb Of God."

2   And this Lamb, he is my (God) Godly true Lamb, that is found of me, forever true. In my most holy, living forever, eternal true life.

3   And forever true life, it is found, in me (God). In my, uttermost, heavenly forever, eternal true presents, that is called life forever.

4   And that true presents, it is, also called: "Heavenly life, that is heavenly true life," forever.

5   And that true life, that is heavenly. And it shall always be ever lasting, and heavenly in me (God), as being forever and ever true, and, forever more.

6   In these, eternal, living forever, true days, they are found in my holy spirit. And I (God), the lord, of both, heaven and earth. I doth desire thee, forever true, O Israel.

7   And I do desire thee forever, even as a man, desireth, his only, true, ever lasting, true bride. When he doth search for her, in a spirit of

righteousness. In the days of his (man) fallen, true youth.

8 And, in these last days, that are found, in this, utterly fallen, unrepentiful, never to receive Christ, true earth. Is found, from me, forever,

9 Is found, end time, righteous, holy and just judgments. That are sent by me forever, into the fallen true earth, forever. And these, end time, just judgments,

10 They are **given,** faithfully of and by me (God), as being eternally forever true, and, as being eternally forever seen, and, forever felt. And they (just judgments called God) are given by me, faithfully forever true,

11 Unto the unrepentiful, true nations, forever. And they (unrepentiful, true nations) are found by me, as being eternally forever true,

12 As being in the worship of unrepentfulness, that is called, Satanism, as being eternally forever true.

13 And end time judgments, they are considered, as last days true judgments, forever true and forever more. And, they are, most certainly, found, given by me, forever,

14 As given of me faithfully forever true. As found given through my eternal, living forever,

true Son. Who is called "Christ," forever and ever true.

15 This **giving,** of me (God), through my own eternal true Son, who is called Christ Jesus. It is, that the giving of end time judgments,

16 They are given from me, as being eternally forever true. As given of me, forever certain, through Christ Jesus, as being eternally forever true.

17 As they (judgments) are given by me forever, unto the unrepentiful true nations. Who are seen in the earth, forever true. As unrepentiful true nations, that are seen and found, by me, forever true,

18 As they are found by me, forever, as being in blasphemous true sins, forever true and forever more. And end time, just judgments. They are given by me, through Christ Jesus, forever,

19 And, those, just judgments. They are given by me, faithfully unto the damned forever, who are found therefore in the eternal true image of blasphemous Satan's true Unrepentfulness, forever.

20 For these, that are the damned, as being eternally forever true nations, who are found by me, in eternal true blasphemy, forever. They are seen, as rebellious true nations,

21 Unto me forever. For they, are found, unto me, as being eternally forever true. As being dead unto me forever seen. And those, same, unrepentiful, seen true nations,

22 They are most certainly seen as eternal nations of blasphemy, forever true. And they are found by me, in eternal true death, forever true.

23 And they, do not, desire, to ever have, Christ Jesus. As Christ Jesus, being their, personal, true savior, forever true. And Christ Jesus, he is sent by me, into the earth, forever.

24 And this Christ Jesus, he is sent, with my eternal, and most true, salvation. That is Christly true salvation, that is, called God forever found, in Christ Jesus, forever.

25 And this Christ Jesus, he is found by me, given unto them, that perish forever true. And this Christ Jesus, he is given by me, forever,

26 Unto them, that perish, that they may repent unto me, as being eternally forever true, in Christ the Son, as being eternally forever seen.

27 And that, by calling upon me, for salvation, that is found given of me, through Christ Jesus, forever. That they, the repentful in Christ Jesus, that they may live, unto me, forever true and forever more.

28 And that they, the repentful in Christ Jesus, that they may live unto me forever true. In all that I Am, as I Am, eternally forever true and forever more.

29 But unto them that do desire me not in Christ Jesus, forever. They are, already dead unto me forever true. And, my holy recompense. It is, given by me, through Christ Jesus, as being eternally forever true.

30 And that holy true recompense, it is called death forever. And it is given by me, faithfully forever true. Unto them, that do desire to be forever true, in unrepentiful true iniquity, as being eternally forever seen.

31 Therefore, end time judgment, it is due forever true, as Godly recompense, unto the unrepentiful true nations, forever true and forever seen.

32 Because these unrepentiful true nations, do not desire Christ as their savior, who is Christ Jesus that is given and sent by me, forever true.

33 Those same nations, they shall die unto me as being eternally forever true, and, they are forever seen, as dead unto all, that I Am, as life forever true.

34 And those, same nations. They shall, most surely, not eternally live forever true, with me

(God), forever, in that heavenly true salvation, that cometh down from me (God), eternally forever and ever true.

35 That salvation, it is a seen eternal true salvation, that is called: "CHRIST JESUS," as being eternally forever true.

36 For, if those, same nations, shall not desire Christ. As Christ Jesus, being their personal savior, forever.

37 Then I (God), the lord of heaven and earth, as being eternally forever true. I shall destroy these unrepentiful true ones, from the earth, as being eternally forever sure, and, forever true.

38 And I, the lord of heaven and of all that is and all that shall be forever,

39 I do dwell forever and ever, and I do dwell eternally forever true. In most eternal, forever true, true holy true righteousness, as being eternally forever true.

40 And my true righteousness, it is a holy forever true righteousness. And that true righteousness, it is given of me (God). As being eternally given, of me, as being forever true righteousness.

41 That true righteousness, it is seen and felt, forever true. As holy forever true, true

righteousness. That true righteousness, it is called, God.

42 And it is forever and ever true, true righteousness. And, it is forever seen. And I Am God forever certain, and for all of true eternity, and, forever more.

43 And, I Am holy forever and ever true, and forever seen. And I shall live, forever true, for I Am the forever, that is forever seen, as God in the fallen true earth, forever.

44 And my true righteousness, as found in Christ Jesus, forever. It is given of me, unto them of the fallen true earth, as forever true and forever more.

45 And that righteousness, in Christ Jesus, forever. It is given of me, as eternally forever and faithfully given, by me, through Christ Jesus, unto the repentful,

46 And the repentful ones, they do desire, this Christ Jesus, as eternally forever and ever seen. And the righteousness of me, as it be found, in Christ Jesus, forever,

47 It is given by me, unto the repentful true ones, forever. And it is given by me, for all of true eternity. And it is given by me, as eternally forever true,

48   And it is given, as eternally forever true righteousness, that is, called God forever. And it is seen, as being eternally forever true, and it is forever seen, as being, ever lasting, forever true, in me, forever seen.

49   And that righteousness, it is given by me, through Christ Jesus, as forever true. And it is given, by me, unto them, of the fallen true earth,

50   As being eternally forever true. And it is given, by me, through Jesus Christ, as being eternally forever, truly seen.

51   And that true righteousness, that is called God in Christ Jesus, as forever true. It is, sent by me through Christ Jesus, unto them, that do love me (God) and do love, my (God) soon appearing, forever.

52   And that true appearing, it is, shortly to come to the earth, as being eternally forever true, and, as forever more.

53   And, it is seen, as ever lastingly forever true, and faithfully forever true. And it shall occur, quickly, in this generation, of end time signs, eternally forever.

54   I and Christ my Son. We shall appear, together as one and the same forever. And we shall appear, soon. For the living and the dead, of this fallen, true earth, forever.

55 And moreover, this Christ Jesus, he is my eternal, living forever, true Son, who is called Christ, as being eternally forever true, and, forever more. And this same Christ Jesus,

56 He shall, execute true judgment, that is, called God in the earth and true mercy, in the earth, forever. And that true mercy, it is my mercy,

57 As found, given of myself, forever true. As given of myself through Christ Jesus, forever true and forever seen and forever known. And my mercy,

58 It is given of myself, as freely given of myself, as I Am God forever true. And, it is given, by me, through Christ Jesus, unto the earth, forever true and ever lasting, forever true.

Chapter 11 w / 53 verses   Unending day

1 My (God) eternal, living forever, true Son. Who is, called Christ Jesus, forever. He shall, soon appear, with the ever most given, true glory,

2 That eternal, just glory. That is, to come. It is me and is of me (God), forever faithful and true. And it shall occur, for them,

3 Who are found faithful, at that true time, in the fallen true earth. Who are found faithful in

Christ, unto me forever. In that great unending true day,

4   That is, a true day, that is seen. As being a eternal true day, that is given of me, as being forever true. And that true day, it is found,

5   As most eternal, holy true truth, as found in me (God), as being eternally forever true and faithfully forever true.

6   Let all understand, as being eternally forever true and forever more. That, this heavenly true Christ, he is made, of my (God) eternal, true hand, as found as Godly true life, as being forever true.

7   And, this Christ Jesus, he is found in me, forever. And, he is, a forever true, living, forever, eternal true truth, forever seen.

8   And this, Christ Jesus, he is seen, in the earth, as being eternally forever true and forever seen, as I Am seen, forever,

9   And this Christ Jesus, he is seen, as a seen truth, who is seen of me, as forever true, and, is forever seen. And Christ Jesus, he is a seen life, from me, as being eternally forever true,

10   And this Christ Jesus, he is seen, as forever true, in me, as forever seen, and forever true.

And, Christ Jesus, he is seen, and felt, as God, as forever sure, and true,

11 And this Christ, he is forever true and forever seen, as I Am God, and as I Am forever seen and I Am true forever.

12 And, this true Christ Jesus, he seen of me, as an undying, ever lasting, righteous true hand. That true hand, it is found, in and of me,

13 As a hand of myself, found in eternal true life, forever. And this Christ Jesus, he is seen, as and is, called God, as being eternally forever true.

14 And this, is because, I walk in Christ Jesus. As I Am God forever true, in Christ Jesus, my Son, as being eternally forever true.

15 And, this Christ, he is found faithful, in me, forever true. And this Christ, he shall always be found faithful, in me forever true.

16 And this Christ Jesus, he is always, in me forever true. And this Christ Jesus, he is, forever true. And he, is, a eternal true truth, of me forever true.

17 And this Christ Jesus, he is found, given of me forever true. And this Christ Jesus, he is seen, as being true and forever seen, as I Am life, as I Am forever true.

18 Christ Jesus, he is my hand, as called life, as given by me, as forever true. And this Christ Jesus, he is true, unto all repentful,

19 Who (Christians) are found in the fallen true earth, as forever true, and, as forever seen. And I Am forever seen, in those loved ones (Christians), who are called Christ Jesus, forever.

20 And this Christ, he is eternal, as forever most, never ending, heavenly true salvation. That true salvation, it is called God, as found given of myself (God), into Christ Jesus, as forever certain and forever true and forever more,

21 That true salvation, called life in God forever. It is, a true, heavenly forever, eternal true salvation, that is God in Christ Jesus, forever.

22 And that true salvation, it is, a eternal, living forever, true salvation, that is seen and called God. And, it is found, in Christ Jesus, as being eternally forever true.

23 And that heavenly, faithful, and seen, true salvation. That is, called God in Christ, forever faithful and true forever.

24 It is, seen, as an ever lasting, eternal true salvation of life and holiness, that is called God as being eternally forever certain forever true.

25   That true salvation, it is called life in me forever. And it is, a true salvation, from me, as being eternally forever true and faithful,

26   As I Am the faithful true life, that is called man (those that are seen and found repentful in Christ Jesus forever) forever.

27   And that true life, it is found in Christ Jesus, forever. And is found, faithful, from me, as I Am thy God, as being eternally forever true and faithful forever.

28   And this Christ, he is found of me, unto all who are found unto me forever true, as being repentful, unto me forever true. As found unto me forever true and forever more.

29   And these, the faithful forever, they are found unto me forever true, as found faithful unto me, through Christ Jesus, forever true.

30   And this, is eternally forever true, saith thy God, eternally forever and ever faithful, truly forever true.

31   My salvation, it is seen, forever true. As a, undying, true, heavenly true, eternal true salvation. That true salvation, it is, Christ Jesus, as he is found in me, as I Am God, as I Am forever true.

32 And that true salvation, it is, called Christ Jesus, forever. And that true salvation. It shall never cease, from before me (God), as being eternally forever and ever true, saith thy eternal, true maker, of men, forever true.

33 That true salvation, it is, called Christ Jesus, as being eternally forever certain, in me, as being eternally forever true and forever more.

34 And, it is, seen. As I Am God, forever true and forever given of myself, as life, unto repentful true men, forever true.

35 Again, that true salvation, it is, most surely, eternal in me. As I Am found, by the repentful. As I Am found, through Christ Jesus, forever certain,

36 As a found, true life, that is, given of myself, unto all repentful, true men, forever true. As eternally forever true. And I Am truly given true life,

37 As I Am found of myself, given through Christ, the Son, who is called: "God forever true," unto them that love me in Christ Jesus forever.

38 For they truly do serve me faithfully forever true, in Christ Jesus, forever. And they truly do love me, as I Am God, as being eternally forever, and, as I Am love, forever.

39 Christ Jesus, he is my own eternal true Son, who is born of my spirit and is born of a virgin. And this Christ Jesus, was not conceived, through sinful true men, as being forever true of sinful true men, forever.

40 But Christ Jesus, was conceived through my spirit, as I Am the creator forever. Therefore, Christ Jesus, was not conceived in the fashion of sinful men, when sinful men are making life, by their natural true course of life, that is made through the will of men, forever.

41 This Christ, he is eternal, of me and by my spirit, as being eternal life, that is found, as true life, as being eternally forever true. And this Christ Jesus, as having put on the garments, that is, called God forever true.

42 He is, therefore, found unto me. As I Am found faithful unto man, forever true and forever certain. And this Christ, he is sent into the earth, with salvation, that is called, God in man, forever.

43 And this Christ, he is dressed, as heavenly and eternally forever true. As dressed in my righteousness and likeness, forever.

44 Christ is forever. And this Christ Jesus, he sent of me, as being eternally forever certain, with all that I Am, as given of myself, as I Am given of myself, as I Am forever true.

45 And this Christ, he is seen faithful unto me, in all that is called God and is granted, as me, forever true.

46 Christ is, seen, as being eternally forever true. And Christ Jesus, he is seen, as eternal of me, as I Am forever certain. And Christ Jesus, he is seen, as being eternally forever faithful, in me, forever.

47 And this Christ, he is a living forever, eternal forever, true forever, unending true salvation. That true salvation, it is called God, forever,

48 And that true salvation, is called God forever. And it is seen as most eternal, as me, as being eternally forever certain.

49 And this Christ, he is seen, as granted true life, that is called God, as being eternally forever true. And, I Am, the life and breath, as found in Christ Jesus, forever.

50 And that true life, it is granted by me, through Jesus Christ, forever. And it is granted by me, as being eternally forever true, unto all repentful true men, as being eternally forever certain and forever more.

51 And that true life, it is my given true salvation. And it is, most surely, seen from me, as being eternally forever true. As a granted true

life, that is granted unto repentful true men, forever.

52 And this Christ Jesus, he is found faithful, in me. As found of me, as given of myself, as being eternally forever true and forever more.

53 And this Christ, he is given by me, as a granted and given true life, unto the repentful, as being eternally forever true.

Chapter 12 w / 52 verses   I Am the life

1 And I, the lord of heaven and earth, forever. I Am the life of the repentful, as found through Christ Jesus. And that, is forever true and forever more.

2 And this Christ Jesus, he is given of me, as faithfully forever true, of me forever certain and forever true.

3 And this Christ (Jesus Christ), he is found, as I Am found, as eternal true truth forever. And this Christ, he is found in me forever true. Even as seen eternal true life,

4 That seen true life, it is heavenly and ever lastingly, forever true. In all that is me, as I Am found in Christ Jesus, forever.

5 And I Am given of myself, forever true, unto Christ Jesus, as life, that is life given unto

repentful true men, as being eternally forever true. And that true life, it is given unto the repentful forever true.

6   And that life, it is found and seen, as Christly true life. And, it is called God, as being eternally forever true, and, forever more.

7   Christly eternal, living forever, true salvation. It is, called Christ, in me, as being eternally forever true and forever seen.

8   And, that seen life. It is seen, and felt. As found in the most eternal, and ever lasting, true righteousness. That true righteousness, it is me (God), as being forever and ever true.

9   And that true, ever lasting true righteousness. It is a ever lasting and eternally forever, true truthfulness, called God. And it is seen and felt,

10   In Christ Jesus, as being eternally forever true. And that righteousness, it is found in me, forever. And I Am, that I Am, as being eternally forever true.

11   And my true righteousness, that is found of me, in Christ Jesus, forever. It is found as given true salvation. That is also salvation that is called, Christ unto the earth, as being eternally forever and ever true.

12 And this true Christ, he (Jesus Christ) is, eternally forever and ever true, in me. For I Am the eternal, loving, kind God. As found, forever, truly given of myself, in Christ Jesus, as being eternally forever true,

13 And I, Am the life, that is given, of myself, forever true. In Christ, the Son, forever true. And I Am given, as eternal true life, forever true. Unto the repentful forever true.

14 And I Am given, even as most forever and ever, true life. That is life, that is found, in all, that is made by me, as being eternally forever true,

15 And that is created, in my true righteousness, and likeness, as being eternally forever seen, and I Am seen, forever.

16 Christ is, truly eternally forever and ever, truly eternal. Even as, ever lasting, eternal true salvation. That doth, proceed, from me (God),

17 Who (God) is seen and felt, as being eternally forever and ever true. And I Am God, and I Am forever seen, and, forever true.

18 Christ, is, Christly eternal, true salvation. And that true salvation, it is heavenly, as eternally forever true. And, as found, given of me, in Christ Jesus, forever.

19 And it is seen, as found, in most eternal, forever true, holy true truth. That true truth, it is seen and felt, from me. As I Am, faithfully with eternal, Christly true life, as being eternally forever true.

20 And that, Christly, true life, called God in Christ Jesus. It is, given, as life, that is called God as being eternally forever true.

21 And that life, it is given of me, through Christ Jesus, unto them, that do, desire me, as being eternally forever true. As I Am found, in Christ Jesus, as I Am seen, as being eternally forever and ever true.

22 Christ Jesus, he is eternal, living forever, heavenly true truth. And that truth, it is, found, given of me, as being eternally forever certain, as, "Eternal, Living, Heavenly True Truth," forever.

23 And that true truth, it is, seen, of and from me. As I Am found of my (God) own, true, eternal, forever and ever, true, unending forever, true presents. That true presents, it is found, in "Most Eternal, Forever, Godly True Life."

24 Eternal, living, forever true, Godly true life. It is, seen, as, "Most Eternal, Unending Forever, And Ever True Life," as being eternally forever true, and, forever more.

25 But, by one's true choice, to not be found in Christ the Son, forever. Then those unrepentiful true nations and their true peoples and their true tongues, that do refuse, Christ Jesus, forever,

26 Then, they are therefore, without my presents, that is called Christ Jesus, forever true and forever without remedy, truly forever. And they, are all, considered of (of means the word by) and by me, as forever true. As being, seen and known,

27 As unrepentiful true peoples, and unrepentiful true nations. Who are considered, by me, forever true. To be unrepentfully forever true. In being unrepentfully truly sinful, forever true and forever more.

28 And they shall, therefore, die unto me, for all of given true eternity, that is called "God forever."

29 And these unrepentiful true peoples and unrepentiful true nations, they shall most certainly, perish in their own unrepentiful true sins, forever.

30 And they shall perish, for all of given true eternity. For those desired in themselves, forever, true sins. As they are seen by me, as being against me (God), as being eternally forever true, in sin forever,

31 And they, do purposely choose to not receive Christ Jesus, as Christ Jesus being their savior, forever true. And they, do therefore, choose to not live in me, as I Am seen as Christ Jesus, forever.

32 They truly do not desire, uttermost true salvation. That is salvation, that is found given of me (God), in my eternal true Son, who is called, Christ Jesus, forever.

33 And these, unrepentiful, true peoples and unrepentiful true nations. They are most certainly, desirethsome, in themselves, as being eternally forever true,

34 In not ever desiring to receive Christ Jesus, who is Christ Jesus, that is seen and known. As my eternal, living forever, true Son.

35 This is, because, that these unrepentiful true nations and unrepentiful true peoples, that do perish. It is from their own, personal, desired, unrepentiful true seen sins,

36 That are unrepentiful true sins, in desiring to not ever accept Christ, in the heavenly true salvation, that is my salvation.

37 That salvation, it is called God for all of given true eternity and forever more. And, it is, my given, true salvation, that is given and sent,

by me (God), as being eternally forever true, as Christ Jesus, forever.

38 And is seen, as eternally forever, truly sent, by me, forever true. And is sent, as Jesus Christ, forever. And is, most certainly, true, in me and of me, forever.

39 And Jesus Christ, he is seen and felt, as most certainly, seen salvation, that is called God forever true. And Christ Jesus, is ever lastingly eternally forever true, in me, forever.

40 Christ Jesus, is even, true, as I Am forever true. For I Am, true eternity. And that true eternity, it is without true end, forever true and forever more.

41 And those, unrepentiful, non Christian, true nations, and those unrepentiful, true, non Christian true peoples, who do perish, forever true.

42 They do not, as eternally forever, ever desire within themselves. To ever receive Christ Jesus. As Christ Jesus, being their seen savior, as being forever true.

43 And, that is a result, of their blindness, to not ever want, to see truth. That is my seen truth, and, my seen righteousness. As it found, given of me, as forever true.

44 And, as to what, is given of myself, forever. It is, my, holy true commandments. That are found, given by me, forever true. And is, concerning forever, true matters, that are concerning, life and death, as being forever true, and, forever more.

45 This blindness, that is found, in them, that perish eternally forever and ever true. It is, found, from their own, personal, living forever, sinful and true, true beastliness. That true beastliness, it is, called, death, as being eternally forever true.

46 And, to live in beastliness, that is called death. It is seen, as eternal, living forever, unrepentiful, desired, true beastly, beguiling true sinfulness.

47 That true beguiling, it is, given, from Satan, who is their spiritual true father. And who is their spiritual true father,

48 Who is found, in earnest and sincere, true death, as being eternally forever true. And they, truly, do desire, to be, without me, forever true.

49 And they, the unrepentiful, they truly do, proceed from Satan, the false prophet, forever true. And they, are of them, that are found in the image, that is this fallen true earth, forever true,

50 That is the earth, as seen, as being beastly and hardened against God, forever. And the earth, as a fallen true image, that is called, desired true death, by the damned, forever.

51 That image, is found, by our true God forever. As being, forever, true in earnest and sincere, true death, forever. And it is found, in uttermost, true, unrepentiful true sins, forever true.

52 And these, the damned, that are found. They are found, as being a Antichrist true image, as found, given by Satan, unto all men, forever. And it is death, forever and is without true end, in sin, forever.

Chapter 13 w/ 42 verses   That glory

1 Therefore, the only escape, from that image of Satanism, that is called death, forever. It is given of me (God) forever. As partaking of Christ Jesus, as Christ Jesus, being one's true savior, forever.

2 Christ Jesus, he is sent, with salvation, from me forever. And Christ Jesus, he is of the uttermost true glory, that is called man.

3 For that glory, called man. It was found in me, before Adam thy forefather, had fell and had transgressed the great commandment, that is concerning life, forever true.

4   And through Christ Jesus, forever. That glory, it is found, in the repentful true ones, forever true and forever made. As given of me, as faithfully forever true, of me forever.

5   And that glory, it is of me, as found of me, forever true. In the repentful, who are found as Christians, in Christ Jesus. Who are, now seen, as eternal man (men), forever.

6   And that glory, in Christ, that is of me, as I Am, thy true Father, forever. It shall never end, in me, forever true. And is eternally forever and ever true, in me, as I Am God, forever true.

7   And Christ, he is ever true life, that is found given of me, forever certain and forever true. And that life, it is found through me. For I Am, the Father of most forever and ever, true life.

8   That life, it is heavenly forever, true life. That is seen, as Godly true life. And is forever found, in me (God). As found, utterly forever and ever, true life.

9   That life, it is called God forever true. Even unto man, as faithfully forever and ever true, saith thy eternal and most holy, true God,

10 And I Am eternally forever faithful and true. Even as forever seen and forever known. And I Am known, as God, eternally forever true. And I

Am he, who is thy breath and life, that liveth forever true.

11 And I do live forever, for I Am the forever. And in me, is life. And I Am the life, saith thy eternal kind God, who is seen and found. As being seen. As being seen of earnest and sincere, true life, forever true.

12 And moreover, I Am, the precious eternal, living forever and ever, true Father. And I Am, the uttermost given forever true life. That life, it is found in Christ, forever.

13 And Christ, he liveth forever true, in me forever true. And Christ Jesus, he is seen. As my eternal, true Son. Who is with eternal true life, that is called God forever true and forever seen.

14 And, I Am seen in Christ, of myself, forever true. As "The God Of Truth."

15 And those, that refuse Christ Jesus, as Christ Jesus being their savior, as forever seen.

16 They are seen, by me, forever true. As "They, who are:" Unrepentiful true peoples and unrepentiful true nations, that shall die unto me forever true. If they deny themselves, to convert unto me, in Christ Jesus, as forever true.

17 And if they shall refuse to receive Christ Jesus, as CHRIST Jesus being their savior,

forever true. Then I shall move upon their seed forever, in death eternally forever true.

18 And I shall cause thy rivers and thy lakes and all that is found as thy land, to subdue thee in death forever, unless thou convert unto me in Christ Jesus, forever.

19 And if thou shalt not convert in Christ unto me forever, then most surely, thy days be numbered unto thee, and thou shalt receive from me, forever, eternal true death, forever. And death, is also granted, unto thy seed, eternally forever.

20 And thou shalt not enjoy thy sinful and unrepentiful true life, in this beguiling true world, that is Satanism unto me forever. For I Am thy maker and eternal judge, forever. And I have and will judge thee, forever.

21 Know ye this, that thou shalt most surely shall die unto me forever, whomsoever thou art, that desirest to not repent for desiring to never receive Christ Jesus, as thy savior forever true.

22 Even now, judgment awaiteth thee, o unrepentiful one, who is found as Satanism, in this sinful true world, forever. And Satanism, it is found unto me, as forever true. In unrepentiful true sin, forever sure.

23 And the stars of heaven, they (the stars) shall change their sizes and eternal true shapes, forever true, unto thee forever. And they, those stars of heaven, they shall seek thee out to destroy thee, forever. If thou shalt not hear me, as I Am found as Christ Jesus, forever.

24 Even thy seas, shall destroy thee, o unrepentiful, non Christian true nations, That are found in unrepentfulness forever true.

25 And though thou shalt cry greatly unto the Christian nations, for survival, as relief from my (God) judgments, that are called life and death, forever.

26 I (God) will limit their hands, in doing so, if those Christian nations, be found unto thee, as helping thee to remain permanently forever, without Christ Jesus, as Christ Jesus, being thy savior, forever true.

27 And those Christian nations, they shall suffer, even greatly, if needed, if they be found, as to be purposely be refraining from my commandment, forever. That is concerning thee O unrepentiful true nation of rebelliousness, forever.

28 And those Christian nations shall suffer, if needed according to their sin, found in not doing my commandant concerning thee O unrepentiful true nation.

29 And they (Christian nations) shall suffer, until those Christian nations, shall conform unto all that is written of me, forever, that is written and being written, concerning thee, O unrepentiful true nation of sin, forever true.

30 Therefore, if thou doth refuse Christ Jesus, as Christ Jesus being thy savior forever, then thou shalt be unto me forever true,

31 As those that do perish, eternally forever true. And thou shalt be lost, unto me, forever true and forever more. If thou, convert not unto me, in Christ Jesus, forever. As Christ Jesus, being thy savior, from me, forever true.

32 And, most surely, O Israel, I do see those unrepentiful true nations, that are seen by me forever true. As being unrepentiful true peoples and unrepentiful true nations, who will not accept my eternal Son, who is called Christ Jesus.

33 And I do see those nations, O Israel, that will never choose thee, as thou being their rightful and true brother, forever true. And I will, most surely, destroy them forever sure and thou shalt enjoy me, as I Am thy God, in Christ Jesus, forever sure and faithfully forever true.

34 Therefore, those unrepentiful, ungodly, true nations. Who are without Christ. As Christ, being not their savior, forever. They do forever perish, unto me faithfully forever true and forever more.

35 And those unrepentiful true nations and unrepentiful true peoples and true tongues, that are found by me, in unrepentfulness, forever true and forever seen.

36 They are seen and are, even considered of me forever. Even as whose coming is after the workings of Satan, forever true.

37 For this generation of the earth, forever true. It is seen, as the days of Noah, to me forever. And are, therefore, found unto me. As whose coming is after the workings of Satan,

38 And that is eternally forever and ever true, saith thy God, forever certain and forever seen, by me, eternally forever and ever true.

39 Again, those nations of unrepentfulness of the fallen true earth forever. They are seen unto me, forever true. As those nations that are found in this Noah's day, type world, that thou currently liveth in, upon the earth, in these days of the fallen true earth, forever.

40 And those unrepentiful true nations, they are non Christian nations of the earth forever. And those unrepentiful ones, they are seen. As being a functional and true part of the beastly image,

41 That is an image called death, that is against me forever true. And it is called a unholy true

image, found in earnest, sincere, true death, forever true.

42 And that beastly image, it is found, in these days, that are of the fallen true earth, forever. And these days, they are considered, as Biblically found in the new Testament, as written, as whose coming is after the workings of Satan.

Chapter 14 w / 54 verses   The beast

1 One must understand, that image has been in the earth, ever since man fell in the garden of Eden. And that while, that image has remained and has continued, in the earth, forever.

2 It is seen, that since the days of Noah, that those days would return in the earth, as the earth being filled with violence against his neighbor, and thoughts of his heart being aimed at being evil, continually forever.

3 Those returning like days of hardened bestiality. Those days are considered to be forever true. As days like Noah's generation, that is seen,

4 As unrepentiful true men and unrepentiful true women and unrepentiful true nations, as they are found in the fallen true earth, forever.

5   In other words, unrepentfulness as the days of Noah, would return to the earth, and would arise in the earth, to the point, that the earth would have to be judged, in end time judgments, forever.

6   And this is because, of fallen unrepentiful true men, that they would chose to never depart from the hardness of heart, that is found,

7   As being eternally unrepentfully and sinfully, against all, that is and is called God, as being eternally forever true.

8   Therefore, mankind has bought himself, to these days, of the earth. That are called "As the days of Noah." And man is now being judged by me (God), in these days, that are of the earth. That is called," "As the days of Noah."

9   And because of these days, mankind shall cease to exist, in his seen sins, forever. Therefore, Christ shall soon come to the earth, and gather the faithful in Christ, unto me (God), forever true.

10   And thou, O little one (Israel), who is in Christ Jesus, forever. Thou shalt, meet me and Christ, in the sky, in that true day. That is a day, that doth, come quickly, to the earth, forever.

11 And, again, unrepentiful beastly true people and beastly true, unrepentiful true nations, that are found in today's true world.

12 They were foretold to occur. And these, Noah type days, they are known, as "That Coming." And these, Noah type days, they are most certainly, seen,

13 As being the days, that are today's, unrepentiful true people and unrepentiful true nations. That are known, as the timeline period of the earth. That is called "The End Of The Days."

14 The word **coming,** in the new Testament, that is found in Second Thessalonians 2:9. It is found, in meaning, that is in reference to the coming of the Days, that like unto the days of Noah, that my (God) Son Christ, had spoken of, to occur, in Matthew 24:37.

15 Those of the earth, they should know, that their day. It is consider, as the days of Noah. For this, present, sinful true world. It is found, in reference to Matthew 24:37 and in Luke 21:25,

16 And these days, they are, most certainly, in reference, to the term: "The times of the gentiles be filled." Those **times** of days, they were fulfilled, in 1967 AD.

17 Then, the beginning for the days, that are called sea and waves roaring, then had began, starting in and from, 1967 AD.

18 That is, in meaning, that the times, of gentiles, are filled. For the term: "Sea and waves roaring." That term, sea and waves roaring, it cannot start, until the times of the gentiles, had first, been filled.

19 Those days, that are concerning the times of the gentiles. They were filled, in 1967 AD. And these days, of the fallen true earth. They are, most certainly, like unto the days, that are like unto the days, that Noah had experienced, in his time of the earth, forever.

20 Therefore, unrepentiful true man (mankind), found in these days of the fallen true earth, is considered being like unto the Days of Noah,

21 That are unrepentiful true days, found presently in this fallen unrepentiful true earth. For many do desire, to not ever repent unto me,

22 As being eternally forever true, as they be seen by Christ the Son, as being eternally forever true and forever more, in their chosen sins, forever.

23 Therefore, they bring unto themselves, forever true. Swift true destruction, that is given

unto them, from me, forever. And it is, most surely, from me, forever true and forever more,

24 And that true destruction, it is given of me, through Christ Jesus, unto them, as being eternally forever true. For they loved, being a part, of the unrepentiful true beast. That is called death, as forever true, and, forever sure.

25 And death, it is given, unto those, unrepentiful true ones, forever. And is, because they, the unrepentiful ones. They chose not to receive Christ Jesus, as forever true of themselves, forever.

26 And they most certainly, have not chosen this eternal, true Christ Jesus, as this Christ, being their personal, seen savior, from me, as being, forever true, saith thy true God, as eternally forever and ever faithful, and truly, forever true.

27 Moreover, those of this fallen against God unrepentiful true world. They shall be eternally forever truly lost, except that they truly repent,

28 Unto me forever. By receiving, Christ Jesus, as this Christ Jesus, being their seen savior, from me, as being eternally forever true.

29 And, if they repent not, then they shall remain, in the beastly, eternal, true image. That is the image of the fallen, who are found by me, as being forever true,

30 In the image, that is called, beastly eternal, dying true death, eternally forever. And, that, unrepentiful, eternal true image. That is made by Satan, and, by the damned, as being eternally forever true.

31 It is seen, as a blasphemous eternal true image, that is the beast, that is called unrepentiful true men, as forever true. And it is, an image,

32 As found by me, as being forever estranged to me, as themselves in earnest and sincere, true death, as being eternally forever true,

33 Instead of themselves, as being found in my true righteousness and my true spirit, as being eternally forever true, saith thy eternal kind God, as being eternally forever seen, and, forever so.

34 And they, that enjoy the spiritual fallen true mark, that is of the fallen true name, that is seen as being of Satan's true unrepentfulness. It is found, in being forever true, in sin, forever seen.

35 And that true mark, it is found, in them, the damned, as being eternally forever seen by me and forever true. And they, the damned, they are truly, of the spiritual true mark, that is of Satan himself, as being forever true,

36 And these, the damned. They are found in that measured true unrepentfulness, that is called measured true death, as forever seen.

37 And they, they are truly, measured, as eternally, truly lost unto me, as forever true. Unless, they repent, quickly unto me. As then, being found, in Christ Jesus, as being eternally forever true, and, as forever seen.

38 Again, they must, come out of their, measured true sinfulness, that is called unrepentfulness forever true. And they must receive me, as Christ,

39 As being eternally forever true. Least they die unto me forever true, in their measured, against God, unrepentfulness, true sin, forever.

40 If they, shall not repent, of their seen eternal true trespassing, that is given of themselves, against me, as being eternally forever true.

41 Then they (the damned) shall die, without Christ, forever, saith thy eternal true maker, who is, called life and breath, as being eternally forever true.

42 That image of the beast, it is unrepentiful true men and unrepentiful true women, forever. And that blasphemous eternal seen true image,

43 It is seen, as being eternally forever true, as Satanism, as eternally forever true.

44 And they, the damned. They, truly do, enjoy, Satan their false idol God, that they have taken

unto themselves, as being forever true, as sin forever,

45 And, as being eternally forever true, as being eternally truly fallen, as unrepentiful true sin, forever more.

46 For they, the damned, they truly do enjoy, taking Satanism unto them selves, as being eternally forever true, as Satan being their false idol God, forever,

47 And they have became unto me forever. As being seen and found, as being blasphemous, unrepentiful, true sin, forever.

48 And, without Christ, as Christ Jesus being seen savior, forever. Then, these blasphemous eternal true ones, as being seen unto me, in death.

49 They are then, therefore, found unto me forever. In dead death, as being eternally forever seen, as eternal death, forever.

50 And they, shall not enjoy hell, and, they shall be cast into hell, as being eternally forever true. For their seen sin, it is seen by me,

51 As I Am found in Christ, the Son, forever. And their seen sin, it remaineth in them, as eternally forever and ever true.

52 And these, without Christ Jesus, they have. Most certainly, chosen Satan and Satan's true ways. And that true choice, it is seen, as being found, unto me,

53 As forever found, as being found, in unrepentfulness, as being eternally forever seen. And, it is seen, as being, against me (God), as being forever true, and, as, forever more.

54 These the damned, they should have believed, all that I have spoken to them, as spoken to them, forever. As it is eternally found spoken to them, by me, through Christ Jesus, as being eternally forever true, and, forever more.

Chapter 15 w/ 90 verses   Unrepentiful sin

1 Eternal, living, unrepentiful, true sinfulness. It is, seen. As being: "Damningly, unrepentiful, true sinfulness," And it is, forever true, as death, forever.

2 And that, unrepentiful, true sinfulness. It is found, in eternal, true death, forever certain and forever more.

3 And, it is, most surely, found. As being eternal unto me forever true. As being, true eternal, true death, as being eternally forever Seen,"

4   And it is seen, as granted true death, that is eternally eternal, greatly forever seen.

5   And is, eternal, unrepentiful, true sin. That is seen and felt, in the damned, forever true. And is, seen and felt. As dead death, forever true.

6   And it is found, as unrepentiful true sin. That is eternally forever true. In being blasphemous unto me, as being eternally forever seen and known, to me, given by the damned, forever.

7   And, living, true sinfulness. It is found, as being a unrepentiful true sinfulness. That is always, found eternally forever true. As being, sinfully,

8   Found in being against me (God). As I Am found, as I Am God, as I forever true, and, forever seen. And I Am seen, as eternal true life, as being eternally forever true.

9   All, beastly true peoples and beastly true nations. That are found, in and of the earth, as being eternally forever true. And they, do follow,

10   Unrepentiful true sin, forever. And each, of them, forever. They are considered by me, as being eternally forever true,

11   As being, of eternal true evilness. And, they are, found unto me, as being eternally forever

certain, and, forever true. As being found unto me,

12 As being true, in most eternal, living forever, heavenly unrepentiful true sin, forever.

13 And, all evilness, is unrepentiful true sin. And it is, most certainly, found. In this fallen, unrepentiful, true world, as being eternally forever true.

14 And it is found, as being, found. In eternal true blasphemy, forever true and forever seen. And it is seen, as eternal, granted, true death,

15 As being forever true. And, it is seen, as true blasphemy. That is, called death, forever true.

16 And true blasphemy, is a granted true death, made by the damned forever true and it is forever seen. As being, a eternal true separation. To be away from me, forever true and forever more.

17 And I do see those things. That are concerning the damned forever true. As being eternally forever seen, in my (God), heavenly, seeing true presents. That is called life forever true and forever seen.

18 And that seeing forever true presents, of me (God), as being eternally forever true. It is found, in the most heavenly forever true life. And that heavenly, true life,

19 It is forever seen, as Godly true life. That is found, as given from me and is in me (God). As being eternally forever and ever true.

20 And that true life, it is forever seen. And it is forever seen, as forever true and forever me.

21 And though, I do give Godly true life, unto the repentful forever true. Those who chose to remain, as seen. As being unrepentful to me, in this world of sinfulness.

22 They are, most surely, found, within the image, that is called: "Ungodly, unrepentiful, true nations", and it's unrepentiful, true peoples."

23 And they shall die unto me forever true, and they shall die unto me without true end, in hell forever. And they are found within the blasphemous eternal true image of death.

24 And, as they are found unto me, in that image of death. They shall remain forever, within their seen, unrepentiful true nature,

25 That is found without me (God) and is found without my eternal true Son, who is called Christ Jesus, as being eternally forever true.

26 And all true people of the earth, who are found in that true image of blasphemous eternal true death, forever. They shall most certainly die unto me,

27　And unto all that is me, forever. That is, if they shall not repent in Christ the Son, unto me, as being eternally forever true, of themselves, to me, forever.

28　Christ Jesus, he is eternally forever found, in me (God), as being eternally forever true, and, forever seen.

29　And these, living forever, unrepentiful true beasts, that are found unto me forever. In most eternal, living, unrepentiful true sinfulness,

30　They are considered of me (God). As a living forever beastly true peoples and beastly true nations. That do not desire Christ Jesus,

31　As this Christ Jesus, being their seen, heavenly forever true, eternal true savior. Who is from me, as being eternally forever true.

32　They who are found willfully without Christ the Son. They are found unto me, as being eternally forever true. As unrepentiful true beasts of the earth.

33　And they are found unto me and by me, in their desired, true, unrepentfulness. As being eternally forever seen, by me, forever true.

34　Again, those, unrepentiful, true, Antichrist beasts. They are seen, as being unrepentiful to me, forever true. As in, not desiring to receive Christ Jesus,

35   As this is eternally forever sure in themselves, and they are therefore, found unto me forever. As dead death, forever.

36   And they, are even seen, as being, Antichrist and anti God, unrepentiful true beasts, of the earth, forever. And they are eternal, living forever, unrepentiful true beasts. That are found unto me forever true,

37   As found unto me forever. In willful, damning, true sinfulness, that liveth eternally forever true, in themselves. As dead death forever true and is, forever seen.

38   That chosen and willful, true sinfulness. It is, found by me forever, in being eternally forever true, in being against all that I Am, forever. And it is against all that I Am, eternally forever.

39   And, those unrepentiful true beasts. They do not ever chose to receive Christ, eternally forever. As this Christ Jesus, being their chosen, seen savior, as being eternally forever and ever true.

40   And they, are seen, before me forever true. And they are found unto me, in all that isn't of myself, as being eternally forever true.

41 Therefore, they are most surely forever true. As being seen and known, to me forever, as death eternally forever.

42 And they, are seen unto me forever. As being unrepentfully against my holy true righteousness. And they, are truly, seen. As being unrepentfully,

43 Found in being against my (God) Holy True Righteousness, as being, forever true and forever seen. As they are seen, in their seen death, as eternally forever true.

44 They are, most surely, seen unto me, forever. As being ungodly, unto me forever true. And they, are, considered of me (God). As being unrepentiful true beasts, forever certain.

45 And they are, found. As, most eternal, living forever, true death, forever true. And, they are, seen. As being, as unrepentfully truly seen, before me (God). In uttermost true damnation, that is called: "Being without me, eternally forever."

46 And they, are, most surely seen. As being, found as being exalted against all, that is called, Godly nations, forever true. And they, the unrepentiful true nations, of the earth, forever.

47 They Shall, most surely be found, in that great day of days. In Hell forever and ever true.

And that, is because of their personal, seen, true choices,

48 That are true choices, that is given of themselves, forever true. In being against receiving the heavenly true salvation. That is salvation that is seen and called: Jesus Christ.

49 And this Christ Jesus, he is sent of me, forever sure and forever seen. And this Christ Jesus, he is seen, as Christ Jesus, from me, forever true and forever more.

50 And this eternal and most true Christ, he is with that message of hope, that is, called God, forever true.

51 Christ Jesus, he giveth me (God) unto the world. And I Am that God, who is forever seen. And I Am, given true salvation,

52 As a eternal true salvation, to repentful true men, and, to repentful true women, forever true and forever seen.

53 Hell is, eternally forever, and Hell is, a place that is found given unto the unrepentfully. Who are willfully by their choices, do desire to be truly lost, unto me, forever true.

54 And those, that do, unrepentiful true evils, in the name of God. They shall find unto

themselves, eternal, true damnation, from me, forever true.

55 That damnation, it is called dead death, forever true. And that dead death. It is and shall be, awaiting the unrepentiful truly lost, forever true.

56 And that true damnation, that is called dead death. It is a given back recompense to the damned ones, forever, as found given from me forever, in eternal, true recompense.

57 As these lost, are truly forever seen and forever felt, unto me, forever true, as death forever.

58 And those that use my holy name, unjustly, as being eternally forever true of themselves, forever. And, if they use my name as if it were an seen instrument, that is of most given, forever true sinfulness.

59 Then, I shall hold him and or her responsible, that useth me (God) and my (God) eternal true name. As if, it were a instrument, to commit desired and willful, ungodly forever, unrepentiful true sinfulness, forever.

60 The unrepentiful, fallen. Who are, of the earth, as being eternally forever true. They shall, soon come, to that great day. That is found, in eternal living, forever true, true rewards.

61 Those rewards, as they are to be given from me, forever true, unto the damned forever. Those are eternal true rewards, as found given, from me forever true. In most heavenly forever and ever, true death, forever.

62 And that is, forever, truly seen. As forever true. And is, a given true reward. As found, according to their personal true choices. That are made, in themselves, as being eternally forever true.

63 And recompense from me forever. It is found, as found given unto the damned ones, forever. As given by me eternally, as given to themselves, from me, forever,

64 As given to them, according to their sinful, desired true choices. That are eternal true choices, that are made by them, as being eternally forever and ever true,

65 And those sinful true choices, that they desire forever. Those true choices, are found, concerning themselves, forever. And granted true recompense,

66 For choosing sinful true choices, forever. It (recompense) is then, found from me, forever. As it (recompense) is found, given faithfully forever,

67 True from me, forever, as found concerning eternal true matters of life and death, as being

eternally forever and ever found, and true forever.

68 Those eternal sinful true choices, are always eternally seen. And they, the damned. They shall be forever rewarded for their sinful true choices, as they truly do desire, to want, Satan, forever,

69 Eternal, living forever, true damnation. Is a given damnation, that is seen and called granted true death, forever. And it is found, as being eternally forever strong, in physical and spiritual true death.

70 And it is a granted death from God, forever strong. And it is seen true death, that is made from their wanting sinful true choices.

71 That are made choices from desiring eternal true sin, forever. As they truly do desire sin, forever. And it is a true life, in sin death, forever.

72 And that life is death forever. And it is seen, as being eternally forever true of the damned, in their wanting sin forever. And it is seen,

73 As being eternally forever, as being eternally forever more. To want Satan sinfulness, forever, as wanting it in one's sinful true life, forever.

74 Therefore, that awaiting, forever true, heavenly true damnation, called death forever true. It is eternally forever true. As given from

me (God), unto them of the fallen true earth, forever.

75 For they, are found, by me, forever true. As being found, in being unrepentfully forever true. In being against me (God), forever true and forever more. As they truly do desire Satan sin, forever.

76 And they, the damned in Satan sinfulness, forever. They are seen, and felt unto me, as being eternally forever true. As being felt unto me, forever,

77 As death forever true. For they are death, unto me, as being eternally forever true. And they shall die forever. If they choose not, Christ as their savior, forever.

78 The sinful, beastly, unrepentiful true earth. It shall be forever true. As being folded up and caste away and caste eternally out,

79 In that, great unending true day. That is a day, that is, most eternal, living forever, holy true life, as being eternally forever true.

80 Christly true life, it is found in me, forever true. And is, a found life. That is most surely, a holy true life,

81 As found given of me, through Christ Jesus, forever true and forever seen. As life in me

(God), as being eternally forever true and forever sure.

82 And that Christly true life. That is, called Christ forever true. It is, seen, as eternal true life, forever. And that life, is called, Christ Jesus, forever true.

83 And Christly true life, is seen, as heavenly forever, true life. That life, it is, called God forever true. And, it is, forever, true life, called God in Christ, as being eternally forever true, and, forever more.

84 And, I Am God, forever true and forever seen. And, I Am, seen, as life, forever true. And, I have sent myself, into Christ, forever true.

85 And in Christ Jesus, I Am, seen, as God, forever true and forever more. And Christ, he is, my eternal, true Son, forever. And Christ Jesus, he is seen, as found in me, as being eternally forever seen, and, forever true.

86 That presents, of me, as I Am found, in Christ Jesus, as being forever true. It is forever true. And, it is seen, as being eternally forever true. As granted, true life, forever.

87 That true life, it is granted in me forever true. And, it is seen, as true life, forever true. And, it is, forever given, in me, forever true.

88 That life, it is, called God, as forever seen. And, it is forever felt, as eternally forever felt and is forever true,

89 For I Am true, forever, saith thy God, as eternally forever sure, and, eternally forever true.

90 That life, it is, Godly true life, found in me (God), forever sure and forever true. And that true life, it is forever true. In all, that I Am, forever.

Chapter 16 w/ 55 verses   Beastly people

1 In this, fallen, against God, and against Christ, true world. Is found, most surely. Unrepentiful, ungodly, Antichrist, beastly true people,

2 Who are the Antichrist, true beast, forever true. And, they are found, unto me. As eternal, granted true death, forever true.

3 And they are found, in all the fallen true earth, forever. And these unrepentiful true beasts, they are found. As the Antichrist true image, that is, called Satanism, forever true.

4 For they, are the damned forever. And they do love, unrepentfulness forever true and forever. And that unrepentfulness, it is found, in themselves, forever true.

5   And unrepentfulness, it is found, given and taught, from the hand of the false prophet, who is called Satan's own image and is Satan himself, forever true.

6   And that blasphemous eternal true image of Satan. That is found in the unrepentiful true beasts, of the earth forever. It is found, as being found, unto me (God), forever true.

7   And it is found, in earnest and sincere, true death, forever seen and forever felt. And is felt and seen, as eternal dead death, eternally forever true, and, forever seen.

8   The Antichrist and anti God, true work of unrepentfulness, that is found in the beastly fallen ones, who are found eternally forever true, as found in and of the true earth, forever.

9   That work of unrepentfulness, it is found, as the spiritual true mark, that is seen. As the spiritual true mark, of the beast, that is called "The workings of eternal dead death," forever.

10 And they (all unrepentiful people and all non Christian nations, who are seen as being unrepentiful, toward God, forever), who are the beast,

11 As they are seen forever true. They are willingly found in Satanism, as forever true, and,

as forever seen, as seen by me, as being forever true, in sinfulness, forever.

12 And that true name and spiritual true mark of Satan, that is called Satanism, that is found in the damned. It is seen as the true work of unrepentfulness, as seen before God, as being forever true.

13 Therefore, these unrepentiful true beasts, that are found in unrepentfulness. They do, chose to be willingly found of (of means the word by) me (God), forever true. As being found in the name and or mark of the beast.

14 The beast, is seen, and is: "Called sinful man and sinful Satan, together, forever, and, for all of the forever, to come."

15 Satan and the unrepentiful true beasts of the earth, together. They are found unto Christ and unto me (God), as forever true. As being found, as the true, Antichrist, true beast, as forever seen, and is, forever more.

16 And unrepentiful true men, they are found eternally, within the sinful hardened stone imaged true workings, that is called beastly eternal true death,

17 As being forever seen, as seen death forever, as found in their desired true sinfulness, forever,

and, it is forever heard, and true, as being eternally forever certain.

18 And beastly eternal true death, is seen, as being, forever truly seen. And it Is, is found, within the beast, as themselves, as forever true, and, as forever seen,

19 And it is seen, as eternal true separation, to be willingly away from God and to be, willingly away from Christ Jesus, for all of given true eternity, and forever.

20 This Antichrist true earth, it most surely seen, unto the unrepentiful forever. As being in true death, forever true.

21 And this sinful true earth, it is found, in them, that do not desire Christ Jesus, as Christ Jesus being their seen savior, as being eternally forever true.

22 And they, the unrepentiful true beast, they are called death. That is, if they shall chose, to remain, in eternal, true death, forever true.

23 And if, they chose to remain without God, forever. Then they shall die, unto me, forever true. And I Am not the author of confusion, which this earth, has become, as being forever true.

24 But I Am the author of heaven, and of all, that is, and all, that will ever be created by me, forever. And I Am the author of creation,

25 And I hold, faithfully forever true, In my countenance, forever. All that was, is, and all, that will ever be made. And that is forever true.

26 Sinful beastly true man, in his desired and true worldliness. Is the author of this sinful, utterly confused, true earth, forever.

27 And all sin, is the error of their sinful true confusion, that sinfully separates men from me (God), forever true.

28 And granted true death, it is due, to their sinful, exalted true nature. That they, the unrepentiful beasts of the earth, do form, against me, as being forever true, of themselves, toward me, forever.

29 And that blasphemous, eternal true form, of eternal true death, as found by me, in the unrepentiful, true beasts, forever true.

30 It is seen, as being against my goodness and being against, my true righteousness, and being against, my true holiness, as being forever true.

31 But all true unrepentfulness, it is found. As being, against my, living breath of the righteous, Godly, true eternity, forever.

32 For my nature, as found, as my righteousness. It isn't found, in the unrepentiful one's, lifeless stumbling block's of sinful true images,

33 That is called wanted true death, as being eternally forever desired in the damned, as forever true.

34 The beast called death, is found unto me forever, as found in their personal, sinful true images. That are found, in being found unto me, forever true, as eternal dead death, forever.

35 And dead death, is found unto me, in being of earnest and sincere, unrepentiful desired sinful true death, forever true and forever seen.

36 All unrepentiful true seen sins, they are found, unto me forever. As being found, as being found, against all that I Am. As I Am and as I Am seen, as righteousness, forever true.

37 And all true peoples and all true nations. That are seen by me, as being unrepentiful. They are found unto me, as being eternally forever true,

38 In being true unto me, forever certain. As being utterly truly perditious. And, they, shall most certainly, be damned by me, forever true,

39 In that great day, that is found, as given true judgment, from me. And it is seen, as being forever true judgment. As eternal true death,

40   As being given by me, as being eternally forever faithful, true judgment, as it called, granted true death, forever true.

41   And that judgment, it is given of me, as forever certain, in being heavenly forever true. As eternal just judgment, as forever seen, and, is forever felt, as from me, as being eternally forever true.

42   That great, eternal, just judgment, it is, called life and death, forever true. And it is given of me (God) and is given of Christ my (God) eternal true Son, forever.

43   And those unrepentiful true peoples and unrepentiful true nations. They are found unto me, and seen unto me, forever. As being found. As being Antichrist and anti God, forever true,

44   As true of themselves, in eternal, just death, forever true and forever seen. And that true death, it is most eternal, and is seen,

45   As seen in the rejected, who are seen by me, forever true and forever seen, as they are eternally seen unto me forever, in their desired true sins, forever.

46   And they are seen, unto me forever. As being found eternal, in eternal blasphemous true death, forever true. And that true death, is certainly

forever true, of themselves, in wanton true sin, forever.

47 And, if, these true Antichrist, unrepentiful true beasts. Do not repent afore hand of their desired, against God, unrepentiful true seen sins. That are, seen sins,

48 That are seen Antichrist true sins, that are forever true. As being seen, as granted true death, forever seen and forever felt. Then, without repenting afore hand, then deathly eternal true recompense, called God,

49 It is, given of me forever, and is felt therefore, by the damned, as being eternal uttermost true judgment, that is forever certain and forever seen,

50 And, in that eternal seen day, that is most eternal, forever. They the damned, they shall find of me (God), in that great day. Recompense empowered ness, that is recompense eternal and seen, empowered ness, forever.

51 That eternal recompense eternal empowered ness. It is final true judgment, that is being carried out by me, and it is forever true.

52 And final true judgment, it is given, by me, forever true, unto the damned forever sure, and it will be forever seen. As granted true death, forever.

53 But unto the repentful true beasts of the earth, they are found through Christ Jesus, forever true. As seen repentful true beasts of the earth, forever.

54 And all repentful true beasts, they are Christly repentful. And they shall, inherit the earth, as my Sons and my daughters, forever true.

55 And they shall live forever and ever true, in me, forever. And they shall never die, again, and forever.

Chapter 17 w / 79 verses   Recompense called GOD

1 Recompense empowered ness, it is seen, from me (God), forever true. And, it shall be seen. As given by me, faithfully forever true, As given at the great white throne judgment. As granted true recompense empowered ness,

2 That is found in all, and complete, and total effect. That is forever true, upon the damned, as being eternally forever certain. As certainly granted true punishment.

3 That true punishment, it is called death forever true and forever more. And it is seen, without true end, in hell, forever true and forever more, saith thy God, eternally forever and ever true.

4   And granted true death. It is, found, with all, Godly, eternal, living forever, true recompense, empowerment. That empowerment, it is seen,

5   As forever true and forever seen. As eternal true death, forever certain and ever lastingly, eternally forever true.

6   And that recompense, it is called God. And is seen, as God, in judgment, unto the beastly eternal true image of uttermost true death, as being forever true. And it is found, as most certainly,

7   Found as granted true recompense. That is, eternal true death, forever true. And, it is given, by Christ Jesus and given by the True Father God. As forever true, unto the beast, forever.

8   And that granted and most true recompense. It is seen, as being eternal true punishment, that is, called death, forever true. And that true recompense, it is, called God, most surely, as eternally forever seen.

9   And it is found, and seen, as concerning, righteous, holy, just recompense. As being forever certain and forever seen, and is truly forever more.

10   That true recompense, it is found, as given true death, forever. And it is found, given of

God. Unto them, that do enjoy, unrepentfulness, forever true.

11 And given true recompense, it is given, because they, the damned. They are found, of (of means the word by) me, as being forever true. As desiring not the heavenly true salvation, that is called Christ Jesus, forever.

12 And they, therefore, do most surely, do deny unto themselves, forever true. The heavenly true salvation, that cometh down from me (God), out of heaven, for the repentful true beasts of the earth, forever true.

13 And they, who are the damned. They are found, by and unto me forever true. As in not desiring Christ. As Christ Jesus, being their seen savior, forever.

14 And that true denial, found within themselves, forever true, it is seen, of themselves, as being eternally and ever lasting, eternally forever true.

15 And their full circle true sins, are seen by me, for all of given true eternity. And that is forever seen, as being forever true and forever more (full circle means to be utterly sinful, forever).

16 My great, given, holy true recompense, it is called GOD. And it is found from me (God), in a

ever most, heavenly forever, heavenly true, most eternal, living forever, true command.

17 That true command, from me forever. It is a true command from me, forever. And it is found of me, eternally forever, as being a forever true command, and, as a, forever seen, true command.

18 And that command, it is seen, as eternally forever found. As given of me (God), as being eternally forever true. In ever most, heavenly, given, true life, forever true.

19 And true life, itself, it is found, as a forever true life. That is ever lastingly, eternal true life, forever true and forever seen and forever more.

20 And that, is a holy true life. That is found given by me (God), in most eternal, living forever, heavenly true life. That life, it is granted true life.

21 That granted true life. It is forever found life, in me (God). As forever seen life, that is, called God, forever. And it is seen, as eternally forever and ever true, in me, forever true and forever more.

22 All unrepentiful true sins. They are, most surely, found by me forever true. As being found, as being against me (God), forever true.

23 And those seen sins, they are found, by me, forever true. In unrepentfulness, forever true. And those seen sins, they are. Seen as eternal true death, forever.

24 And, they (seen sins) are, against my eternal, living forever, true Son. Who is called Christ Jesus, forever true. And those seen sins, they are found and seen, in unrepentfulness, forever true.

25 And, those seen sins, they are always seen by me, forever true. As seen by my spirit, as forever seen and forever known. And, they are to me. As death forever true and forever more.

26 And, in my eternal, living forever, true presents. Those seen sins, they are seen and found. As being damning unto them, who partake of it, forever.

27 And those seen eternal true sins, they are seen as being eternally blasphemous eternal, seen sins. And they are found, unto me forever,

28 As being against me (God). And, they are against my (God) eternal, living forever, holy true Son. Who is called, Christ Jesus, eternally forever.

29 And those damning, unrepentiful true sins. They are most surely, seen, by my (God) eternal, living forever, ever lasting, holy true presents.

That presents, it is, forever true and ever lasting, forever.

30 And unrepentiful true sins. They are seen, as being eternally forever true, sins, forever. And are seen, unto me forever,

31 As a eternal, and most true sinfulness. That shall be caste away from my heavenly and most righteous, eternal living forever and ever, holy true presents, forever true.

32 And this is because, I Am found, in most eternal, never dying, forever true life. For I Am God and there is no other God. And I Am life, that is forever true.

33 And I Am all that is, and all is by me, And that is, eternally forever and ever true, and forever seen.

34 Heavenly forever true life. It is found, in my (God) most holy, mighty forever, heavenly forever, Godly true life,

35 And those, who are unrepentiful, because they chose not to ever accept, Jesus Christ. As this Jesus, being their personal seen savior, as being eternally forever true.

36 Then, those unrepentiful true peoples. They are found, without me (God). And they shall

remain forever. In unrepentiful, damningly, eternal seen sins, forever true.

37 And these, unrepentiful. They do, perish, in their own sinful true choices, that are found, in desiring, this evil true life, as being forever true.

38 And that true desiring true sinfulness, as being eternally forever true. It is, because, they the unrepentiful. They do not desire the heavenly true Son, who is called, Christ Jesus, forever true.

39 And unrepentiful true people and unrepentiful true nations, they are found unto me, forever true. As being eternally lost, unto me, forever,

40 And that is most certainly, forever true. For they, do chose, to be purposely without Christ Jesus, as Christ Jesus, being their seen savior, as being forever true.

41 And these evil lost ones, they shall, most certainly, remain forever true, in their own, personal true seen sins. And that true decision, it is made, by their own, personal true choices, forever true.

42 And that true decision, it is made, by themselves, forever true. As being found, in being against, receiving Christ, as Christ Jesus, being their seen savior, forever true.

43 And because of that true decision, these unrepentiful true one's. They shall create, eternal true recompense, unto themselves forever true.

44 And that eternal true recompense, it is seen, as eternal true death forever sure and forever more. And, it is given by me forever true, unto them faithfully forever true.

45 And is most certainly, seen, for being in unrepentfulness forever. And that true unrepentfulness, it is forever true. And is found as utter true unrepentfulness, forever true. And it is, utterly seen, as death, forever eternal.

46 And, unrepentfulness, it is seen, as a true, sinful true working, of death forever. And it is seen, as a utter true damnation, called desired true death, forever.

47 And that recompense death, it is seen, and is found, as they create within themselves, as being eternally forever true in the workings of eternal true death, forever.

48 And recompense, it is seen, as granted true death, forever true. For they truly do desire, to be, as dead as Satan is dead, unto me, forever true.

49 Therefore, granted eternal, true recompense empowerment, called granted true death, forever.

It is for having within themselves, damningly true sins, forever.

50 And those seen sins, that are of unrepentfulness forever true, they are, seen damnation, as forever true. And that true damnation,

51 It is granted true separation, to be away from all that is me, as I Am found, in Christ Jesus, forever true.

52 And those, seen sins, they are of death forever true. And those seen sins, shall damn the unrepentiful ones, forever. For they truly enjoy the sinful true workings, that are called sin, forever true.

53 And recompense, true death forever, for unrepentiful, true sinfulness. It is eternally forever true, upon and in them,

54 Who are found within the beastly damningly unrepentiful true image of unrepentiful true sin, forever. And it is found, for being against me (God), forever.

55 Nevertheless, most certain, forever eternal, living true recompense damnation. Is for unrepentfulness, that is unrepentfulness, that is seen,

56 For being, as to never desire to receive Christ, as Christ being one's true savior, forever true and forever seen.

57 And, again, recompense true damnation, from me, as being eternally forever true and forever more. It is for being found, in unrepentfulness, forever true,

58 And that unrepentfulness, it is seen. As a living true damnation, that the damned, who have and do, do create back unto themselves,

59 As created forever truly seen, eternal damnation. That is called death. And that, true dead death. It is, forever true. As true death, forever true.

60 And, moreover, these unrepentiful evil true one's. They shall, most surely, perish eternally forever true. If they shall repent not of their personal,

61 Seen true sins, as being eternally forever true of themselves, as they are found unto me forever, in Satan true death, forever,

62 And, they must, quickly, repent in my (God) eternal, living forever true Son, who is called: "Jesus Christ."

63 And all true sins, they are found eternally, as being against my (God) own, very just nature. And those, seen sins, of death forever.

64 They are found, unto me forever true. As being eternally against my (God) own, most holy, true presents, as being forever true,

65 And, those seen sins, they are called death, as being eternally forever true, and, forever seen. And they are forever seen.

66 And those seen sins, they are seen. As seen in true death, forever seen, and true, and true forever.

67 And my presents, is called life, and it is found, given of me (God), forever true. As given in eternal, never ending, Godly, holy true life, forever true and forever seen. And it is seen, as me, forever true and forever seen.

68 Holy true life, shall never perish from me (God), forever true. And that life, it is, found in Christ Jesus, forever true. And it shall never cease from before my (God) righteous and eternal, holy true presents, forever,

69 That presents, it is found, in and of holy forever true life. And it is me, as forever seen. And, I Am seen, as a living forever and ever, true life, as forever seen. And that true presents, of me, as being, forever seen,

70 It is seen, as most heavenly forever true, true life. That is seen, as being forever true, and, forever seen. And that seen true life, it is seen, as granted true life, that is called God, as being forever true.

71 All unrepentiful true sins, they are found eternal, without desired in Christ, true repentance. And they are considered, as damningly, eternal, living forever, true sins, as being forever true.

72 And those unrepentiful true sins, they are seen and felt, forever true, unto me forever. As being found, as being against me (God), forever true,

73 And is found as being eternal true iniquity, that is forever seen by me, as being eternally forever true, and is, forever more.

74 And, when I look upon the unrepentiful true nations, who are of thy enemies, O Israel, they shall most certainly flee seven ways from before thy face, even when none pursueth them, forever.

75 And that is because, my nation called Israel, is found in my eternal, living forever, true Son, who is called Jesus Christ, as being eternally forever true,

76 And thou, O Beloved, great loving nation (Israel), that is found forever true, in me (God),

as being eternally forever seen. Thou shalt, always, be found, in my eternal, unending, holy true presents,

77 That is called, forever true, true life, forever. And that true life, it is a ever most eternal, unending, holy true life, forever.

78 And that true life, forever. It is seen, as being found eternally forever seen, and felt, as found of and in me, forever.

79 And it is found, given of me, as being eternally forever true. As being, Jesus Christ, as being eternally forever true, and, forever more.

Chapter 18 w/ 69 verses   O Israel

1 And thou, O Israel, thou art, greatly in these days, greatly desired of me (God), as being forever true, and, as forever seen. And thou, O Israel, thou shalt be, eternally forever found, by me, forever.

2 And that shalt be found, unto me forever faithful, As being eternally forever found, in my eternal, true Son, who is my holy true Son,

3 And, who is called, Jesus Christ. And, who is seen, as being called: Christ Jesus, in me, forever true. And this Christ Jesus, he is seen, in me, forever true and forever seen. And he is seen, as Godly eternal, in me, forever true.

4   And he is seen, for I dwell in Christ Jesus, as God forever true, for I Am God forever. And the forever, it is me. As I have given of myself, into Christ Jesus, forever.

5   And, in Christ, I Am as seen. As eternal true life, forever certain, and forever true. And in Christ Jesus, I Am seen, in all that I Am, as being forever true.

6   And I, the lord, I do, love thee, O great nation (Israel), that is called by my (God) most, holy, true name. That is seen, as being eternally forever true, in me. As being seen, as Christ Jesus, eternally forever.

7   And, my (God) name, is Christ Jesus, as being eternally forever seen. And that, seen, true name, as it is seen, as being, Christ Jesus,

8   It is seen, as life in my (God) name, and I Am called, Christ Jesus. And, I (God) Am even seen, as Israel, eternally forever seen.

9   And my (God) name, it is, even seen, as called Israel, forever true, and, forever more.

10   And thou, O Israel, thou art found, in this present true earth, forever true, O little one. And this eternal dead earth, in sin forever. It is a sinful unrepentiful, true earth, forever.

11   And my righteous, holy, true judgments. They are found of me, through Christ Jesus, as being eternally forever seen.

12   And those just judgments, they are seen, as being ever lasting, to ever lastingly, "HOLY FOREVER TRUE judgments." As being found, eternal, in me, as being eternally forever seen, eternal true judgment, forever.

13   And those, are end time judgments. And they are called, life and death, forever. And, they are found, and seen. As eternal, Godly, and they are,

14   Seen as being truly given true judgments from me (God), forever. As given by me, through Jesus Christ, as being eternally forever sure, and, forever seen judgment.

15   And those judgments, they are seen and found, in being of me, as being eternally forever true. As being seen and found, in uttermost, most given, righteous and holy, true judgment, forever.

16   And it is seen, as being, judgment that is seen as being eternally forever true. As being seen and felt, as God, as being forever certain and forever true, forever.

17   And that true judgment, it is forever seen, as me as judgment, unto the damned, as being eternally forever true, and forever known. And I

Am known, as God, for all true time, and, as being eternally forever seen.

18 And my seen and felt true judgment, it is called end of the days true Judgments, forever. And I Am seen, as life forever seen. And these judgments, are from me, forever true,

19 And they (judgments) are spoken and written and being written, by me, through Christ Jesus, as being eternally forever true.

20 And my just judgments, they are, even being sent, unto those nations, and peoples, and tongues, and kindred's,

21 Who are seen, as being, faithfully eternally forever true, as being found, as, unrepentfully desiring thy true destruction and thy true fall, O Israel.

22 And these, righteous, holy and true, just judgments. They are just in all eternal true righteousness, that is called God forever. And those eternal end time true judgments,

23 They are seen, before me (God), as being forever true. And they are, given of myself (God), as forever true and forever seen. And they are seen, as I Am seen, as I Am seen as being God, forever true.

24 And they (judgments) are given of me, through my righteous, eternal, living forever true Son: who is called Christ, forever true.

25 And this Christ, is the adversary. That is against all unrepentiful true nations, who unjustly afflict thee, O Israel.

26 And those seen by me nations and their seen by me true peoples and their seen by me, true tongues. They are seen and felt, in the fallen true earth,

27 As being forever true, in death forever. And they are seen and felt, unto me forever. As being unrepentfully, forever true, as eternal dead death, forever true, O Israel.

28 And, in my (God) eternal, living forever, holy true hands. Is my hand of life, that is found with mercy and Godly true judgment. And this is given of me (God), unto whom, it is due, forever true.

29 And ye of Israel, shall see, that "I AM," against the evil affairs of this utterly, unrepentiful, fallen, beastly, against God, waxed old as a garment, transgressing sinful true earth, forever.

30 And this earth, it is seen, by me, forever true. As being seen, as being seen, as being, a "Utterly

fallen, unrepentiful, beastly, Antichrist, perditious, waxed old earth,

31 And this true earth, it is an unrepentiful true image. That is found, as being, in utterly true falleness. That is seen, in being against my (God's) own true righteousness,

32 As being forever sure, and, forever seen, as it is found, as being the damned, forever. For the damned are found in unrepentiful true sin, forever.

33 And the earth, it is fallen forever, in sin forever. And the earth, it is a fallen true image, found as unrepentiful true men and unrepentiful true women,

34 And the earth, as fallen forever, it is found unto me and by me, as being eternal true sin, forever. And this is forever true and forever sure. And it is death, forever certain.

35 And that, is an image found as the earth in death forever. And it is found by me forever true. As being, most certainly, being against my (God) eternal, ever lasting, righteous true plan, forever.

36 And that true plan, it is called, life. And that life, it is found of me forever true. As found, in Christ Jesus, forever true.

37 And that is a lifely true plan, as it is found and given by me, forever true. As found, as a most heavenly, living forever, eternal true salvation. That is forever seen and felt, from me, forever.

38 That true salvation, it is, called God forever true. And that salvation, it is found of me (God), through my Son. Who is called, Christ Jesus, as being eternally forever true, and, forever seen.

39 And all true falleness, it is seen. As being all transgressing unrepentiful true men, forever. And that transgressing, it is found,

40 As being forever true and forever seen, as seen death, unto me, as being eternally forever seen death. And it is, a true death, forever.

41 Eternal true falleness, it is found, as being, all fallen true men and all, fallen true women, as being eternally forever true.

42 And it is seen, as being ungodly. And it is found, as being the unrepentiful true earth, forever true.

43 And that true unrepentfulness, as found in the damned. It is seen as granted true death, as being forever certain. And, granted true death, it is forever true and forever seen.

44 And that true death, it is forever seen. As seen in the fallen, true earth, forever certain and forever seen.

45 And seen death, it is being, seen and felt, as found, by me. As being eternally forever found, as being unrepentiful true sinfulness,

46 That is forever true and forever seen. And it is seen, as eternal true disobedience, unto me, forever true.

47 And eternal true death, it is seen. As being most certainly, found, as. As being found forever certain, and forever seen, in the earth,

48 As eternal true death, that is found as being granted forever true and forever more.

49 Granted true death, forever certain. It is seen, as an unrepentiful true image, that is the damned forever true. And it is an image, that is found, in earnest and sincere, true death, forever certain.

50 And that is a eternal true image, that is the image of the beast, who is called, unrepentiful true men and unrepentiful true women, as being forever seen, and, forever true.

51 These lost ones forever, they are the beast. And they chose to never desire Christ, as Christ Jesus, being their seen savior, forever.

52 Christ Jesus, he is my holy, and true, and sincere, true salvation. That true salvation, it is called Christ, who is from me. And Christ, he is from me, as being forever true and forever seen.

53 And this Christ, he is forever true and forever seen. As seen, as being thy true life, that is found, in and of me, as being forever certain and forever more.

54 And Christ Jesus, he is forever certain and forever true. In all that I Am, as I Am God, forever true and forever seen.

55 My eternal, true salvation. It is most surely, forever found, of me (God). And it is found, in my (God) Son, who is called, Christ. And that true salvation, it is seen,

56 As a holy true salvation, that is most truly forever. And it is given of myself, as being forever seen. And it is seen, from me. As being forever and ever true, true salvation, forever.

57 And my salvation, it is forever seen, as being seen, from me. For I Am the God of heaven, And I Am forever true and I Am forever seen.

58 And I Am seen, as Christ Jesus, as forever true.

59 Granted true salvation, is called Christ. And it is granted by me, as being forever true. And it

is given by me (God), forever. And I Am the righteous, and holy, just kind God.

60 And I Am the God of all, and of all, that is, and shall ever be, and I Am forever. And I Am, most certainly: "THE GOD OF TRUTH."

61 And I Am forever true, and I Am forever seen. As seen Christly true life, that is forever true, true life, forever.

62 And those, seen true nations and their seen true peoples. Who chose to be forever true, to be without Christly true life, as being eternally forever true, as it is true of themselves, as they are found by me, in Satan true death, as being eternally forever and ever true. Then, those shameful true nations and their shameful, true, unrepentiful true peoples,

63 They are found by me, forever. As they are found by me, in their desired, true falleness, forever true.

64 Then, they shall die unto me forever true and forever more. And this is, because, they, the unrepentiful, as they are found by me forever true.

65 They do, chose, purposely to not to ever receive Christ Jesus, as this Christ Jesus, being their personal seen savior, from me (God), as being forever true.

66 Therefore, without Christ Jesus, forever. Then these unrepentiful true nations and unrepentiful true peoples. They are considered of me, as being forever seen.

67 As being seen, as being found unto me forever true. As found in beastliness, forever true.

68 And, that true beastliness, it is found, as fallen true men and fallen true women, as being eternally forever true, and, forever seen.

69 And it is seen, as granted true death, as heavenly forever true and forever seen, and I shall repay all, that truly do desire Satan true death, forever.

Chapter 19 w/ 101 verses   Beastliness

1 Beastliness, it is granted true death, as being eternally forever seen. And it is found, in fallen unrepentiful true men,

2 Who do not ever desire, to ever, accept Christ, as this Christ Jesus, being their own, personal, living forever, true savior, as being forever true, and forever seen.

3 And all, eternal, seen and felt, eternal true beastliness. It is found, and is called, unrepentiful true men, as being eternally forever seen and true.

4   And beastliness, it is found, without my (God) eternal, living forever, holy and great, just presents. My presents, it is called, life forever true.

5   And, without my holy, forever eternal, forgiving eternal, true presents. All unrepentiful true men, they are found, unto me forever. In damning forever, true sinfulness, eternally forever.

6   And, one's (sinner) true, desired true sinfulness. It is called, being unrepentfully forever true, in unrepentfulness forever seen. And it is found, without, myself forever true.

7   And to be found willingly by one's own eternal true choice, to never depart sin forever. That person, shall die unto me forever true.

8   And that eternal choice, it is found in the damned, as being eternally forever certain and forever true,

9   That choice, that is made by the damned, for wanton true unrepentfulness, as being eternally forever seen, and forever felt, as it is seen and felt, unto me, as themselves in Satan death, forever.

10 That wanton true choice, for Satan true death. It is forever true of the lost unto me forever. And it is seen and forever felt, unto me forever,

11 As themselves in eternal true death, as being, eternally forever true, of themselves, as the damned, forever.

12 And that eternal true choice, for them, who want true sin in themselves as death forever. It is found as wanting true Satan death, damnation. That is called dead death, that is given to the unrepentiful true sinners, forever.

13 And Satan death, it is seen and felt, as being eternally forever true, as granted true death, as forever certain. And that is eternally forever true. And, it is forever seen, as granted true death, forever.

14 And Satan death, is seen, as being eternal true death, forever true. And that true death, it is granted unto them, that do hate me, forever true,

15 And that death, is found of themselves in Satan forever. For these, that do hate me, as I (God) Am found, as I (God) Am Jesus Christ, forever.

16 That eternal true choice, it is made by the damned. And it is forever sure and it is forever seen. And it is seen, as to depart from me, forever true and for all of given true eternity, and, forever.

17 Nevertheless, At this time of the earth. I do extend the hand of salvation, that is found in of

me (God) through Jesus Christ, for the remission one's seen sins, forever true.

18 And the blood of Christ Jesus, doth wash away from my (God) holy, true presents, forever true. The sins of the entire true world, forever. And as forever seen, as eternal forgiveness, as eternally forever true.

19 And that forgiveness, it is found from me, forever. And is given of myself, through Christ Jesus, forever true. And is given of me through Christ Jesus, forever sure.

20 And is given of me forever, unto them forever, that do desire me forever sure and forever true. And they, truly do desire me, in Christ Jesus. As being eternally forever true and forever seen.

21 Even though, I forgive these repentful true ones, forever. Yet, even with this hand of me (God), in eternal true salvation, that is called Christ Jesus, for fallen true men.

22 Many shall never come to me, that I may receive them unto myself, in a true spirit of righteousness and holiness, that is called me. As I Am found in Christ Jesus, as forever true, and, as I Am forever seen.

23 And I Am seen, as eternal true life, that is forever true. And I live forever. And I Am the

life. As found, in repentful true men. And that is forever true and that is forever seen, as eternally forever and ever true.

24 My (God) righteousness and my holiness. It is found, given of me (God), unto Christ. And through Christ, is my (God) righteousness and my holiness, found unto them, that are repentful unto me, fully of themselves, forever,

25 And they, the repentful in Christ Jesus, forever. They are found repent fully forever true, unto me forever true. And they are found, and they are seen, unto me,

26 As being, forever true, in the earth. As eternally forever true and forever seen, and I do love the repentful, forever. And my love, it is found through Christ Jesus, forever true and ever lastingly, forever true.

27 And that love, is great, and is my eternal, great love, forever. And that love is most eternal, and it is seen and felt, forever. As seen and felt, as being Jesus Christ, eternally forever.

28 And that great true love, it is called me forever. And it is, great and vast, even as I Am vast. And it is seen, as being eternally forever true, saith thy God, as being eternally forever and ever, and ever true.

29 My true love, it is seen, as granted true life, that is most surely, eternally forever seen, and forever felt. And that felt true love, that is me, in Christ Jesus, forever,

30 It shall never die, and that is forever true. For I can never die, and neither is there anything in me, that is sin, as being forever true.

31 And I do declare, that I love my (God) Son, who is called Jesus Christ, forever. And through accepting Christ Jesus, as Christ Jesus, being one's eternal true savior, from me, forever true.

32 It is, that they of the earth, may live, eternally and repent fully, forever true, in me (God). As being eternally forever forgiven of their seen and felt, unto me, forever true, true sins, forever,

33 And, that had been, true sins. That were forever found and were forever true sins, that were forever seen sins, that were seen eternal unto me, forever.

34 And those seen sins, they were seen and felt, unto me, as being eternally found, as being their desired, true death, forever true.

35 Unrepentiful, eternal, living forever, true sinfulness. It is found, as being eternally forever true. As being found, without having Christ Jesus, as this Christ Jesus,

36 Being in one's true life, forever. And true sinfulness, forever. It is, seen and felt, as death, forever true,

37 And, moreover, true sinfulness, forever. It is most surely, eternally forever, and it is found, as being without Christ in one's true life,

38 As this Christ Jesus, as having been one's true savior, as being truly forever true. Then, without having, Jesus Christ, as this Jesus, being one's seen and felt, forever true, true savior,

39 Then the true cords of death, that is called desired true death, forever. That true death, it shall take hold of the damned, as being forever true and forever seen.

40 And that true death, it is, seen, as their desired true death, forever. And it is, as being forever true,

41 As true, granted true death. And that true death forever. It shall take hold of them, that do forsake, Christ Jesus, as this Christ Jesus, being one's seen savior, forever.

42 And, most certainly, as eternally forever true. They the damned, they shall be damned forever true. And they are unrepentfully forever true, and, forever seen,

43 As seen to be caste away from me. As being eternally forever true and to be forever seen. And to be as dead unto me, for all of true eternity, and, to be forever seen, as dead death, forever.

44 All unrepentiful true sin, it is unholy and is found in the unrepentiful, ungodly, beastly true men, and unrepentiful, ungodly beastly true nations,

45 And those nations and their (ungodly nations) true sinners, as being forever true, in sin true death, forever. They are found unto me, forever,

46 As being eternally forever found as being true, without me (God), forever, And they are found, unto me, forever eternal, in sin, as being eternally forever true, in unrepentiful true sinfulness, forever.

47 And they who are found without me forever true. They are most surely, fallen. And they are seen, as being unrepentiful, to never desire to accept Christ,

48 As this Christ Jesus, being their eternal, true savior, forever. And this same Christ, who is my eternal, true Son. He (Jesus Christ) is found,

49 As given from me (God), who (God) is the most high God, of given, eternal, living forever, true salvation, as being forever true.

50 And, to be without me and to be without Christ Jesus. It is seen, as being, a damning eternal, living forever, true image of unrepentfulness,

51 That is a found image called death, as found within them, that do desire, to be, as Satan is dead unto me, as being forever true and forever seen.

52 And these, the damned. They are seen, as being Satan like men and women. And they, are seen, as being unrepentiful true men and unrepentiful true nations,

53 As being eternally forever true and forever known, as known true death, forever. And these Satan like men. They are seen, as desiring to become apart of the sinful true image of eternal true death, that is forever seen.

54 And that seen true image, that is found, in earnest and sincere, true death, forever true. It is seen, as being a unrepentiful true image, found in death, forever true.

55 And, that damningly true image, of the damned forever. It is seen, and felt, as death unto themselves forever. And it is, damningly true men,

56 Who are found by me, forever true. As being, eternally unholy and unrighteous, as being

eternally forever true. And they are seen, in eternal true death, forever true.

57 And these, in imaged true death, forever. That eternal true image, as found in Satan true death, forever. It is seen, as being found,

58 In unrepentiful true sins, that are unrepentfully forever seen sins. And those seen sins, forever. They are seen, and found, by me, as being eternally forever seen,

59 And those seen sins, in death, forever. They are seen and felt, as eternal true death, forever. And those seen sins, in death, forever,

60 They are found and seen, in and as the damningly true image of death. That is found, made of their own, desired, true unrepentfulness.

61 That unrepentfulness, as being eternally forever seen, and felt. It is, seen, as being, forever true. For they truly do not ever desire, to ever receive Christ Jesus, as this Christ Jesus, being their seen savior, from me, as being forever true.

62 Heavenly eternal true salvation. It is called, Christ in me, the true father, forever. And it is seen, as Christly eternal true life,

63   That is given by me, as being eternally forever truly faithful, as being eternally forever true, unto the repentful, as being forever seen.

64   That seen and utterly true salvation, that is called Christ Jesus. It is seen, and felt, as eternal true life, as being forever true. And that life, it is given of me, and it is found, in Christ, forever,

65   And that true life, that is called God in Christ Jesus, forever. It is given of me (God), as holy forever, and ever, true life.

66   And that true life, it is found most certainly forever true, of me (God), as being eternally forever true, and seen.

67   And that true life, it is, called God, as being truly found, as given of myself, forever. And true life, is found, given of me, forever. As being, eternally forever, and ever true,

68   And is truly faithfully forever, given, by me, forever true. As given, by me, as being eternally forever seen. As being, Jesus Christ, forever.

69   And that true life, forever. It is found, as my (God) only, begotten true Son, who is called, Jesus Christ, as being eternally forever, and ever true. And, I Am, true forever, even as, I Am God, as being forever seen.

70 Heavenly true Salvation, it cometh down out of heaven, from me, for I Am: "The God of most heavenly, forever living, eternal true life."

71 And that true life, it is seen. As eternal, living forever, true life. And that true life, it is, faithfully forever, truly called Christ Jesus, forever.

72 And that true life, that is, called Jesus Christ, forever. It is, seen, by me, forever. And it is seen and felt, forever. As being, eternally forever seen, true life,

73 And it is seen, as being, eternal true life, as being, Christ Jesus, forever. And, that true and ever lasting, eternal, true life,

74 It is, most eternal, and it is found, unto me, as being me, as I Am given of myself, into Christ Jesus, forever. And, it is truly, forever true.

75 That true life, it is seen and felt, as me, forever, as I Am found, as my eternal, true Son, who is called "Christ Jesus," as being eternally forever, and ever true.

76 And without Christly true life, this utterly fallen, true earth. It is found, as being, a unrepentiful sinful true image, of man without God, as being eternally forever true.

77 And those, who are without God, as being eternally forever true. Then true death, it shall take those, that have not Christ, and this, is eternally forever sure.

78 And eternal true death, it is granted most surely, unto the damned. Who are found, as being without God, forever. And to be without God, as God is found in Christ Jesus, forever.

79 That is seen, as being, damningly, Antichrist, true sin, forever. And, that is found, in not, desiring to receive the heavenly true Son,

80 Who is called Christ. As this Christ Jesus, being one's personal, living forever, true savior, as being forever true.

81 And this Christ Jesus, he is sent by me forever. And I Am, "The God of most eternal, living forever, heavenly true truth."

82 And, all utterly, unrepentfully fallen true men. They are seen, by me, forever. As being, a unrepentiful, beastly true, eternal true, true image of dead death, as being eternal true men (men and women), forever.

83 And those unrepentiful true men, as forever true and forever seen. They have chosen, to remain. As being unrepentiful to never receive Christ.

84 And, those seen by me, unrepentiful true men. They are seen by me, as being forever true men. And, they are even seen, as being, unrepentiful true nations of death, forever true.

85 And those, fallen true men, who are found, by their own eternal, true choices, that is seen, as they do desire, to be without Christ, as being forever true.

86 They are considered: As fallen and are, most certainly, Antichrist, perditious true men. And, those unrepentiful true men, they are the damned, and they are found, unto me, forever,

87 As being found, as a damningly unrepentiful true image, of death forever true. And, they are seen, as being found. As being found, as being unrepentfully, truly, earthly. In eternal, true death, forever true.

88 And they are seen, as being, unrepentfully seen before me (God). As always being seen, as death forever true. And, they are always, considered of me (God),

89 As always being seen. As being eternally forever true. As being, truly sinful, as unrepentfully forever true. In earnest and sincere, true death, forever true.

90 The act of unrepentfulness, in never desiring Christ. As Christ being their true savior, forever

true. It is seen, as being unrepentiful, forever true.

91 And they are seen and felt, unto me, forever true. As found, unto me forever. In their desired, true death, forever more. And that desired, true death, forever,

92 It is, seen and felt, unto me, forever true. As themselves, as they be found unto me forever true, as the beast, as being eternally forever true.

93 The beast, is forever seen, and is found, in damningly, eternal, true deathly death. And that true death, it is utterly seen and felt, as being eternally forever true, forever,

94 And it is a unholy true image, of them that perish in unrepentfulness, forever true.

95 That true image, in death, forever. It is seen, as being found, in death, forever true. And these, as they are found unto me, forever,

96 As they, the damned. They are found unto me forever, as found in and as, the unrepentiful fallen true image, found of and is made, by devils and made by, fallen true men and made by, fallen true women, forever.

97 And, that image is death forever. And it is seen forever, as being, unrepentiful true men, and, unrepentiful true women, forever true.

98   Those, that are found, as the beastly eternal true image of beastly true death. They are considered of (of means the word by) me (God). As a living, deathly true working, of eternal true death, as being forever true.

99   And, they, the damned forever. They are seen. As being, sinfully, and unrepentfully, found forever, without me, forever.

100   And, without me, as Christ Jesus, being their seen and felt, true savior, as being eternally forever true. Then, they are found, unto me, forever,

101   As found by me forever. In ever most, certain true death. As being, forever true, and, forever seen. And is seen, as being true death, forever, unless, they repent, quickly in Jesus Christ, forever.

Chapter 20 w/ 73 verses   Damnation against God

1   Those, who are found, in their deathly, forever true, unrepentiful desired, eternal true workings, called death.

2   Those workings, they are found, unto me forever. As being found, in a desired, sinful, true work. That is seen, as their desired true dead death, as being forever true.

3 And that sinful true work, it is found, as their personally desired and true, unrepentiful true damnation. As that sinful true work, is found in themselves, as being eternal death, forever.

4 And that true damnation, it is called working true death forever seen. And it is found by me, in themselves. As themselves desiring to receive eternal true death, as being forever true of themselves, as dead death forever.

5 For they, the damned, they are always, found by me, forever true. In Satanism, as being forever true of themselves. As they are seen and felt,

6 Unto me. As being themselves, as found unto me forever, in eternal true death, forever. And they are seen, by me forever. As being eternally forever seen,

7 As being eternally forever true and forever seen, as being, ever lasting, true dead death, forever.

8 That is a true damnation, and it is made by and given by, the damned, as being eternally forever true, unto me, as forever seen.

9 And it is given of themselves, unto me. As they truly do desire, forever true. To personally give me forever, themselves forever, to be eternal true death, forever.

10 Therefore, I shall not accept them, to live sinfully before me, forever, and I will punish them with granted true death, as being forever seen,

11 That punishment, from me forever true. It is, if they shall not repent unto me in Christ Jesus. As Christ Jesus, being their seen savior, from me, as being forever true.

12 And their desire, to sin, forever. That true desire, it is true of themselves forever, unto me forever true and forever more.

13 And, granted true death. That death, it is seen and called eternal true damnation, forever. And, it is seen and felt, and it is called granted true damnation, that is granted by me, forever.

14 And granted true death, to be as dead as Satan is dead. It is granted to the damned ones forever. That they, the damned. That they,

15 Can be found forever true, to be as dead as Satan is dead unto me, as being eternally forever seen.

16 Even, as Satan is seen and is found, unto me forever, even now, in the earth, in his works.

17 That were true works, that were once given unto him (Satan), as being forever true, as given to him, before he (Satan) transgressed my eternal

true life, that is called Christly true life, forever true.

18 Now, Satan's true works, as Satan being a work of God, before Satan sinned, forever. That true work, it has became, sin forever.

19 And in Satan's likeness forever, eternal true damnation, it is a sinful and a unrepentiful, sinful forever true work, as found made by the damned, in unrepentiful true sin, as being forever true.

20 And Satan, has became, a enemy to the light, that is called God forever. And Satan is and has became, unrepentiful true sin, as desired within himself (Satan), eternally forever.

21 Therefore, Satan, as being unrepentfully forever true. He is seen, as a living in death, true abomination, that is called unrepentfulness, that is forever true and forever seen. And that abomination, it is seen, as being, granted true death, forever.

22 Therefore his (Satan) image, it is called unrepentfulness against God, forever. And that unrepentfulness, Satan doth desire forever,

23 And it remaineth true of Satan and of his kind (demons), forever. For he desireth not to ever repent in Christ Jesus, as being eternally forever true.

24 (As a note: Whatever true part of God's creation, desireth to approach God, it must be done through Christ Jesus, forever.)

25 (Whether it be found in heaven or found in any of God's creation. Any person or angel, or even any other part of God's creation, to approach God forever. It must occur, through Jesus Christ, forever.)

26 Just as it was before Christ Jesus was born, God forgave. And now any part in God's creation, that desireth to repent of it's sin,

27 Whether devil or angel or man or any part that is unseen in God's creation, called created. That repentance, it must be done through Christ Jesus, as being forever true, and, forever seen.

28 Granted eternal true damnation, it is seen and called dead death as being eternally forever certain. And it is seen, as being eternal, in the damned, as being eternally forever true.

29 And that granted true damnation. It is sinfully and unrepentfully, desired by the damned, as being eternally forever true. And that damnation, to be as Satan is dead, forever. It is demonstrated against me, by the damned, forever.

30 And the damned, they are truly, seen unto me forever true. As being, dead unto me (God) as forever seen. And, they are therefore, without me

(God), as I (God) Am found, as I (God) Am found as being Jesus Christ, forever,

31 For the damned, they have chosen Satanism, instead of me (God). And I Am found, as Christ Jesus, eternally forever and ever true.

32 That true death, found in the damned of the fallen true earth, forever. It found unto me forever certain, as being found, sinfully desired by the damned, that do perish eternally forever and ever true of themselves, in dead death, forever,

33 And the damned, they do perish in hell forever, because of their desire, to be as dead as Satan is dead unto me forever. And that true desire, forever,

34 It is seen, as a willful, true damnation, that the damn, do prefer as their own true death, forever. And eternal death, it is seen, in the damned,

35 As being unrepentfully forever true. As they, the damned, as they are found unto me forever. As being sinfully found in being against me,

36 As they, themselves, are found, unto me forever, as they, are forever seen, in deathly sin, as being forever true, of themselves in Satan, forever.

37 And their desired and willful, wanted true damnation, as found in them, that do die unto me, as Satan death, forever. It is found, as their most seen true death,

38 That is their eternal true death. That shall be given unto the damned, as being forever true, even in hell, as forever eternally forever seen.

39 All true death, is dead death, forever. And it is found, without my eternal, living forever, true presents. And that true death, it is found, as being the damned, as forever true.

40 That true death, it is found, in the damned ones true desire. For sinful and true, unrepentiful, true sin, as being forever seen. And that true and ever lastingly, eternal true death,

41 It is found, without my heavenly true salvation, that is called, Jesus Christ, forever. And my granted and most true salvation, it is, called Christ Jesus, as being eternally forever true, and, forever seen.

42 That salvation, it is granted by me (God), in my eternal true Son, who is called Christ Jesus, forever. And Christ Jesus, as salvation,

43 That salvation, it is granted, unto all who are found and seen, as repentful forever true, unto me, forever, in Christ Jesus, forever.

44 But the damned, they are found, unto me, forever true. As themselves, in desiring unrepentfulness, that is called, true sin, forever.

45 And true sin, forever. It shall damn all, forever, who desireth death, eternally forever.

46 And my eternal, living forever, recompense granted true damnation, that is given, unto the damned, forever.

47 It is called, given true damnation, forever. And it is seen, as being, true death, unto the damned, as forever seen.

48 And it is seen and granted, as eternal death unto them who desire unrepentiful true sin, as sincerely desired in themselves, forever.

49 And the damned, they truly do not desire my heavenly true salvation, that is given of me, through Christ Jesus, as being forever and ever heard.

50 And those, the damned, they are eternally and unrepentfully found in being against receiving myself forever, as I Am seen, as being Christly eternal true salvation.

51 And, true death, it is seen. As being truly desired in them, that perish in willful, desired true sin, forever.

52 And, to never accept Christ Jesus, as Christ Jesus, being one's true savior, as being eternally forever true. That is a eternal true work of damningly true sinfulness,

53 True sinfulness, it is found by me, forever true. In them, that do not ever desire to receive Christ Jesus, as Christ Jesus, being one's true savior, as being eternally forever true, and, forever seen.

54 Eternal true death, it is found in them, that do perish in unrepentiful true sin, forever. For the damned, they will not ever desire,

55 To receive the only, approved and true savior. Who is given to all of mankind, who is called, Jesus Christ.

56 And they, the damned. They are most surely found, unto me forever. As being found, as death unto me forever true. And that true death, it is desired by them (the damned), as desired true death, forever true.

57 That true death, it is seen and felt, as being unrepentfully desired within themselves, as forever seen death.

58 And that death, is seen, as being eternally forever true, as true death, that is found, in being against all, that I Am, as I Am God, forever.

59 And these, the damned of the fallen true earth, forever. They are truly seen, unto me forever true. As being against receiving my (God) eternal true Son. Who is, called Christ Jesus, as being eternally forever true.

60 And they, the damned. They shall perish in hell forever, with their desired true unrepentiful true sins, forever.

61 And the damned, they are truly against, receiving Christ Jesus, forever. And, they are truly seen and felt, as being against receiving this Christ Jesus,

62 As ever lasting forever, as of themselves, as they be found, in Satan, forever, and ever lastingly,

63 As being eternally forever true, as being forever seen, as seen and felt, as true death, forever, as being unto me, forever.

64 And the damned of the beastly eternal true image of Satan and Satan's true death, forever. They are the damned, and they are found, unto me, as being forever found faithful, in Satan true death, forever.

65 And them in Satanism forever, they are found unto me forever, as found by me, as themselves, as being found faithful, in the spiritual true mark of the name of the beast, that is both,

unrepentiful true man (all of sinful mankind) and unrepentiful true Satan, forever.

66 And the damned, they are found, unto me, as being eternally forever true. As being, found, spiritually and physically found, as found, granted true death, forever.

67 Given, true damnation, that is given by me, as being eternally forever true, as true unto the beast, as being eternally forever seen.

68 It is seen, as a heavenly forever true damnation, that is called, true death, as being eternally forever seen, true death, forever.

69 And that granted true death, it is granted by me, through Christ Jesus, forever, as unto the damned, forever. And that great death, for the damned, forever.

70 It is granted of and by me forever. Because they, the beast. They truly do not, ever, desire Christ, forever,

71 As Christ Jesus being their seen true savior, as being eternally forever seen. Therefore, the workings, that are called eternal true death, as being eternally forever and ever seen, and true.

72 Then, those workings, shall damn the dead, as being forever true, and, as forever seen.

73 And I shall give death, eternally unto all, that appearth before me (at the great, final, true judgment), forever. As they be found before me, in the image of death, that is called, "The beast," forever.

Chapter 21 w / 41 verses   Blackness of darkness

1 Living forever, true death. It is given by me forever. As a given, true, and utter true death. And true death, it is given, as being a great punishment, from me forever.

2 And it shall be found, given in hell, as given to the damned forever. As they, are living, eternally forever, in the "Blackness of Darkness," forever sure.

3 And that true death, in hell forever. It is seen, as a living forever, true life. As a life of eternal and most true, true punishment, forever,

4 That punishment, it is seen. For desiring and being true. In desiring forever true. To desire forever, to desire to be always, found, in the blackness of darkness,

5 That is seen and felt, as being eternally forever true, as being darkness, that is seen, and called: "Unrepentiful true Sin," forever.

6 For the damned ones, forever. They truly do desire forever, beastly, eternal true life, that is found without Christ, and that is found in the workings of living death, forever,

7 True death, it is given unto the damned ones, forever. As it is given faithfully by me, as being forever true. As given by me faithfully forever,

8 Unto the damned ones forever, for they truly do hold, unto the fallen true image. That is the seen true image of utter true dead death, forever.

9 That image, as found in utter, true dead death, forever certain. It is given by the hands of the false prophet. Who is Satan, that is seen and felt,

10 As the false prophet of earnest and sincere, true death. And that image, as found, as the damned, and yet, even of true devils, forever true and ever lastingly, eternally forever.

11 That image, it is seen and felt, unto the damned. As true dead death forever true. And that is an image, that is made through one's hardness of heart. As seen before God, as being forever true.

12 It is seen, as being hardness of heart. And it is seen, and called, as one's truly desired true death, as being eternally forever, truly seen. And it is seen, as one's true desire, to sin, forever,

13 And, as to sin before me, as unrepentfully forever true, and, that is forever known unto me, as themselves, as dead death forever true. And it is seen death, as being seen unto me, forever.

14 And they are seen, as them, who doth desire Satan's unrepentiful true sinfulness, that called Satan's truly desired true death, forever.

15 That death, it is most certainly, found, as being, unrepentiful, utterly fallen, true man (men), forever true.

16 And that, is a eternal true image in Satanism, forever. As it is found, desired by the damned forever. And it is found, as their desired true death,

17 As it is found in them, as themselves in Satan forever, and they truly do desire, to die before my great eternal true presents, that is called, Christ Jesus, as being forever true.

18 That Satan like true image, found in the damned, forever. It is seen and felt, unto me, as being forever true. And it is felt, unto me,

19 As them, that do die forever. For they truly do desire, Satan's true ways, of death, forever.

20 And they, that are of that Satanism, that is called dead death forever true. That death, is an image, as made as a stone image of seen true

coldness of heart, that is demonstrated coldly toward me, as I Am their God, as forever true.

21 That coldness in living true death, forever. It is seen and felt, unto me forever true. As being truly seen toward me, and is seen, toward, all that I Am as I Am their God, as being forever true.

22 And without me as their savior called Jesus Christ. Then, they shall die, therefore, as being eternally forever true. And that true death,

23 Shall be found, unto them, forever. As themselves, then caste into hell, eternally forever, and ever true.

24 And that is truly given true death, that is death. That is given by me, forever. Unto that wicked true beast, who is forever seen. As being a wicked true beast, of death, as being eternally forever and ever true.

25 And, true death, it is given unto the beast forever, at the great judgment of eternal life, forever. And, at that eternal just and righteous, true judgment,

26 Granted true death, is seen, as being the blackness of darkness, forever. And, granted true death, it is seen, without true end,

27   As being, eternal true death, as being eternally forever and ever true, and, as forever seen.

28   And, that true judgment, it shall remain so, forever. That is, if they, the beast, shall not repent, afore hand, and receive Christ Jesus, as Christ Jesus,

29   Being their true lord and savior, as forever certain, in this life, and as forever true and forever known, of themselves, unto me, forever.

30   Death, is a found true image unto me, as being eternally forever seen. That image, is being, Satan like, forever.

31   And it is, found unto me, as being eternally forever true. As being utter true shame, and utter true contempt, forever.

32   That is death, as seen before me. As thy unrepentiful true self, as a beastly true sinner, when one is without Christ in one's true life, forever.

33   And that death, it is seen before me, as one (mankind) being found unto me forever true. As a unrepentiful true beast, as being found toward me, forever. As I Am found in Christ, the Son, forever.

34 And that true death, it is granted by me, as faithfully forever true, and it is given by me, through Christ Jesus, forever,

35 As given forever, unto all who desire Satan, as being truly forever true of themselves, in the want of unrepentiful true sin, forever.

36 And that death, it is given by me, as faithfully forever true of me, as being eternally forever seen, as seen unto whomsoever thou art, that are found, unto me forever, as being found unto me, forever,

37 As being found, as being eternally desirethsome for Satan, as Satan being thy true savior, to save thee from me, that thou mayest truly,

38 Enjoy his death, as given unto himself, from me, as to be in hell, as it is eternally forever given unto Satan, forever.

39 That death, it is seen and felt, unto Satan, forever true. Even now, Satan thinketh that he can change my mind forever. But in his heart, he knoweth that he has lied to himself forever, in that regard forever.

40 And true death, it is found unto Satan, himself. And it is found, given by me faithfully forever true, unto Satan and unto the damned,

41   As being eternally given of me, as being eternally forever, as faithfully forever true, as faithfully granted true death, forever.

Chapter 22 w / 91 verses   Living forever true death

1   Living forever, true death. It is seen, and heard. As being, unholy, Antichrist and perditious, forever true, true death, forever.

2   That death, it is found given of me forever, with punishment from me, as being eternally forever true. And that true death, it is a beastly image of eternal living forever true damnation.

3   That damnation, it is found for being sinfully against me (God) and for being sinfully found against my (God) own personal true righteousness. And my true righteousness, it is found, in Christ Jesus, as being forever true, and forever seen.

4   And the image of death, it is called sin. And it is a fallen, sinful forever, living forever, damningly, unholy and unrighteous, true image. As it is found in one's own, imaged in sin, true desires, forever.

5   And those, sinful true desires and sinful true lusts, forever. They are eternally desired by the damned, as being forever true.

6   And the damned, they truly do desire sin. As sin being in them, as being eternally forever and always, forever true. In themselves, as death forever.

7   And those sinful true desires, as found in the damned, forever. Those sinful true desires, is found in them eternally. For they truly do desire, this present, sinful, true world, as being eternally forever seen.

8   And this seen true world, in sin forever. It is found unto me. As being eternally forever true. And is found unto me, as death, forever,

9   For it is found unto me, forever. As being truly found. As found in "Bestiality, as being eternally forever True."

10   And this earth as the beast called death forever. It is found, as true death, forever. And it is seen, as one's desired, true bestiality,

11   As it is found, as being desired sinfully forever, within one's, own, true, unrepentfulness, as being eternally forever seen,

12   And it is seen, as being seen true death, as being forever certain, and forever made. As it made, by the damned, as they are found in eternal seen sin, as seen unto me, forever,

13   And that bestiality, that bestiality. It shall damn the unrepentiful true ones, as being eternally forever seen, as seen in granted true death, forever.

14   And they, the damned, who are found unto me, forever. As found, in sin forever. They shall perish unto me, as being forever true,

15   And they shall perish, unto me, as being eternally forever seen, and, as forever more.

16   And the damned, they shall perish forever. And they do perish willfully forever true, of their sinful own true selves.

17   For they truly do not ever desire to accept Christ, as this Christ Jesus, being their seen savior, as being forever true, and, as forever seen,

18   These that do perish in sin, They are considered of me (God), as being found in the judgment. That is seen and called "The Blackness Of Darkness."

19   That darkened and most true judgment. It is found, given of me (God). As being eternally forever true, upon them. Who desire unrepentfully forever, to not ever receive Christ,

20   As this Christ Jesus, being their seen savior, forever. And Christ Jesus, he is sent by me, as

being eternally forever true, as sent by me, into the earth,

21 As sent into the earth, as eternal true salvation. That is heavenly forever true. And this Christ Jesus, he is sent, as eternal true salvation,

22 That is called God forever. And that true salvation. It is forever seen, as seen and given me, as faithfully forever and ever true.

23 The blackness of darkness, it is found and given by me. As being found and given, as being eternally forever true. And it is found,

24 As being given eternally forever. As being found without my (God) most holy, forever eternal, true presents, forever,

25 That presents, it is me. As I Am found eternally forever, in Christ, the Son, forever. And Christ Jesus, he is found in me forever. As found, in most certain, forever and ever, true life, that is called God, forever.

26 Eternal seen darkness, it is called eternal night. And it is found in the damned ones, forever. And it is found, as given by me, unto the damned, forever.

27 And it is found, as being forever true, unto the damned, as being eternally forever and ever true, unto the lost, forever.

28 And, eternal seen true judgment. It is called night, and it is given as hell, unto the damned, forever. And they shall not live forever, without Christ, as Christ Jesus, being their eternal seen savior, forever.

29 And, in hell, they shall know that they have received fair and just recompense, that is called death. And that recompense, it is given by me,

30 As given faithfully forever true, as for one being found, as being found eternally forever true, as themselves. As they are found, in being eternally forever true,

31 In being, eternally against All, that I Am, as I Am found, in Christ, the Son. As I Am eternally forever true.

32 Eternal true death, it is always seen. As being true, against Christ forever. And true death, it is seen. As being true, as eternal true death. That is death,

33 That is true death, in sin forever. And it is seen, as being eternal dead death, as it is found as the damned, forever. And they, the damned. They are always, against me,

34 For they are seen unto me forever, as being seen, as being always, seen. As being truly fallen, as being beastly, Antichrist, unholy, sinful, and unrepentiful, forever.

35 And these, the damned. They shall never desire to accept Christ, as Christ Jesus, being their seen true savior, forever. And, to never accept Christ, as Christ Jesus being one's true savior, forever,

36 That is an image of eternal true death, that is forever, truly seen. And it is seen, and found, by me. As being eternally forever seen,

37 And that image, it is a found, as a true image, as being eternally seen and felt, as being eternal true Satanism, forever.

38 And that image as Satanism forever, as found as the damned forever. And it is found, and it is felt, as being eternally forever true,

39 As a seen, unholy true image, that is and is of the beast, that is even called, true death, forever.

40 And that image as death forever. It is forever true, as a eternal damningly true image. That is them, that do eternally perish, in their own, willful true sin, as being forever seen.

41 As they are seen and found, in unrepentfulness, that is demonstrated and desired, as they truly do desire to be against me, forever.

42 For to love me, is to serve me. In repentfulness (means to receive Christ Jesus, as

lord and savior, forever), forever, as saith, thy eternal true God, forever.

43 The Antichrist image. It is a unholy true image. As it found, to be Satanism, as being eternally forever and ever seen, and felt, as given unto, true death, as forever seen.

44 And it is seen and felt, and it is known, as eternal dying true death. And it is seen,

45 As being seen, as found in and is, the damned. Who are found unto me, as being forever true. And the damned of the earth, forever,

46 They are found, by me forever. As being, unrepentfully fallen, within themselves, as being eternally forever and ever true.

47 And that is because, they the damned of the earth, forever. They truly do desire, as personally desired, the true wanting, of granted by me forever, true death, from me, eternally forever.

48 Therefore, as they the damned, are seen and felt, unto me, as Satan like, forever. Then, they truly do, forever true, desire true death.

49 And true death, is seen and felt, as being eternally, dead death, as it is given by me, unto the lost ones, forever,

50 And dead death, is given by me, faithfully forever true, unto themselves (the damned ones forever), as being eternally forever and ever true.

51 And they are truly seen unto me, forever. As being seen and felt, unto me, forever. As being dead unto me, as being eternally forever seen, and, forever true.

52 And the unrepentfully, they are found by me, forever. As being eternally dead unto me, forever, And they are found by me, in the sinful true works,

53 Of death forever. And they are found, in death eternally: "As being beastly eternal true sin" forever. And they, the damned.

54 They are seen unto me, forever. As being found to me, as being eternally forever, estranged to me, as being eternally forever estranged.

55 As they, the lost, as they are truly found by me, forever. As being themselves, as being estranged to me, as being forever seen, and felt,

56 As they are seen and felt, unto me, as being eternally forever true. For they are found unto me, forever. As being eternal, in being found, as being, eternal dead death, as being eternally forever true.

57 And they are seen, unto me forever. As being unrepentfully seen, as being the unrepentfully, truly lost of the earth, as being forever true,

58 As they are found in eternal seen unrepentfulness, as being forever seen, and true in themselves. As being true to Satanism, forever.

59 And, they are the rejected of me and of Christ Jesus, forever. And they are seen and felt, unto us (God and Christ Jesus), forever.

60 As they are the rejected, that are found in being unrepentiful, as being seen and felt, as being the truly dead, unto me, forever.

61 And the damned, they are unrepentfully dead unto us (God and Christ Jesus), as being forever true. And they are, seen and felt, unto me forever.

62 As being eternally forever true, and forever seen, as they are seen and felt, in death, before me, as I Am found in Christ Jesus, forever.

63 And the dead, as they are given of themselves, unto Satan, forever. They are the unrepentiful, truly dead, who are damningly seen,

64 As being unrepentiful, truly dead unto me and unto my Son, Christ Jesus, as being eternally forever, in Satan death forever.

65 And the dead in Satan death, forever. They are seen and felt, as dead death, forever. And they are seen and felt, as death, for all of given, true eternity,

66 And, as being forever true. And they are dead, in unrepentiful true sins, forever, as unto me forever, and unto Christ Jesus, forever.

67 And, moreover, they are seen and felt, unto me forever so. As unrepentfully seen, as true death, as being forever seen, true death, that is a seen, granted true death, unto them, forever, from me, forever.

68 And that death, it is granted unto them, as being forever true. As being granted unto themselves, forever. As granted to them, at the last, final true judgment,

69 As it given unto the damned, forever. And at, the great white throne, true judgment. Then, eternal just judgment, it is seen, and it is called, "Final true judgment," as being forever and ever sure, and, forever more.

70 They, the damned, forever. They truly do desire, the spirit of error, rather than me (God),

who has created them, to love me (God), as being forever sure.

71 And they truly do desire, Satan's true self, as he (Satan) is seen as eternal true death, forever. And they are seen and felt, as death unto me. As being eternally forever certain, and, as forever seen.

72 And true death, it is seen. As a true, unrepentiful, true beastly eternal image. As found in and is, the damned, as being eternally forever found, and seen.

73 As a seen image, as being, eternal true death, as being eternally forever certain, and forever true in Satanism, forever.

74 That is, eternal death, that is a forever imaged true work, as it found, in being true unto me, forever. And it is a eternal, true work, that is called unrepentfulness, as being forever true.

75 And, dead death, it is seen and felt, unto me. As them, that doth, desire Satan, as being forever true, of themselves in Satan forever. And, that death, it is seen and felt, unto me, as them in Satan death, forever,

76 And, as a result of their willful and true desire, to sin unrepentfully, as being eternally forever seen, Then, Satan, has became,

77 Their false idol God, for all time. And, dead death, it is forever seen, as death forever true, and, it is, forever more.

78 Eternal true death, to be as Satan, as Satan is found as being unrepentiful, as being eternally forever true.

79 It is seen and felt, as dead death. That is seen, as the blackness of deathly night, that is called deathly forever true judgment, as being forever true.

80 And, the blackness of darkness, is found without me, as forever true. And, the blackness of eternal dead death eternal true night.

81 It is seen, as being without Christ, as Christ Jesus, being their savior, as being forever true, and, as forever seen.

82 That blackness in death forever. It is seen, as a, eternal true image, of granted true death, as being eternally forever seen, and felt, as being forever true.

83 And that blackness of eternal dying true night, forever. It is seen, and felt, in the utterly fallen. Who are seen and felt, unto me. As forever sure, in Satanism, forever.

84 And eternal dead death, it is felt, as granted true death, as being eternally forever true, in the damned, forever,

85 For they truly do, do desire, to be away, from me. As I Am found, in Christ Jesus, as being eternally forever and ever true.

86 And, to be felt unto me, as being eternally seen, as being eternal dead death, as being eternally forever sure. It is, seen and felt, as the true image, of Satan's own true likeness, as being eternally forever seen.

87 And it is found, as being found in the spiritual true mark of the beast, who is called, Satan and unrepentiful true men, as being forever certain.

88 And that image of the damned. It is seen, as a, unholy, beastly eternal, true image. As a eternal image, in death, forever. And, it is, surely,

89 Found unto me forever. As being given sinfully forever true, unto me, as found unto me, as being eternally forever true, of the damned, forever.

90 And true and ever lasting, eternal dead death. It is, found, as being eternally forever certain, as found in one's sinful, true sinfulness, forever.

91 And, true death, it is desired, by the damned, forever. As being eternal true death, forever certain, and, forever more.

Chapter 23 w / 52 verses   The beastly image of death

1 The unholy, beastly image of death. It is seen and felt, as being Antichrist. And that image, it is seen as Satan himself, that is found in all persons,

2 Who are found unto me forever, as being found unto me, as being, forever true death. And they are found unto me, as being forever true. As being found, in the fallen true image of Satan, as forever seen.

3 And they are found unto me, as being forever true. As being found unto me, as being unrepentfully, sinfully forever true. In the workings of Satan's true spirit, that is found in Satan's true death, forever.

4 And Satan's true death. It is a seen image, found as being true Satanism, as being forever true, as found in the damned, as forever seen. For they, the damned, they are Antichrist, as being forever true.

5 And they are the damned, with Satan and Satan's kind, forever. And these, the damned.

They do enjoy their unrepentfulness, as being sinfully forever true.

6 And they, the damned, they are seen, as being of the beastly image of true death, forever. And they truly do enjoy the false imaged miracles of heavenly, false fire,

7 That the false prophet of death, giveth as eternal true life, unto them, that are found in and of the beastly eternal true image, as it forever true of themselves, as it is found by me, in their desired true death, as being eternally forever seen.

8 For his miracle of life from heaven, it is granted in true death, from me forever, in recompense forever, as forever seen. Unto the damned, as being eternally forever sure.

9 And this false prophet, who is called Satan the deceiver. He wroughteth miracles of eternal true death, unto the fallen true earth, from heaven,

10 As forever sure. Instead of life, as life is found, in Christ Jesus, as being forever true and forever sure, as given by me, for I Am, God the father, with eternal life, forever.

11 And neither, can Satan give the pure rivers of eternal true life, that is called Christ, unto the world forever.

12 For Satan is fallen and shall be punished, as forever true of me (God). For Satan is found by me (God), as being unrepentfully, sinful, and, as being forever true, in sin, forever.

13 And they, the Antichrist true beast, forever. They truly do desire, to be always true. In never desiring Christ Jesus, as Christ Jesus, being their seen savior, as being forever true.

14 That image, is called Antichrist. And, it is always found, as being against receiving all and complete, total knowledge,

15 That is concerning the Son, who is called, Christ Jesus. And who is Christ Jesus, that is given of me (God), as being eternally forever and ever true.

16 And, even in the body of Christ, in these days of the earth, forever. Is found unto me forever true. Are chaff, that are seen, as being Antichrist, as being Antichrist, truly forever.

17 And those Antichrists, along with the Antichrists of the earth. They are them, that are found unto me forever true, as who are found, as whose coming in these days of the world, is after Satan's own sinful true heart of eternal true unrepentfulness, as being forever seen.

18 And the Antichrist true spirit, it is seen and found unto me, as being found unto me forever

true. As being found forever true. In one's desired, true sins, as forever true, and, as forever seen. And is seen, as death, that is forever desired, in the damned, as being forever true.

19 The Antichrist true spirit, it has been in the earth, since the fall of Adam and Eve, and has always remained in the earth, and shall always remain in the fallen true earth, forever. And it shall continue in hell forever, and is the damned, forever.

20 And this Antichrist true spirit, it was foretold to occur in the last time. Which is seen as the timeframe of the earth, that is called "The last days."

21 Therefore, the timeframe of the earth, that is called the last time. It is seen, as the complete timeframe, from start to finish, of the timeframe of the earth, that is seen and called "The Last Days."

22 And during these days, that are called the last days, the early church knew, that man would reject Christ Jesus and that man would reject Christ Jesus, as Christ Jesus, then being born in the earth, as savior for Israel, forever.

23 And when the early church dealt with this rejection seen in Israel as rejection in not believing that the savior for Israel had been born

and that this Christ would change the customs and laws regarding things of God.

24 Then, the early church looked upon this rejection by Israel, as being an Antichrist true spirit, that was foretold to occur in the last days (The last time).

25 Of course, the last days, they began with the birth of Christ Jesus and Christ's resurrection, and so forth.

26 And the early church, had to deal with that Antichrist true spirit, that is found in a number of ways, such as not believing that Christ had actually, been physically born in the earth, in Israel.

27 And the early church knew that during the complete timeframe of the earth, that is seen and called the last days, that at some point in time, during that timeframe, that is called the last days,

28 That unrepentiful true man (men) would in fact, become in his behavior, as the days of Noah, and those days have become the timeframe, that is seen and called "The end of the days" as noted in Daniel 12:13.

29 Therefore, in these days, unrepentiful true man (men), is seen as a true unrepentiful true Antichrist, Noah's day type person, forever. And

who desires to be as Satan is unrepentiful toward God,

30 Even as Satan is seen and heard, as heard and seen, as sin, as being forever seen, and, as forever, truly heard, as sin, forever true.

31 And, in the body of Christ, in these days of the world, it is seen, true chaff, who is seen and heard, unto me, as being beastly eternal true Antichrists,

32 And they are unrepentfully fallen against me (God), and they are spiritually seated in the blood of Christ for Christ and I, to accept them, always,

33 In my eternal true presents, of heavenly true life, while they remain in their seen and felt, true sins. As those seen and felt, true sins, are seen and felt, forever true, by me, forever.

34 And they are truly found of (of means the word by) me (God) and are found, of (of means the word by) Christ Jesus, As found in being found as being not totally repentful unto, both me (God) and unto Christ Jesus, as being forever true,

35 And they, themselves, they are found, as desiring, the wanting of true death, as forever eternally forever true of themselves, as forever seen by me, as being forever true,

36 And while they are found unto me forever, as they claim, Christ Jesus, as savior, as forever true. They do claim Christ Jesus as savior, forever,

37 But I know them not and my name, it is taken away from themselves, forever true, while they remain falsely forever, in not being Christ like, in the body of Christ Jesus, forever.

38 For they do desire to remain forever, in Christ Jesus. As being forever true of themselves, in their desired true death, as forever certain, and forever true, of themselves, forever.

39 And they are chaff forever. And they are seen, as being Antichrist, and they have fallen away, while seated in the blood of Christ Jesus, forever,

40 And they have fallen away, while they are found unto me, in the body of Christ, as being fallen in Satanism, as found forever certain, and, as forever true.

41 And they are fallen away from me (God), as forever true, of themselves, in Satan's true image and in Satan's true likeness, that is called unrepentiful true sin, forever true.

42 And I Am found, in Christ Jesus, as being eternally forever seen. And these (the unrepentiful forever), true Antichrists,

43 They shall be spewed of me (God) and of Christ, as being forever true. For they have gone, in the way of Baal, as forever true of themselves, in Satanism, as eternally forever true of themselves, as death forever certain, and forever seen.

44 And they have gone, most surely, gone away from Christ, and, gone away from me, as forever true of themselves, as Satanism, as forever true, and, as forever seen.

45 And these Antichrists, they are truly seen, unto me, forever. As being found unto me forever, in a state of being lukewarm, Christ like, true creatures. That are found unto me forever, in true death, forever.

46 That death, it is true in themselves, as being forever seen by me, as being eternally forever true, and forever more.

47 And these Antichrist true creatures, they are called Satanism. And they truly do desire. To be as dead as Satan is dead unto me, forever.

48 And they are truly considered of me (God), as being fallen away from Christ and fallen away from me (God), as being forever true of themselves,

49 As they are found, unto me, forever. As found, in the deathly eternal true image of true

death, forever. As it is found, as being, earnest and sincere, true dead death, as being eternally forever seen, true death, forever.

50   These Antichrists, they are seen, as being, antigod, forever. And they are seen, as being, not Christ like, as forever true and forever seen.

51   And these Antichrists, true beasts, as found by me, forever, as found in Satanism, as being eternally forever seen.

52   They are not holy creatures, unto me, forever. And, they are not found, in my (God) eternal created creation. That is to be Christ like, as forever seen, and, as, to be true forever, in Christ Jesus, forever.

Chapter 24 w / 62 verses   Repentance

1   When one has repented, in Christ Jesus, as being eternally forever true. As in repenting of his or of her own, seen, true sinfulness, that is called death, as being forever true.

2   That repentance, as found given to me, in Christ Jesus, as forever true, that is concerning the repentful true beast, who was seen before their repentance,

3   As the true beast of death, as being eternally forever sure of themselves, while they were, in

the true workings of beastly eternal true death, forever.

4 Unto me, they are accepted in their desired repentance in Christ Jesus, forever. And they, truly do desire, forgiveness from me, as being eternally forever seen.

5 And I shall accept them in Christ the Son, forever, as they are found unto me forever. As desiring me, as I Am found in Christ Jesus, forever.

6 And forgiveness, that is called God in Christ Jesus. It is, most surely, found unto the repentful beast. Who was, at one time, before. Had been seen, as being, a true beast of death, forever.

7 And they, the repentful true beasts of the earth. They are found, as being repentful true beasts with Godly true kindness, now and forever, instead of being forever,

8 As once was true beasts of death, that was forever true of themselves, as they, the beast, were found in Satan's true name and true mark, that is found in Satan's true death, as being eternally forever true of the damned, forever.

9 And when, these true beasts. Do truly, accept Jesus Christ, as this Jesus, being their personal true savior, forever. And, as being eternally forever seen. Then, their desired true repentance,

unto me, to receive Christ Jesus, as Christ Jesus, being their personal true savior,

10 It is, then granted of me, as being forever certain, and, forever true. And their true repentance, to receive Christ Jesus, forever.

11 It is seen, by me forever. As being seen forever made of themselves, as being made and seen before me (God), as being forever true of themselves, forever.

12 And, in Christ the Son, for all of true eternity, and, as forever seen. Is granted Christly true life, as granted to the repentful true beast,

13 Who was, once was sinfully seen, when eternal sin had once been found in themselves, as themselves, being eternally forever true,

14 As they were found in eternal dead death forever. And they had been seen, as death before my great presents, that is called Christly true life, as being eternally forever and ever true.

15 And when, these repentful true beasts of death, are seen repent fully walking, as faithfully found of themselves, forever true,

16 As being eternally found unto me forever, as walking faithfully in my Son, who is called Christ Jesus, as forever seen,

17 They are then, most surely, forgiven. And my true righteousness, it is called, Christ Jesus. As that righteousness, is found, given eternally by me, as given of me, as given faithfully forever certain, in Jesus Christ, forever.

18 That true righteousness, it dwelleth by me in Christ, as given of me through Christ, unto themselves, as life forever. And that true life, it shall live forever true,

19 For that true life, is me, as being eternally forever true. And it is seen, as being forever true, in Christ Jesus, the Son, as forever certain, and, as forever given by me, as being eternally forever true,

20 And true life, is faithfully forever true of me forever. And it is, truly given by me, as I Am seen, as I Am seen as being eternally, the eternal kind God, forever.

21 And I Am forever true, and, I Am faithfully forever true. And I Am seen, as the life, that is called God, as being forever true, and, as forever seen.

22 And these repentful true beasts, in Jesus Christ, forever. They are eternally forever, as forgiven of their seen sins of death,

23 As being eternally, truly forever, forgiven. And they shall walk in Christ, as being forever

true, and, as being eternally forever seen, even as I Am seen, as the life, that is called God, forever.

24 And when, as a result of walking in me, in Christ Jesus, forever. Then, these repentful true beasts,

25 They are then found unto me, as being forever true. As walking in and of me (God), as faithfully forever and ever true, and forever more,

26 As they are found walking in Christ, as forever true of themselves, unto me, as forever seen.

27 But, when anyone particular true beast, is found by me, as walking Without Christ Jesus, as Christ Jesus, being one's eternal true savior, forever true. Then these without Christ, back sliding true beasts,

28 They are seen, as being unrepentfully and being seen faithfully of themselves, as being forever true. As being, eternally forever true,

29 And they are seen by me in sinfulness forever. As being corrupted in themselves, in their wanted true desire, for true death. That is called, to be Satan like, as being forever seen,

30 And, they are truly seen, as forever seen, as themselves, in the image, that is called, to desire hell, as being forever true, and, as forever more.

31 And, again, in Christ Jesus, are seen chaff, as forever seen by me. As they are seen, as being, eternally, faithfully forever true, in sin forever. And these eternal chaff, they may even say, they know me and know Christ,

32 As Christ Jesus, being their seen savior, as forever seen of themselves, while they remain in their seen sins, as being forever true.

33 But spiritually, they are liars and the truth of me, isn't found in these, that do, and most certainly, shall and do, profess, to know me, forever true,

34 Yet, inwardly, they are devils and not holy Christian like creatures, as found of my planting of righteousness and holiness, as being forever true.

35 And they are seen before me, as being forever true and faithfully forever true, as the damned, as being forever certain, as death, as forever seen.

36 And they are seen unto me forever. As being eternal chaffly true beasts of death, unto me, forever. And they are seen by me, eternally

forever. And they, are forever true, in unrepentiful true sin, forever.

37 And those beasts, as chaff, they are known, unto me, as being in death, as being eternally forever true of themselves, as being dead unto me, as being forever seen, in eternal dead death, forever.

38 And, they are seen, as being forever true, in Satan, as eternally forever true. And, they are forever seen, by me, as I see them, through Christ Jesus, as being forever true.

39 And those chaff, they are most surely, corrupted, in their sin offerings, that called "Deeds meant unto repentance," unto me, as being forever true.

40 And these true chaff, they are spiritually and physically seen, as being seen, as being fallen and being unrepentfully seen before my (God) eternal, living forever, true presents,

41 That presents, of me, as being forever sure. It is seen, as life, in Christ Jesus, forever. And it is seen, as Christly true life. That is life, that is seen, in me, as being forever true.

42 And that life, in Christ Jesus, forever. It is seen, as being forever true life, that is called God, as forever true, as me, forever.

43 And my life, forever. It is found, given by me, in Christ the Son, as being eternally forever true, and, as certainly forever true,

44 And, that true life, it is given of me, forever. And it is without true end, as being eternally forever and ever seen.

45 And those seen chaff, as found by me, in the body of Christ. They most certainly, do show forth, the works of eternal true damnation, that is found of Satan, within themselves, as being forever seen,

46 And they, as eternal true chaff, forever. They are of the damned, as being forever true. And they are considered by me, as dead death, eternal chaff.

47 And these chaff. They are not of my righteous, holy children, who are of Christ Jesus, as being forever true,

48 And these chaff, in Satan, forever. They always refuse my eternal true disciplining, and my eternal, true correction, while they remain in the body of Christ.

49 Therefore, in the body of Christ, whosoever, willingly shall, desire, the unrepentiful true damnation,

50 That is called Satanism as forever true. They shall, therefore, die unto me and die unto Christ Jesus, as being forever true, and, as forever more.

51 And, whatever true chaff, shall partake, willingly forever, of this damning true matter, of refusing complete and total knowledge, of both,

52 Christ and me (God), that they may sin forever. They shall die in hell forever, unless they repent quickly, of their Antichristism, as forever true.

53 And in refusing to repent in Christ, then these seen true chaff, they shall most certainly, perish forever true, and, as forever seen in hell, forever.

54 These chaff, if they shall try to sinfully satisfy their own lust, for the evil thirst of damning unrepentiful true sinfulness,

55 As it given unto them of Satan forever. Then they shall die unto all, that is me, forever.

56 And if, they shall repent not, then they are found of Satanism, in this beguiling, sinful Satan imaged against God, true world,

57 And this true world of sin, as being eternally forever seen. It is found, as being a eternal true world of earnest, and sincere, true death, as being eternally forever seen.

58 And if, they repent not, then these chaff shall be with all certainty, eternally forever spewed and forever damned, by me, forever,

59 Unless, these chaff in Christ, repent quickly of their desired sinful true deeds, that they do, do against my holy true name,

60 And, as it (true deeds) is found as being sin, as it (true deeds) is given unto me forever. As of themselves, as they are found unto me, forever,

61 In being against my (God) true holiness, and as being eternally forever seen, in unrepentiful truly desired, seen sin, forever.

62 Then, these true chaff. They shall die unto all that is me, forever. And they shall be damned forever, and they are found without me and without Christ Jesus, forever.

Chapter 25 w/ 92 verses   Antichrist damning sins

1 All true chaff, they are fallen from my grace, that is called Christ Jesus, as being forever true. And they are, as a result, without the heavenly true salvation, as eternally forever seen,

2 For they truly, have rejected that true salvation, that is called God, that had been placed in them, of me (God), as found given of me, through Christ Jesus, as being forever sealed,

3   And, these true chaff. They are found unto me, as being forever true, as found in Antichrist damningly true unrepentiful true sin, as forever true of themselves, in Satan forever.

4   And, these chaff, they must repent quickly, least I move upon them, to destroy them, in hell forever true,

5   That is, if they shall not repent as forever true of themselves, as they are found by me, in the works of eternal true dying true death, forever,

6   For without repentance unto me forever, then these chaff, they have most surely, as eternally forever true. They have returned unto their former damningly true sins, forever.

7   And that return, it is unto Satan forever. And it is seen, as being, in Antichrist damningly true sins, as being eternally forever true,

8   And it is true of themselves. As they are found by me, forever. In unrepentfulness, as being forever true.

9   And that return, to death. It is known by me, as them, desiring true death, as being forever true of themselves, for they truly do desire,

10 To be Satan like, forever. And that is forever seen by me. As themselves, as being forever true, in death, forever certain.

11 And, as result, of returning to Satan's ways of eternal seen death, forever. They shall die forever. And they shall die. For these chaff, they do most certainly, forever,

12 Truly desire, damningly true, Antichrist, damningly, true sins. As it is sought, by them, forever. For their desired true death,

13 As that death, is found, forever. As being seen, as the deathly eternal true want, in themselves, as being desired forever true, of themselves,

14 To want Satan's true death, in them, forever. For they truly do desire. To be as dead as Satan is dead, unto me, as being forever true.

15 These chaff, they are seen, as wandering true stars, that shall never come to complete and total knowledge of Christ and of me (God),

16 Even though, they have a form of Godliness, but they do deny the power of me (God), forever.

17 As, they truly do desire, Satanism as forever true of themselves. For they truly do desire, eternal seen true death, as forever true of themselves, as wanted true death, forever.

18 And that true death, as to be as dead as Satan is dead unto me, forever. It is sought by the chaff, as being eternally forever true,

19 And it is eternally forever sought by the chaff ones, forever. And it is sought by them, as eternally forever and ever true, to be death before me, forever.

20 And that is a eternal deathly true work of eternal seen death, as it is found in themselves, as forever seen in them, as being forever true.

21 And they are seen, unto me forever. As being wandering true stars (chaff in Christ). And they are found unto me forever, as dying, as eternal, as ungodly, and as forever true.

22 And they are seen by me, as death, as forever granted true death, as eternal seen death, as being eternally forever true, true death, forever.

23 And they are, considered of me (God), as unrighteous true stars, but these dying true stars, they do resist all righteousness and all knowledge, that is found concerning me (God),

24 As I Am found, truly in Christ, and that I have shared with the world, as concerning Christ Jesus, forever.

25 These chaff and tares, they are found by me, as being forever true, Among the wheat, as found in the body of Christ, forever. And they are unrepentfully fallen, as being eternal seen true stars, forever.

26 And they are seen, as being Antichrist, and being in damningly true sin, as being forever seen. And they are seen, with eternal true death, forever.

27 And that true death, it is found within themselves, as being forever seen death. And that true death, it is forever seen, and it is seen by me, through Christ Jesus. As being eternally forever true, and, as forever seen, true death, forever.

28 And that death to be as Satan is dead unto me forever. It is seen as being dead for all of true eternity and is forever true. And that death, it is found within the chaff and the tares, forever.

29 Eternal death, it is found in all peoples, that truly do not desire, Christ Jesus, forever, as Christ Jesus, being their seen savior, forever true.

30 Therefore, these chaff and tares. They are considered of me (God), as being seen. As being seen, as dying blackened stars. As found by me, as forever true. In most heavenly forever, true death, as forever true.

31 And that death, it is seen, as being of never ending, forever, eternal true death, as forever true, in the damned, as forever seen.

32 These Antichrist, beastly true chaff and Antichrist, beastly true tares. They do indeed, desire sinfully forever true, within themselves,

total, unrepentiful forever true sinfulness, forever.

33 And that is desired by them, as being true sinfulness, that is called Satanism, as unrepentiful true sinfulness,

34 That is found as being against me (God), and it is found, as being against my eternal Son, who is called, Jesus Christ.

35 Yet, they are seen, as being blackened true stars, forever. And they are faithfully forever true,

36 In resisting true conviction, that is given of me, through Christ Jesus. That is called, to completely repent of one's true, seen sins, forever.

37 Therefore, they do resist, complete and total change, unto me (God). And I Am seen, as the God of most eternal, forever living, heavenly forever, Godly true life,

38 And as a result, of resisting true conviction, that is called "To completely repent unto God, forever." Then these chaff and tares, who are found, in the body of Christ,

39 Then they, most surely, do resist me and they do resist Christ, the Son, forever. And this is

done willfully within themselves, for their chosen and desired, true Satanism, forever.

40 And they have, as unrepentfully, they do desire sinful exaltedness in themselves, as being exalted against me (God), and they do remain,

41 As being sinful unto me forever true. And they shall, most certainly, die unto all, that is seen, and is, me forever,

42 Therefore, as they are found by me, as being sinful, and are seen, and are found, as being eternally sinful unto me, in their own, desired true unrepentfulness, as forever seen,

43 As true unrepentfulness, as it is found, within themselves, forever. It is seen unto me, as themselves, as they are seen and found,

44 As found of themselves, forever, as in never desiring to accept Christ. As this Christ Jesus, being their eternal seen savior, as this savior, being called, God forever.

45 And I Am God forever, as found in Jesus Christ, forever. And Christ Jesus, he is my eternal true Son, forever. As this eternal, true Christ Jesus, is found given and sent of me, as being eternally forever true,

46 As sent, and as given, as sent with my life, forever, unto all men, forever. And Christ Jesus,

he is sent with all, that is me, forever, as saith, thy eternal true one, as I Am "Father True," forever, as I Am God, heavenly forever, eternally forever true.

47 And this Christ Jesus, he is found, given. As given true salvation, that is found in and from me, forever. And that seen. true salvation,

48 It is, seen truth, that is called God, forever. And that eternal, true salvation, that is called seen life. It is given, of me, forever. In all given true knowledge, that is concerning me, forever.

49 And these chaff and tares, that do deny unto themselves, forever. To not ever accept all and complete knowledge, that is found concerning this eternal true Christ, forever. And is concerning me (God), forever.

50 Then, these true chaff and true tares. They are called Satanism, forever. And, they most surely do, refuse my true correction, as it is found, of myself, in Christ Jesus, who (Christ Jesus) is of my (God) truth, forever.

51 And these seen true chaff and seen true tares. They most surely do, refuse true correction, unto themselves, as it given and sent, by me, forever. As to walk completely in the light of Christ, as Christ walketh in all, that is called God, forever.

52 And Christ Jesus, he most certainly, doth walk in all that is me, forever. And this eternal and kind, Christ Jesus.

53 He (Christ Jesus forever) doth, walk in all that is eternally commanded of me (God), and is me (God), as I Am found, as the life, that is called God, as being eternally forever true.

54 These chaff and tares, they do walk, only partially in all that is commanded of me (God). And, as a result, these chaff and tare,

55 They do, therefore, deny unto themselves forever. To accept all and complete, total knowledge. That is concerning Christ and that is concerning me (God), as I Am forever seen and felt, as I Am forever true.

56 And that rejection by the chaff and tares, it is seen, therefore, that these unrepentiful true chaff and unrepentiful true tares, that they do refuse, unto themselves, forever,

57 To walk completely in the light of me (God), as I Am found in my eternal true Son, who is seen and called, Christ Jesus, as being eternally forever true.

58 And these chaff and tares, they do desire within themselves, forever. To refuse whole heartedly, to ever walk in all of my righteous true spirit,

59 That is found, in all of my true righteousness, that is given of me, as Christ Jesus, as being eternally forever seen, and, as being, forever true.

60 And these chaff and tares, as seen in the workings of true death, forever. For they do reject, all of my holy, true commands, that are placed by me (God), through Christ my Son, as being forever true.

61 For they, have desired, unrepentiful true sin, as being eternally forever true. Instead of desiring me, the God of righteousness,

62 As I Am found, in Christ, the Son, as I Am seen, as being forever true, and, as being eternally forever seen.

63 I Am, a most holy, true God, who is a God of true righteousness. And these chaff and tares. They most surely, do refuse, to walk completely and faithfully forever true,

64 In all that is of me, as I Am found in Christ, the Son. As being eternally forever certain, and, as forever seen.

65 Therefore, these chaff and tares. They do not ever desire me (God), who (God) is seen, and is, the God of truth. And these chaff and tares. They will not walk righteously before me (God), as

Christ is found, walking faithfully before me (God), as eternally forever true.

66 Christ Jesus, he walketh in all my true holiness, and in all my true righteousness. That is most certainly, given of myself, forever, unto all men, forever.

67 And this Christ Jesus, he is given of me (God), and is, therefore, called God, and is of me (God), as being eternally forever true, for I Am God, who is found in Christ Jesus, as being eternally forever seen.

68 And, as I Am God, forever. All shall walk before me in Christ, as walking faithfully forever true, as concerning themselves, unto me,

69 As being faithfully forever true of themselves, to me, as being forever seen, by me, as being, faithfully forever seen, and true, as true, forever.

70 And all men and all women, they shall walk faithfully, in all that is called of (called of, it means the word seen) me, as I Am God, forever. And that is in meaning,

71 To walk in all that is concerning what I have command the world, in the light of myself (God), as being eternally as forever found, as found of me, through Christ Jesus, as being forever seen of me, forever.

72 Nevertheless, willful against God, Antichrist and anti God, true sins. They are seen by me, as being eternal true sins. That are against me (God),

73 Are those seen sins, they are seen, as being, eternally forever, as in being eternally against me, as being true of the damned forever.

74 And those unrepentiful true sins. They shall most certainly, damn them, who desireth such forever. As those seen sins, are seen unto me, forever,

75 As being seen eternal, as being damningly forever, true sinfulness, as being forever seen, true sinfulness, forever.

76 That sinfulness, it is called death forever. And it is found, as being, against all that I Am. As I Am God, as forever seen, and, as forever heard.

77 And all true chaff and true tares. They shall fall back into their previous, damning Antichrist true seen sins, forever. Unless,

78 They repent quickly, of their seen, unrepentiful true sins and unrepentiful true sinfulness, as being eternally forever seen, and true, forever.

79 And if, they shall not repent quickly, of these evil, unrepentiful, true treasures. That is seen and called, eternal living, forever true damnation. Then, they shall die unto me, forever.

80 That true damnation, it is found in being against me (God), as being eternally forever and ever true. And, it is forever seen by me, as faithfully forever seen. And it is a true damnation, forever.

81 And again, that desired, unrepentiful true damnation, that they (chaff and tares), the fallen do desire unrepentfully forever true,

82 As being against me, who (God) is seen and felt, as the God of eternal, forever heavenly, forever true truth.

83 Eternal seen true damnation, it shall, most certainly, and most surely, shall damn them who desireth such unrepentiful true evil. That is found in the false images of the false hopes. That are found, in: Living Unrepentiful, Forever True, True Life."

84 That true life, as it is found in Satanism, as being eternally forever true. It is found, in being, as being a unrepentiful, damningly forever, true life.

85 That true life, it is called God, in Christ Jesus, forever. And it is, forever seen, as true life, forever.

86 And that true life, that is called God in Christ Jesus, forever. It is seen, as a unrepentiful true sinfulness, that is eternally forever true, as found by me forever, in the damned, forever.

87 And that sinfulness, forever. It is forever seen. And it is, a chosen true death, as being eternally forever true, as being of the Antichrist true spirit, forever

88 That true death, it is seen, as them, who are lost unto me, as being forever true unto Satan forever. And they are, truly lost, unto me forever,

89 And they are lost forever. As being forever true unto the beast, that is themselves in Satan forever. And they shall remain lost for all of true eternity, and, as forever lost.

90 And they shall remain, as the eternal rejected of God, forever. For they truly do desire, Satan and Satan's kind, forever.

91 And, in hell, they shall not be ever comforted, for they chose death, rather than me, as I Am found in Christ Jesus, as forever true and forever more, as saith, thy eternal kind God, as being eternally forever true, as unto the lost, as forever true.

92   Those things, they are true of the damned forever. And those things, they are seen in their desired true death. That is called Satanism, as being forever true, as it is found, in themselves, forever.

Chapter 26 / 34 verses   I Am

1   I Am the God of most eternal, ever living, forever heavenly, forever and ever, true life. That true life, it is found. As being forever seen, as I Am seen as forever true life.

2   That true life, it is found, given of myself, as I Am God, and as I Am forever true, and, as I Am forever seen.

3   And that true life, it is called God, as being forever true, in Christ Jesus, as being forever seen. And it is found, in the most eternal, true, true love, that is me, forever.

4   And that great love, it is given, as being faithfully forever true, of me. As being forever seen, as seen eternally seen unto all, who claim the name of Jesus Christ,

5   As this Jesus Christ, being their chosen, true savior. As Christ Jesus, being given of me. As given by me, as given and sent by me, as faithfully forever true, and, ever lastingly, forever seen.

6   And Christ Jesus, he is given by me faithfully forever true, and, as forever seen life. That life, it is called, God, as being eternally forever seen, and true.

7   And I Am true life, as given of myself (God), as forever true. And it is given unto the repentful of the true world, as being eternally forever and ever seen.

8   And it is, seen given true life, as it is given by me forever, unto the repentful true beast, as being eternally forever and ever seen. And it is seen from me, as being forever certain, and, ever lastingly, forever true.

9   And that true life, it is given, faithfully forever true, of me, in (in means the word through) Christ Jesus. Unto the repentful true beasts, as they are found by me of the earth, forever.

10 And that true life, it is given eternally of myself (God). And it is given true life, as found, given of myself, through Christ Jesus,

11 As forever faithful, from me, as I Am God, as I Am forever seen, and true, and as forever true.

12 And that true life, it is seen, unto all of the world. And is for all of given true eternity, and is, forever and ever true, as saith thy eternal true kind God, as eternally forever and ever true,

13 And, that true life, it is forever seen life. As I Am seen, as I Am seen as God, and as I Am, forever true, and faithful, and as I Am being seen, forever.

14 Even, as I Am seen as the life, that is called man, as being eternally forever sure, and true.

15 Therefore, in this world, without that true love. That is me (God), then unrepentiful true sin.

16 It shall damn them, who enjoy such evil pleasures, that are found in being against me (God), as being forever true of the damned, as forever seen.

17 And, this being against me (God). As it is found by me. As being, most surely forever true. As being truly against receiving my (God) Son,

18 Who is called Jesus Christ, and who (Jesus Christ) is seen with eternal true salvation, that is called God. As being forever sure.

19 And is, true salvation, in me. As being forever found of me. As being forever true. And, it is seen, as a heavenly true, forever and ever, true salvation. That is called God, as being forever certain, and, forever true.

20 That salvation, it is me in Christ, forever. And through Christ Jesus. I (God) have given

that salvation, unto the fallen true world, as forever seen,

21 That man, may know me, truly as his God. As they, who are seen, as being repentful true men, that doth rise up, in my true garments, that are found, in Christ Jesus, forever.

22 And those true garments. They are, most surely, me. And I Am found, in Christ Jesus, as being eternally forever true, and faithfully forever true.

23 And those true garments, they are found. As being my true righteousness, as, forever seen.

24 And, Christ Jesus, he is found with my true garments, as they (true garments) are called true life, forever. And this Christ Jesus, he is truly seen. As being my approved, and most true life,

25 As being eternally forever true life, as found given by and in me, forever. And he (Christ Jesus) is, forever seen life. And he is seen, as being the life of men, as being eternally forever true, and, as forever sure.

26 And Christ Jesus, he is found faithful, unto all repentful true men, forever. And this Christ Jesus, he is seen, as their savior. As being eternally forever true, as true of me, forever.

27 Eternal, seen, true salvation. It is, heavenly, and it is given of me (God). And, the eternal, unrepentiful, sinful true image, as found, as being the damned, as who are forever seen, by me, in death, forever.

28 They are seen, unto me, forever. As being seen, as being, truly fallen against me, as being forever true, of themselves, as being sinful true men, forever.

29 And, that true image, it is seen, as a Antichrist unholy true image, of Satanism,` as being forever true.

30 And that true image, as death forever. It is truly found within the damned, forever. And the damned, they truly do enjoy the fruit of eternal dead death, forever.

31 And dead death forever. It is found, as being Satanism, as forever found, as given by the hand of Satan, who is the false prophet of death, unto them, that truly do worship, the image of Satan, as that image of granted true death, that is found within themselves, forever.

32 And they, the damned. They truly do enjoy, partaking of Satan's sinful true mark, that is called dead death forever. And that spiritual true mark, that is from Satan. It is placed within the damned, forever,

33 And it is found, given in true death, unto the unrepentfully truly lost, forever. And this, is because, of found unrepentfulness,

34 As it is forever found, as being eternally true, forever. And it is found, in being eternal, true death, forever. And it is found, in the damned, forever.

Chapter 27 w/ 74 verses   Truth

1 **I Am** truth, and I Am the life. As found of me (God), forever. As found of me, forever, as found in repentful true men, as being forever true. And he, that desireth, to never love me, as I Am found in Christ Jesus, forever.

2 That person, shall be found forever true. In the worship of his own, beastly imaged, personal seen true sins. As those seen sins, are seen unto me,

3 As being eternally forever true. As they, the damned forever. Are found in sin, forever. And they are found unto me forever, as being dead in Satan, unto me, forever.

4 And they, the damned ones, forever. They are seen, unto me forever. As being seen, as being forever true, in unrepentiful true sin, forever.

5 And that person, in Satan death, forever. That person, shall be seen forever true, by me. As

being eternally forever seen, as seen in their own, true death, forever.

6 And those, in Satan death, forever. They do prefer, to worship, the image of the beast, that they may die unto me, forever.

7 And, they the damned. They have exalted themselves, as a heady minded true work of unrepentfulness, as it is a seen true sinfulness, forever.

8 And, in this seen headiness. The damned forever, they are found, unto me forever. As seen by me, as being forever true, as:

9 Being truly marked, in their forehead of their innermost, true self. As being marked, in unrepentfulness. As being forever true of themselves. In their desired true death, forever.

10 That is true death, as given to them, from Satan, as being forever true. Then, they are found, unto me. As being forever seen, as being seen as eternal true death. That is forever true of the damned, forever.

11 And true death. It is given unto all (unrepentiful to God forever, true people), who are called Satan. And that true death, it is seen, as Satanism, as being forever true.

12 And Satan doth encourage the sinful true image (unrepentiful true people), to speak blasphemy unto God forever, and to live unto God, as being forever found, as being forever seen and true, by loving death, in hell, forever.

13 For Satan, doth not encourage mankind, to ever repent forever true, as in Christ Jesus, forever.

14 Therefore, because of all these things. Satan and his kind, that are called demons. They shall receive the greater judgment. As it given by me and given of Christ Jesus, in the great judgment. That is called: "LIFE."

15 And as Satan doth not encourage mankind to repent of it's seen sins. He shall be held greatly responsible for the works of the image that Satan has encouraged all unrepentiful true men, to serve from Satan unto me forever.

16 For Satan, the false prophet of eternal true death, forever. He encourageth, all men. To buy and sell in the works of utter true shame, that is called "Wanted true death,"

17 And, it is seen forever true, unto me, as being eternally forever true. And, it is, forever seen true death, unto me, as being forever true. In the damned, forever.

18 And these, that doth, follow Satan and Satan's encouragement. To want death, forever. They shall have placed that sinful true mark of utter true shame and death,

19 As found from Satan within themselves (the damned), as being placed of themselves (the damned) and of Satan, as most surely. As placed forever true, in themselves, forever .

20 And they, the damned. They should not have place that sinful true mark of earnest and sincere, true death. Upon themselves and in themselves. At all and as, being forever true.

21 And these, the damned. That do and have placed their hands, to be marked forever, in the true hands of the beastly image of Satanism, as being seen forever true, then:

22 As that image as the damned in Satan forever. Is placed of themselves, through Satanism, as being forever true, in themselves, forever.

23 Then, that mark of earnest and sincere true death. That is given from Satan and Satan's true kind,

24 It is found given and given unto the damned, as given by their false prophet of eternal life, as given unto themselves, from Satan and Satan's kind, as being forever seen.

25 And these, the damned, they are greatly deceived by Satan forever. For he (Satan and Satan's) giveth the power of death unto them of the eternal true image of the beast,

26 And Satan, he sayeth unto the damned. That they truly do enjoy the work of unrepentiful true sin, as it is found, in one's unrepentiful true life. As it is seen before God, as being forever true.

27 And, unrepentiful true sin. It is placed by Satan and by Satan's true works of death, into their sinful true lives. That they, of the earth,

28 That they should continue in unrepentiful true seen sin. And that they should make a continuing true image of the work of unrepentfulness. That is already found in their fallen true lives, forever.

29 And that they should place that image, that is a speaking true work of continuing work of seen unrepentfulness, as seen before God, that is found, in them, forever,

30 That they should place that imaged true work in (in means the word of) Satan forever. On and into the true image of granted true death, that is granted from God, forever.

31 And that, is already found. As working within the damned, that is being seen by God, as being forever true.

32 And, that they should speak and perform, blasphemy unto God, as being eternally forever true, as true of themselves. In the service of unrepentiful true sin, forever.

33 And Satan desireth them to do this blasphemy, by placing that speaking blasphemous eternal true image of death forever, on and into the image of the damned,

34 Who are already found in the earth, since Adam fell in the garden, and that is most surely, seen by me, as the fallen true earth, as being forever true.

35 Again, the entire true earth. It is a fallen blasphemous eternal image of speaking and performing true blasphemy. That is continually being spoken unto God, forever. As spoken by the spirit of Antichrist, forever,

36 And, true blasphemy. It is forever seen, as the works of unrepentfulness. As it is found in the damned, as being forever true of themselves, in death, forever.

37 The fallen true image of the earth. Is a blasphemous eternal true image of death, forever.

38 And it is found, as being all unrepentiful true men, that have given of themselves, to serve death in Satan forever. And it continues to be made, by the damned ones, as being forever true,

39 And that image of the earth. It is seen, as being, a transgressing true earth. As It is made by devils and by the unrepentiful true men, as being forever. And it lives in death, and speaks in death,

40 Unto all unrepentiful true men, as being forever true in death, forever. And is forever sure, in the damned, forever.

41 That image, it doth live as death forever, in all unrepentiful true men, forever. And it does live, since the fall of Adam and eve. That occurred, long ago.

42 The beastly image, is a man made blasphemous eternal true image in Satan true death, as being forever true of the unrepentiful toward all that is God, forever.

43 And, it is a man made sinful true image, that is seen as being the beast, as being forever true, and it is most surely, made, by the unrepentfully damned and is the damned,

44 As they give of themselves to Satan, as they and the beast, who (beast) is called Satan. Are one and the same, in death, forever true.

45 And that image of death, called the beast. It is seen, as being in Satanism, as being forever true, of the damned ones, as being forever seen.

46 And that image called the beast. It doth live blasphemous unto God. As truly desired true death, by the unrepentiful ones. As being forever true of themselves. In the buying of sin, that is called true death, forever.

47 And that blasphemous eternal image of devils and of the unrepentiful, who are the damned. They shall be judged of God through Christ, in the great judgment of judgments, forever.

48 And they shall be judged forever. And the false prophet of death shall be judged, for even he hath, caused and encouraged them, who are found, in the beastly image of devils and unrepentiful true men,

49 To persecute and even kill them of the earth, forever. As to kill them (them is Christians), who (Christians) desire to not remain within the sinful true crafts of utter true death, forever.

50 For many repenting in Christ, and many repenting true nations, and many repenting true peoples,

51 They have chosen Christ, and they have been persecuted and or even killed, by Satan's true image. That is called, death forever.

52 And many, are: killed and or have been persecuted. For believing and accepting, Christ Jesus, as Christ Jesus, being one's savior, from

me, as being forever true. And, many, do accept me, in Christ Jesus, forever.

53 And many do accept me forever. As accepting me in Christ Jesus forever, as accepting me as Christ Jesus, unto themselves, forever,

54 As truly accepting me, in all that I Am, as I Am found, in Christ Jesus, as being forever certain, and as I Am found with eternal, approved life, that is called God, that is me forever.

55 And approved true life, it is forever true, and, it is forever more, and it is found as me, in Christ Jesus, forever.

56 And, again, the false prophet hath encouraged the beastly eternal Satan true image, that is seen as being made, as being unrepentiful true men, forever, and is demons forever, as to kill, and or, as to persecute, forever.

57 That is a eternal blasphemous seen image of the damned and of devils, forever, and they truly do encourage them in the image of death, forever,

58 To kill and or persecute all, who will not faithfully serve the image, that is found of Satan and of the damned, that is found as an image,

59 That is found with the power of life, that is life as found without God, forever, and that is called "Speaking granted true death, from God, forever."

60 And, the false prophet with the power of life, that is called eternal true death, forever. He doth deceive them of the earth, with his miracles from heaven, that are called granted true death, as given of God, unto the damned, forever.

61 And though the false prophet, desireth them of the earth, to be willingly found forever, as partaking of the sinful true mark of unrepentfulness, as being eternally forever true.

62 He (false prophet called Satan) doth wonders and miracles of giving true death, from God, unto the earth,

63 That the fallen true earth, may truly, enjoy their sin, that giveth the joy of eternal seen death, unto the damned, as being forever true and forever more.

64 And death, it is seen from the false prophet, as given of himself, forever. As given unto the fallen true earth, forever. And it is given, of Satan, forever,

65 As a given true speaking, true blasphemy, as given unto God, as being eternally forever seen. And it is seen and found,

66   As seen in the want, as I Am a fallen true sinner, that I (the fallen) may ask for death, as being forever faithful of myself (the fallen), forever.

67   And, at that great, end of the age, great judgment. The damned shall be smashed through Christ Jesus, as being eternally forever true and forever seen.

68   And that image of the damned. It shall live in hell, for all of given true eternity. And, that given true judgment. It is found, without true end, as being forever true.

69   Therefore, if these, true beasts. Shall not repent of their seen sins, by accepting Christ Jesus. As Christ Jesus, being their seen savior, forever.

70   Then, they shall die, unto all, that is me, forever. And they shall die, without true end, in hell, eternally forever and ever true.

71   And my Son, who is called, as being: Jesus Christ, forever. He is sent unto the beast, that the beast, may repent.

72   But if the beast, shall not repent of it's seen sins, that are given unto me, forever. And that is given, unto me, as themselves, in eternal seen death, forever.

73 Then, they shall most surely, die unto me, as being forever true, as true of themselves, forever.

74 And, they shall never depart, hell, as being forever true, saith thy kind God, as being eternally forever and ever true. For I Am true, and I Am the life, that is called God, forever.

Chapter 28 w / 53 verses   Unholy nations of death

1 Unholy nations of true death, they are seen as being, unrighteous true nations. Who will unrepentfully never accept the holy salvation,

2 That is eternally from me (God). And these fallen, unholy nations of death, and their unrepentiful true men. They are always seen. As being against me (God), as being eternally unjust, forever. And they are seen,

3 As being truly unrepentiful true men. And these fallen, unrepentiful true men and their true, unholy, Antichrist true nations of death.

4 They are seen, unto me forever true. As being: "Most Eternal, Living Forever, Holy true Death."

5 That true death, it is seen. As being holy true death, unto them that perish in their worship of the beastly eternal true image of devils and of fallen true men, forever,

6   And that true death, it is seen, as being seen. As being a forever "Great Eternal Granted True Death," As being obtained by the damned, as being eternally forever sure,

7   And that sure true death, as it is found forever, in Satan true death, forever. It is seen, and is seen. As being, a certain living forever, true damnation. That true damnation, is desired in the damned, forever.

8   And it is considered of me (God), as being found by me forever true. As being found, as being: "Most Eternal True Damnation."

9   That most eternal, true damnation, is called death forever. And it is seen, as being true. As one being found, as being found. As one living unrepentfully forever true,

10   As in not ever accepting Christ. As Christ Jesus, being one's personal, living forever, true savior, as forever seen.

11   Unholy unrepentiful true sin. It is seen, in the damned, as being forever seen. And that death, it is seen, as being their personal, seen true work, that is forever and eternally seen,

12   And is seen, as being a unrepentiful, true work of eternal true seen sin. And it is, a living forever true work, of seen and desired, true unrepentfulness, that is forever true.

13   And true unrepentfulness. It is found, as being eternally, the damned as forever seen. As they are seen, in all, that is Satan forever, as Satan is seen, in true death, forever.

14   And that, true Satan like, true death, forever. It is found in the damned ones, as being forever seen. And it is seen, as Satan beastly true death, forever.

15   And it is seen by me, as being forever true of them, that die unto all, that I Am, as I Am God, as being forever true.

16   unrepentiful true seen sin, is seen. As being, seen unrepentiful true sinfulness. That is a seen, fallen, unrepentiful true damnation, found in the damned, as eternal true death, forever.

17   And that eternal, living forever, true damnation, called death in the damned forever. It is most surely found in the damned. As being their eternal seen true life, that is called Satanism, forever.

18   And Satanism is seen, as being justly forever true, in the damned, as they are seen. As being seen, in death forever. And it is seen, as eternal true death, forever.

19   That is, a forever seen death. As being forever seen unto me, as being forever true. And that true death. It is found given from me (God),

20 As being forever true, unto "the beast," as being forever seen. And the beast, is seen. As being fallen true men and fallen true devils, as being forever true.

21 And, unrepentiful true damnation. It is forever and ever true, without forgiveness. As forgiveness as found in Christ the Son. That is, if that unrepentiful true damnation,

22 Is found in that great day, that is most eternally forever holy. In uttermost, heavenly, final true judgment. That is, forever true judgment.

23 Therefore, repentance must occur before the great judgment day. And during that judgment day, eternal granted true repentance, to receive Christ, then as savior. It shall not occur, during that great, holy, true judgment.

24 Therefore, let all, non Christian true nations, understand. That they must be holy unto me forever, and not be found desiring Satanism as forever true of themselves, forever,

25 Least I break forth upon their stubbornness. That is found in denying unto themselves, forever. To not repent in Christ, as being forever true of themselves, as they are seen in death. As being forever true.

26   Fallen unrepentiful true damnation. It is considered a beastly unrepentiful true image of devils and unrepentiful ungodly true men. And it doth contain,

27   The workings of unrepentiful true spirits. As they are found in uttermost, ever lasting, forever true, unrepentiful true damnation.

28   That sinful, unrepentiful beastly true image. As found as a unrepentiful true damnation. That is made by the lost, unto Satan forever.

29   It is a eternal, living forever, unrepentiful true damnation. And that unrepentiful true damnation. It is always seen and found, as being eternally against me (God) and against Christ, forever.

30   And it is seen, in being against me forever, as they that are seen as being the beast, and they are the beast, forever. And the beast, is seen,

31   As being a utterly, fallen, perditious, true man (the word man is in meaning of all true men), as being eternally forever true, in unrepentfulness toward me (God), forever.

32   And death, is eternally desired by the damned, as a true and uttermost, given true recompense. That recompense, is a seen damnation, that is sent and given by me, forever, as unto the damned, forever.

33 And it is given unto the them, that hold unto their unrepentfulness, as being eternally forever true of themselves. As they are found by me, in their desired true sins, forever,

34 And at the great judgment. I shall not grant Christ Jesus unto them forever. As they are found unto me, in that great judgment. As being found by me, in the true death of Satan, forever.

35 And I shall damn them forever true, at that judgment. If they shall be found dwelling eternally forever true, in Satan's true death, forever.

36 And, they shall found caste into hell forever. I shall not hear them, eternally forever. As they, then plead with me, for Christ to be their chosen true savior, forever.

37 And most surely, the fallen unrepentiful beastly true image. It is a seen true image. That is seen, as being a seen, eternal true image,

38 Found in true Satan death and his (Satan) true likeness. And it is seen, as being a true abomination, as being forever truly desired by the damned ones, forever.

39 And, all non Christian true nations, of the earth forever. As being seen and found in Satan's bestiality forever. They shall not go unpunished, by me, forever,

40   And as they are found in that bestiality forever. They shall die in unrepentfulness forever, if they shall not ever repent in Christ Jesus, forever.

41   And as these unrepentiful true nations in Satanism forever. Are seen, as being seen as being an image of fallen true men, forever, and fallen true devils, forever,

42   And it is seen, as being a true image of fallen true men and fallen true devils, as being forever true. And it is seen before God, as a image found in the damned, forever.

43   And that true image, is made in "Lifeless Satan," forever. And that unrepentiful true image of man without God, as made by man's own true choices, forever.

44   It is a true choice. As made and seen, as being a unrepentiful beastly image, found in most certain, forever, heavenly true death, as being eternally forever seen by me (God), forever.

45   And that image, that is found in the damned, and made by the damned, As being, truly made, truly unto the image of Satan, that is called, Satanism, forever.

46   It is seen, as being a unholy, damning, Antichrist, perditious true image, of the men of

sin, forever. And they, themselves. They are most surely,

47 Seen as being unrepentfully fallen against God. As a fallen, true, unholy true image. That is seenly made of eternal true damnation. That is called true death, as being forever seen,

48 And that damnation. It is a seen granted true death, as forever seen. As seen unto them, that are seen as being dead in Satanism, forever true,

49 And it is seen, as a granted true death, forever. And it is seen, and found, because they as a man of sin, they have exalted themselves, against all, that is called and is, God forever,

50 And, these days of the earth, as forever true. I do reveal from heaven, that these, the damned. That they are being revealed by me,

51 As being revealed by me, as themselves, in being seen. As the unrepentiful true ones of the earth. Who are being revealed by my spirit, as a man of sin, who are trying live after Satan's own heart of true rebel lioness,

52 And they are them, that are seen and felt, unto me, as forever true. As them, that are, truly Antichrist. And they are seen, as being antigod, forever certain.

53 And they, willingly do forsake, all that I Am. As I Am their true creating God, forever.

Chapter 29 w / 67 verses   That image

1 Concerning the dragon, who is the false prophet, that giveth the power of eternal true death, unto man, as being forever seen. That unrepentiful true man, may die unto me (God), and unto my Son, who is called Jesus Christ, forever.

2 And, all men, who will not serve Jesus Christ forever. As Christ Jesus being their seen savior, who is Christ Jesus that is with life, that is from me (God), forever.

3 Then, they shall die unto me, as being forever true, in their desired true death. That is found in them, as they truly do desire, to remain within their fallen true worship, that is found in wanting to remain in the worship of Satanism, forever,

4 And, all, whose name shall not be found recorded in the book of eternal true remembrance, that is called God. Then, they shall remain in the image of Satan's true death, forever.

5 And they shall, most surely, remain in the deathly true worship of the fallen true beast, who is the beast, that is seen and called:

6 "Unrepentfulness," that is forever found. As to be forever, as being both, one, is: Satan and demons, and secondly: "unrepentiful fallen man" (all unrepentiful true men), forever.

7 That image, it is found. As being, a fallen true damnation. That is seen, as being fallen true man, himself and Satan himself, and Satan's (demons), forever.

8 And that image, is found in death forever. And is a seen image of Satanism as forever sure. And it is a seen, as a eternal true image of Satan and the unrepentiful ones, who are mostly seen and are: "The beast forever."

9 And that image, is most eternal, as the damned, as being forever true. And it is a seen image. That is a heavenly true image of the damned forever.

10 And they are found by me, in the bottomless pit of true death, forever. And they are given over unto damning forever, true death. As being forever seen before God, as being forever true,

11 And that pit, it is a true destruction, unto the damned. As they are found in Satan forever. And I shall lay hold unto them, as being forever true,

12 And I will chain them in their seen sins, forever, as to be in hell, forever. And without

true end, in hell, as being eternally forever and ever true.

13 And, in hell, hell is given of me (God), unto them who desireth the beastly forever true image. That is called unrepentiful to not ever accept Christly true salvation. That salvation is called Christ Jesus, in the Father, forever.

14 That salvation, it is found, as Christ Jesus forever strong and forever true. Therefore, they the damned ones forever, they shall remain forever,

15 In unrepentiful true death, as being eternally forever and ever true, as true of themselves, in the buying and selling called sin, forever,

16 And as it found as being the spiritual true mark and being the spiritual true name, as it is found as being Satanism, forever.

17 That name, it is spiritually seen. As being: "desiring true death," that is forever true. And, it is desired by the lost forever.

18 And that they, the damned of the earth forever, that they may enjoy their eternal seen true death, forever. And it is found unto me, forever.

19   And it is found, as themselves as given true death, as they do give themselves, to Satan, forever.

20   This eternal true image, in as given true death, as themselves to Satan true death, forever, as forever true death. It is found, in the unrepentfully fallen unholy one's, who are eternally forever true,

21   As being against me (God), in earth. As they are forever seen, as seen true death, as being eternally forever true, as true of themselves, as true in Satanism, forever.

22   And true death, it is granted of me (God), unto the beast, forever. And I (God) shall repay, all that chose Satan and his (Satan) ways of death, forever.

23   These that are fallen, as fallen in unrepentiful true seen sin, as being without Christ Jesus, forever. They are, then found without my true salvation,

24   That is salvation. That is a seen true salvation, as being eternally forever seen. As a seen, heavenly true salvation, that is eternally from me (God), forever.

25 And I shall grant my true salvation, that is called Christ Jesus, as it is eternally forever true, and as it is eternally forever,

26 As a granted Christly true salvation, as it is seen and given from me, forever. And it is called God, as given true salvation, unto all, who will accept me. As I (God) Am found, as being, Jesus Christ, as being forever true.

27 The image that is Satan true death, forever. It is a sinful true image. As it is found in being, true, damningly true, unrepentfulness, as forever seen,

28 And that true image, in Satan true death, forever, and as it is being forever seen. It is seen and felt, as death forever,

29 And this is because, they the damned of the fallen true earth, forever. They do not ever desire Christ Jesus, forever,

30 As this eternal, seen, true Christ Jesus. Being their, seen savior, from me, as being forever true, and it is true of and from me, forever.

31 And that true denial, to never accept Christ Jesus, forever. It is a sinful true image, made in eternal true death, forever,

32 And it is found, as being, a utter true death image, as the damned ones, forever. And it is seen forever, as eternal dead death image, as eternal dead death, forever.

33 And it is seen, as being, an eternal true image, as found, in being a unholy true image, as being the damned, as they are found by me, in Satan, forever. And, it is seen, as being, antichrist and antigod, forever.

34 And it is sinful true image, in Satan, forever. And it is, a eternal, living forever, unholy true image.

35 That damningly true image. It is seen, before me (God). And is a unholy, forever true, true living forever, eternal true image. As it found, by me, forever. In most certain, forever true, living forever, true death.

36 That death, it liveth as true death, forever true. And it liveth as eternal true death, for all of given true eternity, and is, forever seen, as seen death, forever.

37 And death, it is found in not desiring to ever receive from me (God), the eternal living forever true waters, that are found of me, in Christ Jesus, forever,

38 Those waters, they are seen of me, forever. And they are pure of me, forever. And they are true, forever. For I Am true, forever.

39 My eternal true water, it is seen. As being: "Eternal, living forever, heavenly true life." And it is seen, as being Jesus Christ, in me,

40 For I Am the true Father, who is the Eternal True Father, as the Father of the water of life, as being forever true.

41 Christ Jesus, he is seen, as being, the water of life, that is called God, forever. And I do send, Jesus Christ, as being forever sure, as sure, unto the world, forever,

42 And Christ Jesus, he is forever true of me, as being forever seen, and is eternally forever seen. And Christ Jesus, he is seen, that the world, may truly live,

43 As true unto me, in Christ Jesus, as being eternally forever true, as saith, thy eternal, kind God, as being, eternally, and, as forever sure.

44 And I, the Lord of heaven and earth. I Am found, most certainly. As being, eternally forever found, as found in Christ Jesus, thy savior. Who (Christ Jesus) is from me, as being forever true of me, as being forever seen.

45 And this Christ Jesus, he is seen. As being, my eternal, living forever, true Son,

46 And again, I the Lord, do declare, that this sinful eternal true image, that is the damned. As they are found by me, in Satanism, as being forever true,

47 They are found unto me forever. In most certain, living forever, true death. That true death, it is given of themselves, to me,

48 As given in being eternally forever found, as they are found, as being found against me (God), as being forever true, as true of themselves, in Satanism, forever.

49 For the damned, they have desired forever. To never accept Christ, as Christ Jesus, being their seen, true savior, from me, as being forever seen.

50 Granted true death, forever. It is a seen true death, in the stone cold heart of bestiality. That is called unrepentfulness, as being, forever seen,

51 And granted true death, forever. It is seen, as being, a true forever, heavenly of God, given damningly true death. That is granted by me, unto the damned, forever,

52   And granted true death, to be as dead as Satan is dead unto me, forever. It is given of me (God), in heavenly holy recompense. For not receiving Christ,

53   As this Christ Jesus, being one's, eternal and personal, living forever, true savior. And who, is Christ Jesus, that is sent by me, into the earth. As being eternal true salvation. That is, called God, as being forever true.

54   For Christ, he is sent unto them of the earth, forever. That they may have life and have it more abundantly, as given by me (God), for I Am the God of most heavenly, forever eternal, living forever, true life.

55   True living forever true death. It is found in the fallen true earth. And it is given, as eternal, true recompense. As it is found, in not ever accepting Christ, as this Christ Jesus, being one's personal, living forever, eternal true savior, forever.

56   And this given true recompense. It is unto the fallen, who are found by me, forever. As being forever true. As they are found in being against me,

57   As they are seen before me, forever. As in not accepting Christ Jesus, as this Christ Jesus, being their seen savior, forever.

58 And they are seen unto me, for all of given true eternity, forever. And they are a fallen true image in Satanism, as being forever found.

59 And that true image, it is true death, to them, that do worship Satanism, as being forever seen. As they truly do worship, unrepentfulness,

60 As it is eternally forever true, as true in themselves, as eternal seen true death, forever. And that true worship, of Satan, forever. It is found, within the damned ones, forever.

61 Therefore, unto these unrepentiful ones, who will never accept Christ Jesus, forever. They are, therefore, reprobates unto me forever. And they are reprobates, in both, spirit and body, forever.

62 And, they are found, in most certain, Godly forever and ever, true destruction. That true destruction, it is called "Death Without God And Without Christ Jesus, Forever."

63 Godly, everlasting, true destruction. It is surely, found, in both, body and spirit of the unrepentiful fallen. Who are fallen against me (God),

64 As being eternally forever and ever true of themselves. In death, as being eternally forever true, and, as forever known as death, unto me.

65   Godly true destruction, it is found, in both, body and spirit. And, it is forever, truly seen. As seen, in being, a Godly true recompense true destruction,

66   That is given from me, forever. And it is forever true, from me (God). For I (God) Am seen, as: "Recompense for one's seen true sins, forever."

67   And I Am the God, of most eternal, living forever, holy true life, as being eternally forever and ever true,

Chapter 30 w / 133 verses   Perditious sin

1   Unrepentiful true death, is a living sinfulness. That is found as being, a eternal seen unrepentfulness. That is found, as being sinfully forever true,

2   As being found, as being a ever lastingly, forever true, true death. That is eternally forever seen and felt, unto me, as death forever

3   And that true death, as in nevering to desire to accept Christ, as this Christ Jesus, being one's personal, living forever, true savior. It is a perditiously seen, eternal, true life, as found in sin, forever.

4   That evil true life as perdition forever. It is seen, as being, utterly perditiously forever seen.

As one being given unto all, that is: complete and total, seen and final, true ruin, forever.

5 And perdition of ungodly true men, forever. It is found, in one's, unrepentiful and unthankful, true seen spirit. As it is eternally forever seen, and is seen, as seen in the damned, forever.

6 And the damned forever. They are a perditious true beast, found unto me forever, in death, forever. And they shall most certainly, pass on back into death, forever. And they shall not see me, as I Am found,

7 As I Am found, as true life, forever. For they have decided and have chose Satan, forever. Rather than me, as I Am eternally found, in Christ Jesus, forever.

8 Therefore, sinful true life, it is, seen. As being, a unrepentiful true life. And it is found, in the sinful, unrepentiful eternal true workings, of eternal true death, forever.

9 And that tainted true life as death forever. It is found, in being seen, as sin forever. And it is seen, as being in true death, that is called Satanism. forever.

10 And, all unrepentiful true sinfulness. It is faithfully forever found, as found in the lost, as being forever true. And it is true,

11 As the perditiously lost, who are perditiously lost unto me forever, as lost in utter true perdition. That is seen, as being eternally, Satanism, forever.

12 And, to be lost unto me, as being truly lost unto me, as being forever true. As true in utter true perdition, that is found in ungodly perditious true men, forever.

13 That perdition, it is found in Satanism, forever. And it is, utterly true perdition of the utterly beastie ones. As they are found by me, as being eternally forever true,

14 As true, in being against all that is me, as I Am found in Christ Jesus, forever true.

15 And utter true perdition. As concerning all, who are seen, as being: ungodly Satan like men, and, ungodly Satan like women, forever.

16 That is utter, true, damning eternal, true perdition, forever true in the damned forever. And it is seen, by me, as forever seen, as seen as their faithfulness,

17 As being faithfully forever seen, as their desire for true death. As that true desire for eternal true dead death, is found by me, forever,

18 And is found in the damned ones, as being eternally forever true. And this is eternal of

themselves in Satan forever and in Satan's true death, forever.

19 And utter true perdition. It is called granted true death, forever. And it is found, as true in the damned ones, as they are found by me in Satanism, forever.

20 And that death, is most surely seen, as being eternally found. As being a eternal, utter true perdition, that is true of themselves (the damned ones forever),

21 As they, the damned forever. Are found unto me, in their desired, true Satan death, forever. And that, desired in them, true death. To be dead as being like unto Satan himself, forever,

22 It is found by me, faithfully in themselves, forever. And it is found by me, as being eternally forever true. And the death in Satanism forever. It is found by me, for all of given true eternity, and, as forever more.

23 As these, in Satanism forever, they truly do worship the beast and the beast's true mage of Satan and unrepentiful true man (all men), together and forever true. Even, as the false prophet of death,

24 Doth encourage all, to blaspheme God forever. That they may remain, truly in

unrepentfulness, as being forever true. And, that they may remain,

25 In eternal dead death, forever. And that they may appear in death, forever, even as Satan is dead unto me, forever. And that they, the damned. That they, may die unto me, as being forever true, as saith, thy eternal, kind God, as being eternally forever true.

26 And that is true forever, of the beast, and of it's seen false prophet, who (false prophet) is the eternal sinful true prophet of eternal true lies, forever.

27 And that they, the damned in Satan, forever, and who are seen by me, as being forever true. As being, the damned ones, of the fallen true earth, as being eternally forever seen.

28 That the damned, may die unto me for all time and forever. And they the damned, they truly do desire, to be seen. As being seen, as being found unto me forever true,

29 As truly found, as being: "Antichrist, perditious true sinfulness," forever true. And these anti Christ true ones, they are dead unto me already,

30 And they shall remain dead unto me forever. If they receive not, Christ Jesus as their true lord and savior, forever.

31 And the damned, are found, as the lost unto me forever. As they themselves, being found, as being eternally forever seen. As being, against all that is called, me (God). As it forever seen and felt of me, forever.

32 And granted true death. It is granted unto the lost, as forever true. For they, are truly the damned, as being eternally forever seen,

33 And they are seen by me, in their true death, as it is found to me in Satan forever. And it is found, as being, earnest and sincere, true death, as forever seen.

34 And they, the lost forever, in Satan forever. They are, truly seen, by me, who (God) is the God of truth, forever. And they are seen, as being in true, spiritual true falleness, as being forever true. And, as they, are seen,

35 As being forever true, in utterly spiritual, final seen true ruin. As it is found, as eternally forever seen.

36 And it is seen, in their own, utterly, Antichrist, perditious true life. As it is a found, as being a damningly true life, that is called death, forever.

37 That damningly true life, as it is found in Satanism forever. It is seen, as a fallen true life, to be as Satan is found in granted true death,

38 As that life, to be like unto Satan forever. It is found in being eternally forever true, as one desiring to be eternally like unto Satan himself, forever.

39 And it is seen as being true death. And it is death, as it given of me forever, unto the damned forever. And that deathly eternal seen life,

40 It is, most surely, eternally from me, as being eternally forever certain, as given by me faithfully, unto the damned ones, forever.

41 And, utterly, final, true perditious, true death. It is a forever seen true death, as found given by me in Satan forever and in Satanism, forever.

42 And that true death in sin forever. It is granted truly from me (God), forever true. And, it is a true, eternal true death. As found, in all: "True perditious true Satanism."

43 And that is forever seen, as being true perdition, of ungodly true men and ungodly true women, forever. And that true perdition, it is seen. As they, the ungodly,

44 As they, are found unto me, as being forever true. In eternal, true Satanism. And Satanism, it is, utterly true death, as being forever found, as found by me forever, in utter true perdition, forever.

45 And, Satanism true perdition. It seen, by me, as being forever true. And it is seen, as being eternal true perdition, that is called the utterly true damned ones,

46 As the utterly true damned ones, are seen by me forever, as being eternally forever seen. As they are seen unto me forever true,

47 As they are seen, as being the eternal damned, who seen by me, as they are found unto me, forever, as found in Satan, forever.

48 Recompense called granted true death. It is found, upon the head of the perditiously seen wicked, as being a just judgment, forever. And that, true judgment, it is called God, forever.

49 And that just judgment, it is called God forever. And it liveth in me, upon the damned, as being forever seen true judgment.

50 That judgment, it is called God, unto the wicked ones, as being eternally forever seen, and, as being eternally forever true.

51 My eternal, "Just True Judgment." It is given of me forever true. And it is given, because of unrepentiful desired true sin. As it is found, in not ever desiring,

52 To ever accept Christ, as Christ Jesus, being one's personal, living forever, true savior, as being eternally forever seen and forever more.

53 Therefore, desired, unrepentiful, to never accept salvation from me (God), forever. It is seen, as being, utterly seen perdition. That is seen, as being:

54 A True, eternal, true perditious sinfulness. And it is, eternal, living forever and ever, true unrepentfulness. And it is a seen, as a living forever true perdition,

55 That is found, as being the damned, as they are forever seen and felt, as death, unto me, forever. And the damned shall die unto me forever, unless they repent in Jesus Christ, quickly and forever.

56 And, unrepentfulness. It is seen, as being a eternal seen and true abomination. As it is seen before me (God), as being forever true, as being the damned, as the damned, are found unto me forever,

57 As being eternally seen and felt. As seen and felt, unto me, as being true death, that is a true death, forever. And true death, to be like unto Satan, forever. It is called, true Satanism, forever,

58 Utterly unrepentiful, true perditious, true sinfulness. It is always found in being against

receiving me as their savior called Christ Jesus, forever.

59 And utterly unrepentiful, true perditious, true sinfulness. It is considered of (of means the word by) me (God), as being anti Christ,

60 As in meaning to be always being eternally against receiving Christ Jesus, as Christ Jesus, being their savior, forever. And that is considered of me, forever,

61 As being against receiving me (God), forever, as that is true forever. And I do see them forever, as death forever, and as to be like unto Satan himself, forever, as Satanism, forever.

62 And, utterly unrepentiful, true perditious, true sinfulness. It s seen by me (God). As being a utterly fallen true image, as the damned, as being eternally forever seen.

63 And the damned, in Satanism forever. They are seen, unto me forever, as I see them, forever, through Christ Jesus, forever.

64 And I do see them through Christ Jesus, forever, as a seen eternal true image, that is made, as being a perditious true image, as they are the damned, forever.

65 And that image, it is a image found in being eternally forever, as being eternally forever, truly

seen. As being, seen and found, as found unto me forever, in being of earnest and sincere, true death, forever.

66 And the image as Satan himself as the damned forever. It is a eternal deathly true image, found in given true death, as being eternally forever seen, and true forever.

67 And eternal Satan true death, forever, It is seen, as being eternally the damned forever. As they are felt and seen, unto me forever true, as being eternally, true death, forever.

68 And death, it is seen, as being eternal, as the damned ones, forever. And the image, is found by me forever, as being the damned in Satanism, forever,

69 That image, as death. It is forever. And it is tainted true life, forever, as death eternally forever, and ever true death, forever. And that image, it is found unto me forever, as being Satanism, forever, as they themselves, as dead death, forever.

70 That image, it is them, themselves, and as result. They are found in being eternally forever found, as being blasphemous eternal seen true image, that is as and is of Satan forever,

71 That is a found true image, as being found as being, dead unto me, forever. And that true

deathly eternal true image, it is unholy to me, forever.

72 And that image is the damned in Satan himself forever. And it is found in being a unholy true image, as the damned ones, as they are of Satan himself and of Satan's true sinfulness, that is called death, forever.

73 And the image is eternal true death, forever. And it is always seen, before me forever. And it is found, in being against me (God), as being forever true.

74 And they, the damned ones forever. They are most eternal, as being the beast, that is called unrepentiful true man, forever,

75 And that image, that is the damned forever. It is utter true perdition, and it shall live forever, and it is forever eternal, and shall live in hell, forever.

76 And the image is found in Satan's ways of granted true death, forever, and it is eternally forever seen. And it is considered by me (God), forever,

77 As being a image that is of Satan himself, forever. And it is eternally forever true. As a deathly eternal living true damnation, that is called death,

78   And it is found forever. As being eternally forever found, as one being found before me, forever, as found. In being in eternal and willful and true, disobedience, unto me, forever faithful.

79   And they the damned, they are truly seen. As being unholy true beasts. As they are found by me, forever. As they are found by me forever true. In eternal true damnation, that is called desired true death, forever.

80   Eternal true damnation, it is a living forever unrepentiful true damnation, as it found in desiring to not ever receive Christ, as Christ Jesus, being one's seen savior, forever.

81   And they, the unrepentfully found, as the damned, forever. They are found without Christ Jesus, as Christ being their seen savior, forever.

82   And, as a result, in not believing to accept Christ Jesus, as savior, forever. Then they shall perish without me (God), as being forever true,

83   As true of themselves, as they are seen as being found unto me forever, as being Satanism, forever.

84   And they are seen, as being eternal true beasts. And, they are antigod, in all that is called God. And I do see them, as death, forever.

85   And, those deathly living forever, heavenly true, unrepentiful true beasts. They are, and shall always, be found by me, in most heavenly, forever true, true death, forever,

86   And they, as death, forever. They are seen, and felt, as being eternally forever true. As being, seen and felt. In eternal, true, granted true, perditious true death, forever true.

87   And those beasts, they are most surely, eternally forever found. As being, without my eternal, living forever, true presents. That true presents, it is, called God as being forever seen, and true forever.

88   And my true presents, it is shown, in Christ, faithfully forever true of me, as surely forever true. And it is faithful, of me, as being forever seen, as I Am seen, as I Am God, forever.

89   And I Am the forever. And I Am seen, as the life. That is called Christ Jesus, as being forever true, and, I Am forever seen. And that seen life,

90   It is seen, as being, seen eternal and most true life. And that life, it is given, faithfully forever true, of me. As given, by me, freely of mine own, eternal true heart, as, forever seen.

91   That heart, it is my eternal, true heart, that is my eternal true grace. That I Am forever, as I Am God, forever.

92   And I, truly do love, mankind, as being forever seen. And I do, love man, forever true, and faithfully forever true. Even, as forever, truly seen, and true, and as forever true and forever known, as I Am known, as I Am God, forever true.

93   And though, I truly do love all men, forever. Many will not ever come unto me, in Christ Jesus, who (Christ Jesus) is my (God) Son, as forever seen.

94   And, as a result of them, not coming unto me, in Christ Jesus, forever. Then, ever lasting true damnation, that is called granted true death, forever,

95   It is, then granted as a granted and true death, unto the damned, forever. And eternal, true damnation, it is therefore. As a found judgment, granted in eternal, true death, forever.

96   And it is granted unto the utterly lost, forever. And it is seen, as being, a living forever true damnation, and is granted by me, faithfully forever true,

97   As granted unto the lost, who are found by me, forever. In Satanism, as being forever seen. For they truly do desire, to worship their false prophet, who is called unrepentfulness, as being forever seen.

98 And I shall damn them forever, who willingly shall partake of that willful against God, damning, Antichrist, true worship of utter damningly true seen sin.

99 That worship, it is found in Satan and in his (Satan's) unrepentfulness, as forever seen. And it is called, eternal true death. As it is found, as being without me (God), and, it is without Christ Jesus, as being eternally forever true.

100 And they, as found in Antichristism forever. They are seen, as being, truly unrepentiful true men, and, unrepentiful true women, forever.

101 And they shall, most certainly, as eternally forever true. They shall depart from this world, forever true. And they shall be found in the lake, that burneth, in all, that is called God, as being forever true.

102 And these Antichrists, they are seen by me, forever. As being, perditious against my righteous ways of most eternal, forever true, true life,

103 And they, the damned as being Antichrists forever. They are found, unto me forever. As found in, unrepentiful, damningly true damnation, that is forever true, as being of Satan and Satan's true ways of death, forever.

104   And it is found, because of their personal and true desiring, as to personally desire Satan's falleness forever, as it is given of themselves, forever,

105   And it is eternally forever true and forever more and ever lasting, forever seen and felt, as death unto themselves, forever.

106   And the damned forever, they are seen unto me forever, as being those, who are seen. As being, faithfully forever true. As being devoted, as true Antichrists. For they are most surely, eternally forever and ever true, in Satan death, forever.

107   And the damned forever. They are always seen in being perditious against all, that is found of me, in Christ Jesus, as being forever true. And, they are, most surely, found unto me, forever true,

108   As even found, in being eternally forever true. As reprobate with all that is seen, and is called unrepentfulness, as being eternally forever and ever true,

109   As that is true of themselves (the damned ones of the fallen true earth, forever), as they are found unto me, in Satan, forever.

110   And they are, most surely, eternally forever true. In being against me (God), and, they are

sinfully against Christ, and they are found, in Antichrist perditious sinful true transgressions,

111   That doth damn them, forever. For they truly do desire unrepentiful true evil, as it is demonstrated of themselves forever,

112   As it is demonstrated against me (God), as being eternally forever true, as true of themselves. As it is given of themselves, to me, forever,

113   And it is sent of themselves, forever, towards me and towards all that is me, forever. As it is truly eternal and willful, of themselves, to me, forever,

114   And it is given faithfully certain to me of themselves. As they as being eternally forever true, do desire, Satanism, forever,

115   And they are seen, in being, unjustly forever certain. As being ever true in unrepentfulness, as being eternally forever true of themselves,

116   As that unrepentfulness, is demonstrated of themselves, forever. And it is demonstrated to me, as they truly desire Satan true unrepentfulness, forever. As they desire that to remain in themselves, for all of given true eternity, and forever.

117 And it is seen, as being eternally forever true, as true of themselves, forever. And they are forever seen, in their desired true death, as being eternally forever true, in Satanism death, forever.

118 All willful and true Antichrists, who are willfully found in wanton true sins. That are unrepentiful sins, to never accept Christ, as Christ Jesus, being their savior, forever.

119 Then, they shall die in hell, as being eternally forever true, and they shall die unto me forever. And they shall die, for all of given true eternity, as being forever seen, and true. And I Am true, forever.

120 And, as a result, of that desired, within themselves, forever eternal, seen and felt, as given of themselves, unto me forever true, true death,

121 As it is seen, in being eternal, true defiling ness, forever. It shall move me, to final true judgment, forever true,

122 And that death, as the damned ones forever. It is found in being eternally forever seen, in being eternally sinfully against themselves, forever.

123 And that true death forever. It is seen, by their true desire. In disregarding my command to receive Christ as one's true savior, forever.

124　And, they are found truly forever. In the wantonness of desiring, Antichristism, as being eternally forever true. And, it is desired, sinfully forever true. As desired willfully forever, by the damned, forever.

125　And that desired true wantonness, for eternal deathly true sinfulness, as being eternally forever true, of and in the damned ones, forever.

126　It doth, damn the lost ones in Satan forever. And these are fallen from my grace, that is called life that is called God forever. And these fallen,

127　As they are truly fallen, as being eternally forever seen, as being seen and felt, as being forever true, as being true in Satan's true death, forever,

128　And these fallen, they do drink of that given, forever lethal, ever lasting, holy unrighteous true damnation, that is a eternal true death, forever.

129　And that, is a true, desired true death, that is eternally desired forever, by the damned ones, as being eternally and faithfully forever seen, and I Am seen, as eternal just judgment, to themselves, forever.

130　And they, the damned ones forever. They are most surely, eternally forever seen. As being true death, as that death, is found, in being:

131 True men and true women, who are seen, as being: Ungodly evil true men and ungodly evil true women, forever.

132 And these, are damned by me faithfully forever. And they do drink, from their unrighteous true sins. That are seen, as true sins.

133 As those, true unrepentiful true seen sins, they are found as their desired, true damning forever, true unrepentfulness, as it is seen forever. And it shall kill them, forever.

Chapter 31 w/ 72 verses   Recompense

1 When unrepentiful true men, shall and do, create Damningly true sin. It is called heavenly unrighteous true sinfulness. And, it is found,

2 As being a deathly death, as a forever true damnation. That is called and seen. As dead unto God forever true.

3 And, when I giveth, recompense, for heavenly unrighteous damningly true seen sin, forever. It is seen, as being a heavenly eternal righteous true damnation. That is given unto the wicked of the earth, as forever seen.

4 And recompense, that is called God in Christ Jesus, forever. It is, most certainly, found of me (God). As a given true recompense. That is called "Granted true death," as forever seen.

5   And recompense, that is called death from God, as being found eternally forever found, as found of me forever, through Christ Jesus, forever.

6   It is seen, as being a granted true death, forever. As granted by me through Jesus Christ, forever. And it is given of me forever, unto the unrepentiful true ones,

7   Who are found unto me forever. And they are found by me, in the fallen true earth, as forever seen in Satanism, forever.

8 And granted, holy and righteous, heavenly true recompense. For not believing in the Son of God, forever. As in never accepting Christ, as Christ Jesus being one's true savior, forever,

9   And who is Christ Jesus, that is sent by me, forever, into the earth forever. As salvation, that is called God, forever.

10   Then, by refusing Christ Jesus. As Christ Jesus, being one's true savior, as given by me, forever.

11   Then, in that great unending holy day of most given, forever heavenly, true judgment, that is forever true. It shall be found forever, that in being without God and without Christ,

12 This shall cause many, to be eternally lost unto me and unto Christ Jesus, as being eternally forever true. And they shall be lost unto me, forever.

13 And they shall be lost unto me, in that great day, that is most holy, unto me, as being eternally forever true.

14 And, they shall be lost, unto me forever true. In that eternal living, forever righteous, holy recompense. That is called holy true judgment,

15 As that eternal great judgment, that is being forever seen from me, as being eternally forever faithful, of me forever. And that great judgment,

16 That is called God in Christ Jesus, unto the damned forever. It is given of me, forever, as through Christ Jesus, forever. And it is given of me, forever faithful, as a faithful seen true judgment, that is called God, unto the damned ones, forever.

17 And if the damned ones, shall not repent afore hand of their seen sins, by calling on the name of Jesus Christ, for the remission of one's seen by me, true seen sins, forever.

18 Then, they shall be caste away, by me and by all, that is called God forever, into hell forever. And they, the caste away true beast,

19 As they shall be found, as found eternally forever, with granted true death, as being eternally forever seen, and is eternally forever sure.

20 Then, they shall die forever. And true death, it is most surely, eternally forever true. And that granted true death, it is granted by me,

21 As being eternally forever true. Then, they shall be found, most surely, in hell, without true remedy, as being eternally truly forever true.

22 Again, living forever true life. As found in Satan's true unrepentfulness, forever. That is eternal true death, that is granted by me unto the lost, forever.

23 For the damned forever, they chose not ever receive Christ, as Christ Jesus being one's personal, living forever, true savior,

24 Therefore, they are found unto me, as being eternally forever certain, as certainly forever, in unrepentiful damningly forever true sin, as being forever seen, as seen in eternal dead death, forever.

25 Damning forever and ever, unrepentiful true seen sin. It is found in Hell forever. And in hell, hell is found eternally forever true, for the unrighteous, and, for the unholy one's, forever.

26 And hell, is a given as a great eternal true judgment, as it is found eternally forever true, as it is given from me, forever. And it is faithfully given of me, forever,

27 And is a given true judgment, that is called true death, forever, and it is forever true unto them, as they are found by me forever, in Satan true death, forever.

28 And death, it shall be found given of me forever, in that great unending true day. That is most eternal, living forever, holy true light, as being forever seen. As Christ in me, the true Father, forever.

29 And that light, it is me (God), in Christ Jesus, as being eternally forever true, saith God, as being eternally forever true, and, as forever seen.

30 Recompense that is called God. It is seen, as being, true everlasting, eternal, living true death, as being eternally forever seen.

31 And it is seen by me, as being eternally and faithfully forever seen, and granted true death, shall be granted by me forever, unto them, Forever,

32 And true death, is due unto them forever, as a granted true recompense. And this is because of their sinful, true, unrepentiful true desires,

33 As it is found by me forever, in their personal true trespasses and true sins, forever. Therefore, they are found unto me forever true, as being eternally, found as being the damned, forever,

34 And they are found unto me forever, as I look forever at them, as I seen them through the eyes of my eternal true Son, who is called, Jesus Christ, forever.

35 And I see their personal, true, unrepentiful true iniquity, forever. And they are found by me forever, as being eternally forever true,

36 As being found, in being against me (God), and being eternally found in being against my (God) eternal true Son (Christ),

37 Who is called, Jesus Christ, forever. And this Jesus, he liveth forever true, in my (God) holy true presents, forever. And this Jesus,

38 He is seen, of and from me, forever. And he is most eternal, as forever and ever, eternal living, forever, heavenly true life,

39 As being Christly, eternally forever seen, and, forever heard, as me, forever.

40 Heavenly true life, as it is seen and felt, as being heavenly. And it is seen, and it is felt as being Jesus Christ forever. And it is forever true

of me (God), and from me, as being eternally forever seen.

41 And that is seen true life, that is it is most certainly, as being eternally forever found, in Christ Jesus, forever.

42 And that life, it is most surely, seen and felt, as being eternal, living forever, true life, that life, it is: "GOD FOREVER."

43 And I Am God as found of myself forever, in Jesus Christ, forever, and that life. It is eternal life, and is seen and felt, as me (God), forever.

44 That life, it is called God as forever seen, and felt as life forever. And that life, it is seen, as being, heavenly, never ending,

45 And it is seen, as being, even yet. As being, uttermost, forever and ever, most holy, living forever, eternal true life, that is me (God) forever.

46 That life, it is found in me (God) and of me, as being forever true, as saith thy God. For I Am the life, as it is found, in mankind, as it is being forever seen. And it is seen, as being eternally, Jesus Christ, forever.

47 And that life, that is called God in Christ, forever. The utterly fallen, shall never experience

it personally forever. If they shall continue forever,

48 In being found unto me, forever. As being eternally found, as being. Found against me (God), and as being eternally forever seen, as seen, true death. As it is seen, as being, unrepentiful true sin, as forever seen.

49 The forever true workings, of unrepentiful, damningly seen, eternal seen sin, as it is seen by me, forever, as it is being truly seen as sin forever,

50 That work, it is seen, as being, as true death. And that work, it shall receive, great recompense. That is called God forever. And that recompense,

51 It is found, as a granted true death, forever. And it is seen, as being, recompense in most certain forever heavenly true death. And that death, it shall come to the wicked of evil deceiving true devices, forever,

52 As they, the damned, are found by me, forever. As they are found unto me, in fighting against me, forever. As found and seen, unto me forever,

53 As seen by me forever, in their own personal true decisions. That are made of themselves, forever. As they, do chose to remain in unrepentiful true sin, as being eternally forever

true of themselves, as they are true unto Satan, and unto Satanism, forever.

54 The unrepentiful, as they are found as the beast, that is called fallen true man, as being forever seen. They, the beast, that is called men. They shall never pass into all heavenly true life, forever.

55 For righteous of myself, forever. They are found unto me, with eternal heavenly true life. As it found, given by me to them forever,

56 As it is given by me, faithfully forever, as it is given faithfully of myself (God). As they are found unto me forever. In Jesus Christ, forever,

57 And they shall live eternally forever. And without true end, in me forever. And they shall be as my heavenly true angels, forever. And they shall live,

58 In my true and righteous, true spirit, as, forever seen. That spirit, it is called, and it is seen. As being, eternal, as being: "Eternal true life," as forever seen, and it is true, forever. For it is my spirit, as I Am found in Jesus Christ, forever.

59 Eternal life, it is called God as forever seen. And it is seen, as being, given of myself (God), as eternally forever true. Unto all, who are found most certainly, forever true. As being found

faithful unto me, forever. In Jesus Christ, eternally forever.

60 These that do walk within the grace of me (God). That is eternally found forever, as certain in Christ Jesus, forever. They do walk without true spot, and without, true wrinkle.

61 They are found in Christ Jesus, forever. And they do refrain from uttermost damning forever true sin. And they, shall be found unto me forever,

62 In that great unending true day of days. That is eternally forever seen. As being seen, as: "Most Eternal Living Forever True Grace, That Is Called God," forever.

63 Heavenly true life, it is a forever eternal true life. That is given of me, (God) in Christ Jesus, forever. And that true life, it is found of me. As being forever faithful, in all that I Am. As I Am God unto mankind, forever.

64 And, eternal living forever true life. It is found forever true, in me (God). And that eternal living forever true life. It is seen, as being, forever and ever true. In all that is made by me, forever, as being Christ Jesus, forever.

65 But those, who forsake me, as being eternally forever seen. They are seen forever, without

eternal living forever true life, as being forever seen.

66 And they are seen, by me faithfully forever true. As being, the rejectful of me. As I Am found in Christ, as being forever true,

67 In these days, forever, I shall come to the earth, soon, and, forever, as truly seen. And though no man knows the day nor hour of my coming unto man, forever,

68 Thou can know that though Biblical true signs, forever. That it is in these days forever, as saith thy God unto all of mankind, as forever seen.

69 And soon, eternal living forever true life. It shall come to the unrepentfully fallen and unto the righteous of the earth,

70 And they, shall receive their heavenly true rewards. As found given by me, forever. In the most, heavenly forever, true life. As found given by me. As forever faithful. As forever seen.

71 And the righteous shall enter in to heaven, but the unrepentfully lost. They shall receive, their heavenly eternal, living forever, true life,

72 In the eternal, living true rewards. As found, as given unto the damned, as forever seen. As

being seen, as death forever, to be in hell, forever.

Chapter 32 w / 78 verses   Unending holy light

1   In my (God) unending holy light, is found, given of myself (God), as being forever true. Is my (God) eternal, living forever, true Son. Who is: called Christ,

2   And this Christ, he is seen. As being eternal of myself. As I Am given of myself, as being forever true, in Christ, unto the world, forever true.

3   And this Christ, he is found, in my (God) great, eternal, forever heavenly, true light. That light, it is of myself (God). As I Am found in my Son, who is called Jesus Christ, forever.

4   This Christ, he is seen of me (God), as being eternally forever true. And this holy one, called Christ, he is Jesus Christ, forever.

5   And that Christ Jesus. He is of my (God), most eternal, holy true presents, that is called: "Eternal Living Forever True Life."

6   That life, it is seen, as being, most heavenly forever seen life. For I (God) Am, most holy, true life, forever. And I (God) Am eternal, and I (God) do live, forever and ever, truly eternal of myself. As I Am God, forever.

7   And this Christ, he shall most surely, live eternally forever true. In all of my eternal, living forever, holy true presents, that is called life.

8   And that true presents, it is seen. As being: "Most Eternal, Living Forever, True Life.

9   For this Christ, doth live in me (God), as being eternally forever true. For this Christ, he is found, of me (God). And I Am, Christ's, living forever, holy True Father.

10   And I Am the life, as it is found given of myself, forever. And I Am God forever. And I Am found, in and as Christ Jesus, as being eternally forever and ever true.

11   And I, the lord, I Am "Godly True Creation, forever. And that Is me," And I, doth create, new heavens, and, a new earth. And the former, old stone imaged, hardened sinful true world,

12   As it is found by me forever, in and of sinfulness, as being eternally forever seen and felt, as it is being seen, as eternal seen death, forever,

13   It shall, depart from me forever, in that great day, as to depart away from my eternal, living forever, heavenly true presents. As that true presents,

14   Is found, in most eternal, living forever, unending, holy most true life, as being forever true, as truly eternal, for I Am eternal as says the lord, forever.

15   Christ Jesus, he is a unending, holy, most true life. And this eternal true Christ, he is eternal, of me (God). And this Christ, he doth live in me, forever.

16   And this Christ, he is greatly anointed by me, as being eternally   faithfully forever and ever true, and, as forever seen, as I Am seen as being God, as I Am eternally forever. And most surely,

17   Heavenly true life, that is heavenly true life. As found given in and of me (God), forever, as says the creating true God,

18   For it is eternally forever and ever true. As being, eternally forever and ever true of me, and in me, forever. For I Am the life, that is called, Jesus Christ, forever.

19   And this Christ Jesus, he is my only begotten true Son. And he is seen, as my (God) holy one, that is of my (God), eternal, living forever, true righteousness.

20   And this Christ, he shall, as being eternally forever true. He shall live forever true. In my (God) eternal, living forever, true presents, that is called, "Heavenly Forever, True Life."

21 Christ Jesus, he is my (God) eternal, living forever, true Son (Christ). And this Christ Jesus, he shall always be seen. In them, who are of the body of Christ,

22 As they are found by me, forever. As being eternally forever true, as true of themselves, in me (being seen as Christian forever) as being seen, as seen in Christ Jesus, forever.

23 These of the body of Christ, that know me, in Christ Jesus, forever.

24 They are known of me (God). In my most eternal, living forever, living true righteousness. And, they are known, to me, forever. As being,

25 As being found in my most holy true light. That light, is called Jesus Christ, And this Christ, he is most eternal, in me, as being forever true. And this Christ, he is seen,

26 As being seen, in my most holy true light. That light, it is found, in Jesus Christ, forever. And it is seen, as being in Christ, as being forever true,

27 And, it is forever seen, as I Am seen, as I Am seen, as being the true life, that is called God, as being eternally forever true, and, as being, eternally forever seen.

28   And this Christ, he is seen and felt, in me (God), who (God) is the True Father, as being eternally forever sure. And, as faithfully forever true, as I Am true. As I Am seen, as life forever. And I Am seen, as being the eternal kind God, forever.

29   Christ Jesus, he is my holy true one. And this holy, lighted in my righteousness, true Christ. He doth, live, in my (God) holy true righteousness. For all, of given true eternity. And that true eternity,

30   It doth proceed, from me (God), as being forever sure, and as being eternally forever true. For I Am, thy eternal true maker. Who has made, heaven and earth, as being forever sure of myself, as I Am God, forever.

31   This Christ, he is surely, in my holy, most eternal, living forever, true presents, as being forever true. And, this Christ Jesus, he is found, given of myself,

32   As given true salvation, for the repentful of the fallen true earth, forever. And that salvation. It is seen, as being forever seen, as seen of and in me. As seen faithfully forever and ever true.

33   And this Christ Jesus, he shineth in the darkness, that darkened true sinners, may come to the undarkened true light, that is called God, forever.

34 And that forever, true light. It is called God, forever. And it is, as being eternally forever and ever found, as found. In being, undarkened true light, forever.

35 And I (God) Am found, in Christ. As being eternally forever and ever true. And, I Am eternally forever seen. And I shall live, as God, as being eternally forever true.

36 For I Am, true forever. And I Am, the forever, that is called God, forever. And, there shall never be a true end, to me.

37 And that is, eternally and ever lastingly, forever true, and, as forever seen. And I Am seen, and felt, forever. And I Am true forever. And I shall live, eternal of mine own true self, as my own eternal true power, forever.

38 And, as I live, as saith thy God, as forever true. All unrepentiful true sinners. They are found by me forever. In most eternal, living forever, true darkness.

39 That darkness, it is called death without God, forever. And Christ Jesus, is found, as forever true, in me, forever. And Christ Jesus, he is sent unto these lost sinners,

40 That they, as the beast. That is called the man of sin. That they, may truly repent, in the

heavenly eternal true light. That has never known, true darkness, forever.

41 And that heavenly true light. It shall never know, eternal living true darkness. And sinners, may repent, in that great light, and, that they may live, as being eternally forever and ever true.

42 And that, they may live, in that great eternal heavenly true light. That is called God, in Christ Jesus, forever. And, that they, as repentful true beasts, as found, of the earth, forever,

43 That they, may repent unto me forever. And never die again, as being eternally forever and ever true. Therefore, as they are seen, unto me, forever.

44 As they are seen, as being, repentful unto me, as being eternally forever true. Then, I shall hear them, in Christ Jesus, forever.

45 And, those, once darkened, repentful, true beastly, seen true sinners. They are now, saved in the precious glory of me, who is the most eternal, living forever, true Father,

46 And, they shall never die again. In this earthly true darkness. That is seen, as being, eternal, living forever, true darkness. And that, they,

47 As repentful true sinners, had once known in the eternal living true workings of sin, that is sin, as found as darkened, most certain, living forever, true death.

48 All, darkened, sinful, unrepentiful against God, true death. It is seen, as being, eternal. And that, eternal dying, true death. As found in all that is, Satanism, forever.

49 It is a beastie eternal true death, as found in Satan, forever. And it is seen, as being, a true death, in Satan, as being eternally forever seen, and true.

50 And, that death, in Satan, as being the damned, in Satanism, forever. It is seen, as being a true death, in Satan, forever.

51 And that true death, it is found, in Satanism, as being forever seen, and it is seen, by me, as I Am God, as I Am eternally forever true,

52 That death, forever. It is, seen, as being, a sinful true death. And, it is, forever seen. As a seen darkened beastly true image. As it is found by me, forever. And, it is found, by me, as being, forever seen,

53 And, it is seen, as a true death, forever. And it is seen, as being: Granted true death, forever. And, it is seen, as being, true death,

54 That is forever true, and forever seen. As seen, in "Most Eternal, Antichrist, darkened Forever, unrepentiful, blackened True Sin."

55 And that true death, as it is found by me, and as it is seen by me, as being eternally forever true, as being eternally true in the damned, forever. It is seen, as being, Satanism, forever. And it is forever seen, as seen,

56 As seen in the damned, as forever made, as made by the damned ones, forever. And it is made, as being eternal, by the damned, as being, forever true, as true in death, forever.

57 And all true sinners, they are found unto me, forever true. As being, found in darkened true unrepentfulness. That unrepentfulness, it is seen,

58 As being: "To never accept the eternal, living, holy true Son, who is the eternal, true Son. Who (Jesus Christ) is the everlasting eternal true Son of God, as being eternally forever seen, as I (God) Am seen, as I (God) Am God, forever.

59 And this eternal Christ, is called "The Christ." And who is the heavenly lighted Godly true salvation. That is given of me, forever. And that, true salvation,

60 That true salvation, it is called God forever. And it is sent of me (God), as being forever

certain, in me. As found, given of me, as being forever true, in the earth.

61 That salvation, it is, even yet, greatly called, Christ Jesus, as being forever seen. And this seen Christ Jesus, he dwelleth in me. For I Am, the Pure Father, of the water of life, forever seen.

62 The blackness of darkness, it is seen, as being, a unrepentiful, eternal, sinful, beastly, darkened fallen true image of them, as they are found by me, in Satan death, forever.

63 And that blackened true image, as found, as Satanism, forever. It is seen, as being: "A Darkened True Death, in the blackness of Satan true night," as forever seen night.

64 And the eternal, most true, blackness of death. It is, "A Fallen, Unrepentiful, Beastly, Ungodly, darkened true Image of Spiritually Darkened, Antichrist True Men," as being forever seen, in wanted true death forever.

65 And the damned of the fallen true earth forever, they are found, forever true, in "The Blackness Of Darkness," as being forever true of themselves,

66 As they are found unto me forever. In the mark and in the number of the name of eternal true shame. That is called Satan, forever.

67 And, they are seen, as being, without God. And, they are, even seen, as being without Christ, as being eternally forever seen. And they are seen,

68 Unto me, as eternal true death, as being eternally forever true, as they found unto me, forever. In Satan true death, forever.

69 And, they are seen, unto me, as being forever seen. As being without me, as forever true of themselves, as they are found by me, forever,

70 As they are found eternally forever, in their Satan desired true death, forever. And they do hold fast, unto that true Satanism,

71 As it being forever true of themselves, as they are found by me, forever, in Satan, forever. And, they shall die, unto me, and unto all, that is found,

72 As being found, as found in and as being Jesus Christ, as being eternally forever true, as saith thy eternal kind God, and I Am kindly forever,

73 And I shall never die, and they that serve me faithfully forever, in Jesus Christ, forever, and they shall live free of Satan, forever,

74 And they shall live, in all that I Am, as I Am their kind, redeeming, true God, forever. And

they shall never know, the pain of eternal true separation, ever again,

75 And I shall love them, for all of given true eternity, forever. And without true end, to my kind love, forever. And I shall be found of them, forever.

76 For these, do love me and serve me, as being eternally, faithfully forever true, as being eternally forever true, as true unto me, and always, forever true.

77 And they, are true forever, and they are found by me, forever, in Jesus Christ, forever. And they shall live eternal, in me, forever,

78 And they shall live, without true death, ever again, and, as being eternally forever true, and that is, true forever, without true end, forever. For I Am the forever, and I Am God, forever.

Chapter 33 w/ 57 verses   Eternal death

1 Beastly eternal true death. As it is found, as being Satanism, as being forever seen. It is seen, as being, darkened and being, truly, deathly eternal true death, as being eternally forever, in death, before me, forever.

2 And, eternal true death, it is found, as sin, as being forever true. And, that eternal true

sinfulness, as it is forever seen and true. It is, a eternal, most true, eternal reproach,

3 As made by the damned ones. As being forever seen and true, as given of themselves forever, unto me, eternally forever. And they shall die unto all, that is Godly true life. As it is found, given by me,

4 As given faithfully forever true, of me, in Christ, for all, of given, true eternity, and, as being forever seen, as I Am seen, as the life, that is called God, as being forever true.

5 The damned, who are found, by me, as being forever true. As being, found in Satanism, as being eternally forever true. They shall, all appear forever, at the judgment seat,

6 That is, of Christ and of me (God), forever true. And Christ Jesus, he shall give them, the due eternal true reward of true death.

7 As they are found unto me forever, as in, desiring and partaking of the true mark of sin, as it is found by me forever, in Satan's true sins, forever.

8 Eternal true death, as it is found. As being true unrepentfulness, as being eternally forever seen, as seen in eternal true death, forever.

9   It is seen, as being found in the beastly worship of the image of Satan and of the damned ones, forever.

10   And the blasphemous eternal, true image of dead death forever. It is, eternally seen and felt, as true death, unto them, that are measured unto me, as measured to me forever, as seen sin, forever.

11   And I shall measure, unrepentiful true seen and unseen hidden true sin, as it is found by me forever, within the damned. As it is their seen sin,

12   That is seen unto me, forever. And I shall measure that granted true death, back unto them, forever, in hell, forever,

13   For I Am the lord of the harvest of souls, forever. And, if they be found, as worldly true chaff (worldly means them [sinners] that hath not believed upon the Son of God, for salvation, that is called God, in the earth, forever), unto me forever,

14   Then I shall damned them forever, as saith thy t rue God unto the beast. As the beast, is found. In his desired, true death. As being, found in Satan,

15   As being eternally forever true. And that true death, is truly found unto me, as forever seen.

16 The damned, they do desire, Satan forever. And they are found and seen. As being seen eternal unto me, in all, that Satan is, as forever seen, in Satan true death, forever.

17 And, as eternal death. Is found in the beast, as they are seen unto me forever, as being forever felt, as being damningly true sins, forever. That sin, it shall separate the damned, from me, forever.

18 Therefore, let the beast, that is called the Son of perdition and the daughter of perdition, let him and her, repent unto me, quickly,

19 Least I move upon them of the perditious beastly true image of death, with death from me forever, found in hell forever.

20 Therefore, let them come and repent, in Christ Jesus. Unto me forever and quickly, least I kill them and their seen and unseen children, with death in this world and in hell, forever.

21 And, in hell fire forever. I shall never hear them, in their seen sins. As they shall be found in hell, for all of true eternity. And that is forever seen. Therefore, they should have chosen Christ, and not, Satanism, forever.

22 These, as they are found in eternal true death, forever, and as being forever seen, as being seen dead unto me, in all that is Satan forever.

23   They are seen, as being fallen, and unrepentiful. And, they are, quite beastly, as being forever seen as true dead death, forever.

24   They, the beast. They are called unrepentiful true ones of the earth. As being, seen as Satan is seen, as being seen as unrepentiful true seen sin, forever.

25   Satan and they, who are the brute beast. They and their damningly true image. They shall die unto me forever,

26   And they shall die and their seed shall die, as forever true. And mankind, in Satan, shall die unto me forever. And I shall determine the true course of Godly true angels, whom, are called men, forever.

27   Eternal seen true death, it is seen, as evil without true end, forever. And they that enjoy Satan forever. They shall die in hell and they shall not, live in all that is Christ Jesus. As Christ Jesus, is seen as being a true Son of me (God), forever.

28   Satan is seen, as a angel of divine, true light. As unto them that doth hold eternally forever true, unto the image as made of Satan unto the beast, that is called man, forever.

29   And most surely, those in Satan forever. They are seen as being antigod and Antichrist

Jesus, forever. And that brute image of slow bellies, forever,

30 They shall die in hell forever. And their cries for Christ Jesus shall not succeed unto obtaining Christly true salvation. That is called God, as they be found in hell forever,

31 Where their worm dieth not and the flame of judgment. Is seen as payment for granted true death, forever.

32 Eternal death, it is a darkened true image, as it is made in Satanism, forever. And it is called: "death that is against the light,"

33 As that light, is found by me, forever. In Christ Jesus, as given of me, as faithfully forever given by me, forever.

34 Christ ruleth the heavens forever. And hell, shall not be found in heaven, at all and forever. And darkened true death, it is sinfully seen, as being those, that are found unto me, forever,

35 As they are seen, as being eternally forever true, as being seen, as being beastly true men, who are found unto me forever. As being against my holy true plan,

36 As my plan, is found as being eternally forever seen, as seen of most eternal, heavenly, living forever, true salvation. That salvation, it is

found of me, in Christ Jesus, forever true. And, it is seen, as being, "The Light Of God," forever.

37 My holy plan, it is called "The Light Of God," and is given of my (God) eternal, living forever, righteous holy hand.

38 And, that plan. It is called God in Christ Jesus, forever. And it is found, in the most eternal, living forever, heavenly true life.

39 That life, it is called God, as forever true. And, it is, heavenly of myself, as forever seen.

40 Christ Jesus, he is given of me (God), unto all men, who are found unto me forever, as being repentful true men, as forever seen.

41 And they, who are seen, as being, unrepentful true men, as forever seen, they are seen unto me forever. As being unrepentful beastly eternal true men, forever. And salvation, that is called God in Christ. It is given,

42 Unto all repentful true men, as forever seen. That they, the repentful in Christ Jesus, forever. That they, may know me (God), "The God Of Eternal, Forever Living, Unending, Holy True Truth."

43 That truth, it is called God, in Christ Jesus, forever. And it is seen. As being, holy and undefiled, eternal true truth, that is called, God,

44 And that truth, that is called God, forever. It is forever true, and, as forever seen. For I Am seen, forever, in Jesus Christ, forever.

45 Again, that truth, that is called God, as being forever seen. It is seen, as being, true forever. And it is seen, as being me, as forever seen. And I Am seen, as Jesus Christ, forever.

46 And that is a holy truth, that is me (God). As I Am most assuredly, forever true. And I Am found, in the repentful. As their personal true God, forever. And that truth, it is, Christ Jesus, in me, forever,

47 And that truth, that is concerning me, as it concerning Jesus Christ, my Son, forever. It is given (Christ Jesus is given by our kind God forever to them that are repentful forever) by me,

48 As being eternally forever true, as given from me, to the repentful, as being eternally forever seen truth, that is called God in Christ Jesus, forever.

49 And that truth (Christ Jesus is given by me [God] forever), it is given, to the repentful true ones, forever, and, as they, truly do receive, my eternal, living forever, true Son, who is called "The Christ."

50 Christly true truth. It is given, of my holy, most pure, undefiling, holy true presents. That presents, it is, called life forever.

51 And that life, it is found, given by me, faithfully forever true, in Christ Jesus, as forever seen life,

52 And this Christ Jesus, he is my eternal true Son. And he (Christ Jesus) is found of me, as being forever seen. As seen, in all that I Am, as I Am God, as I Am forever true.

53 And I Am true forever, and I Am forever seen, and I Am seen with eternal true life, that is called Christ Jesus, as being, forever seen, true life, forever.

54 Christ Jesus, he is seen of me, as being forever true. As he is given of me forever, unto all repentful true men, as being eternally forever seen.

55 And, Christ Jesus, is that life, that is called "The Son of God," as he is found, of me. As I Am the True Father God, forever.

56 I Am that true Father God, who is forever eternally seen, as seen with granted true life. That life, it is, my life, forever, as saith thy eternal true God,

57   Unto them, that shall love me, faithfully forever true of themselves, forever. As they shall love me in Jesus Christ, the Son, as being forever seen, and, faithfully forever seen.

Chapter 34 w 62 verses   The darkened beast

1   Sinful men, they are seen, unto me forever true. As being, "The Darkened True Beast," And these, unrepentiful beastie, darken true ones,

2   As they, are found by me, forever, as being forever true in Satan, as being eternally forever, in sinfulness, forever. They do not, ever desire, to ever accept, the lighted one,

3   Who is, called Christ Jesus, forever. As this Christ Jesus, being forever true, as their, seen savior, from myself, as seen and being, eternally forever and ever true.

4   And Christ Jesus, he is given faithfully forever, true of me, as one's personal, lighted forever, true savior.

5   And this Christ, he is found, faithfully forever seen, in all that is seen, as it is seen in and being found as true Godliness, that is called God, as it is forever seen.

6   And that true Godliness, it is my (God) true presents. That is of me, forever. And my true

presents, it is called: "Most eternal and ever lasting, and, unending, forever true, true life."

7   That true life, it is seen and felt, as being: "Uttermost heavenly true salvation." That true salvation, it is my eternal true love,

8   As given of me, forever faithful. And it is given, unto all, all of true creation, as forever true.

9 That true, heavenly true salvation. It is me, as I Am found, in Christ Jesus, forever. And, it is, a heavenly true, eternal seen salvation. As it is found, as given of me (God), faithfully forever true.

10 And it is given forever, as true righteousness. That is my righteousness. And it is forever true. And it is, eternally called God, and it is forever seen. For I Am seen, as being God, forever.

11 The darkened true beast, as found, in death, as being, forever seen, as seen in Satan's true death, forever.

12   That beast, it is seen, as being faithful unto Satan, as being eternally forever true, as true to Satan himself, eternally forever.

13 And that beast, is considered, of me, as being eternally forever seen. As being, each person, as they are found unto me forever, in unrepentiful

true falleness, as it is forever true. And, each unrepentiful, fallen true person,

14 That doth not desire, to ever accept, the heavenly true Christ. As this Christ Jesus, being one's, personal, living forever, true savior. Then, they shall die in Satanism, forever,

15 And Christ, he is given of me, as being eternally and faithfully forever true, as true unto the beast, forever,

16 That the beast, may repent forever, and be cleansed, forever. And, to be simply, cleansed from of all it's true seen sins. As those eternal, seen true sins, are found unto me forever, in eternal Satanism, forever.

17 Therefore, all utterly fallen, unrepentiful true persons. They are each, considered of me forever. As a hardened, against God, true sinfulness.

18 That true sinfulness. It is found, in utter true damnation, as it is forever true, and, it is forever seen. And they, the damned ones, forever.

19 They are seen, unto me forever. As themselves, as they are found by me, forever. In being a granted true death, as to be found in hell, as being eternally forever true, of themselves, forever.

20   And they, are the damned forever. And that damned, they are called the beast, And that beast, is called: "The man of sin." And, that beast, shall receive hell,

21   As being forever true. In that, great given, true judgment. That is called life, as it shall ever seen, in that great day of truth, as being forever true.

22   And that darkened true image, found as the damned, in Satanism, as forever true. It is seen, in earnest and sincere, true death, forever.

23   And these, that find that sinful true joy, as the darkened true Satan, who (Satan) is the dark serpent of true death, forever,

24   They shall die unto me forever, as they are found in Satanism, as being forever true and forever seen. As it is seen of themselves, in Satan himself, forever. And that is a true darkness, that is called true death, forever.

25   And, as the damned ones, forever. Are spiritually bitten with true Satanism, forever. That deathly eternal true bite, it is a incurable sore of true death, forever,

26   As it is given unto them, forever. As they truly do desire Satan, as Satan being darkened true death, in themselves, forever.

27 All, who shall reject me, as me being their chosen true savior, who is called Christ Jesus, forever. They shall serve Satanism, as being truly forever true. And they, shall remain, as being dead, unto me, forever true and without true end, forever.

28 And that is the image of Satanism forever. And it is found in Satan forever. And that true image, is found in the unrepentiful, sinful true workings of death, as being eternally forever true.

29 And I Am life forever and Satan is death forever, therefore, chose this day, whom thou shalt serve forever. For If thou, shalt not, chose me, as thy savior, forever. Then thou and thy seed, shall die, forever and without true end, in death, forever.

30 Eternal granted last days true judgments. They are found unto the damned, as being forever true. And those true judgments. They are given, unto all nations,

31 Who hate me as I Am found in Christ Jesus, forever. And I shall destroy them in hell forever, and in this world forever. And they shall have death, even now,

32 As being poured out upon and unto themselves, as being forever true from me,

forever. And it is a poured out true death, as it seen, as being, a granted true death,

33 As being eternally forever true and forever seen. And I Am seen and felt as God forever, and I Am seen, as God, eternally forever true.

34 And I shall cause that death unto all, who shall refuse forever, Jesus Christ, as Jesus Christ, their being seen, true savior, forever.

35 And those, who are faithfully forever seen, as they do reject me, as I Am found, as being Jesus Christ, forever,

36 They shall die unto me forever true. And those rejectful, they are darkened in Satan true death, forever,

37 And they are seen, as Satan is seen, as Satan is dead unto me, forever. And Satan is dead unto me forever. And he shall remain dead forever,

38 For he hateth me, as I Am Christ Jesus, forever. And he, therefore, repenteth not, in Christ, forever true.

39 The beastly darkened damned in Satanism forever. They are seen, as being utterly true, in unrepentiful true sin, forever.

40 That sin, is dark and it is darkness forever. And it shall damn them, forever, as to whosoever

shall desire the dark drink of that, sinful, fallen, unrepentiful true image of perditious beastie darkened true men and true devils, forever.

41 And, they are forever seen, as seen. As being eternally forever true. As being true daughters of perdition and true men of perdition, forever.

42 And they are seen. As being a true darkened true beast. In Satan true death, forever. And they are Satan himself, forever.

43 And, when they are found unto me forever, as being beasts in Satan forever. They are found, as being dead in sinfulness. That is called rebellioness, as being forever seen.

44 And darkened true death, in Satanism, as being forever seen. It is found, in the false images of the false hopes, for ungodly true life, forever.

45 And that forever true tainted true life, it is seen. As being in and as the damned, forever. And it shall be found, in hell, forever.

46 And, in this fallen true world, is found, the damned in Satanism forever. And they have no love for God, and this shall damn them,

47 Who desireth such evil, as being eternally found against me (God), as being unrepentfully

forever true, as true of themselves, to me, forever.

48 I Am the maker of heaven and earth, and I do hold, heaven and earth, in my eternal, living forever, true hands. And those hands, they are found, in "Most forever Heavenly True Life," as being eternally forever true.

49 And these the damned. They do declare their sin, openly in this fallen true world, forever. Even as, if my eternal true laws, means nothing at all, and forever. And they live their true lives, as if these darkened one's, should live forever, and not die forever,

50 But they, they are of the given forever true darkness. That is called unrepentiful true sin, as it is forever seen, as seen by me through Christ Jesus, forever. And they shall perish, most surely,

51 In that great, true day, that is called: "Most eternal true light, forever." That great light, it is great forever true punishment,

52 As to be given by me through Christ Jesus forever, unto the beast, that is called "Unrepentiful, beastie, eternal true man, forever," as he (sinner) is found in unrepentfulness forever.

53 That true punishment, it is called "Eternal, Ever Lasting, Holy true Judgment," as forever seen. And it will be seen, in that great, lighted true day, that is, forever.

54 Eternal true darkness, is fallen true man. As he is found by me, forever. In his true transgressions, as he is forever seen and felt, as he giveth those eternal seen and felt, true sins, to me, forever.

55 Darkened true judgment. It is called recompense from me (God), forever. And I Am, the God of eternal true truth,

56 As being eternally forever seen, and felt. And I Am the life, that is forever seen, and felt, as I Am the heaven of heavens, eternally forever.

57 And that true life, it is me, forever. And it is given of myself (God), unto whom, it is due, as being eternally forever true, and, as forever seen.

58 And this darkened true world, that is the darkened true workings, that is called Satanism, forever. It is, called sin. And it is, forever seen,

59 As seen and felt, as seen and felt before my (God) great, eternal living, true presents. And that presents, is forever.

60 I Am, most eternal, living forever, true life. As being forever seen, and felt, as God forever.

For I Am God faithfully forever seen, and felt, as the true life, that is forever true.

61 And, in me, is the true life of men. And that true life, it is seen, as being, Jesus Christ, as being eternally forever seen.

62 Therefore, come unto me, forever true. In Jesus Christ, as forever seen, as saith, thy eternal true God, as being eternally forever and ever true, and, as forever seen.

Chapter 35 w/ 86 verses   Antichrist nations

1 This corrupted earth, with all of it's corrupted, ungodly, Antichrist nations. They are seen, unto me forever. As being non-Christian nations of the fallen true earth, forever.

2 And those forever nations, they are even considered of (the word of is the word by) me, as being eternal seen nations of Satanism, forever. And those nations,

3 They know not Christ, as Christ Jesus, being their seen savior, as Christ is given of me. And this Christ, he is forever faithful, as I Am faithful, even as forever sure.

4 Those nations, they are Antichrist, forever. For if, they chose to deny Christ, forever. Then they have become Antichrist, forever.

5   And, they are seen, unto me, forever. As being unto me forever true, as Satan forever. And they shall die unto me, as forever true. And, if those Antichrist true nations, as they are found by me, forever, in sin, forever,

6   If, they shall not repent afore hand, unto me, as faithfully forever true, in Christ Jesus, as forever seen. Then they shall die unto me, as forever true, as saith thy eternal kind God, as being eternally forever seen, and felt, as I Am true life, as forever seen and true.

7   Those Antichrist, true ones. They are seen, unto me forever. As being death, that is forever and without true end, forever.

8   And they shall be caste away by me and by my true Son, who is called, Christ Jesus, as caste into eternal, and most true, hell fire, as being forever seen, and, forever true,

9   And in that great day, I shall repay, all anti Christ true nations with the deeds, that they have recompensed unto me. As I Am their God forever.

10   And that recompense of them towards me, it shall be burned back unto those Antichrist nations, as forever seen. And they shall remain in Satan true death, forever.

11 For they have recompensed me, by denying unto themselves forever, to never, truly partake of the salvation. That is called Christ Jesus, forever.

12 For they **have willfully** forsaken me, **by intentionally** hurting me forever, by never loving me in Christ Jesus, forever. For they, **have purposely,** chosen not to love me, in Christ, forever,

13 And, as I have given them, me in Christ and have shown them love and consideration. That is called my life, as found in Christ Jesus, forever,

14 And, as I **have given them**, me, and **have encouraged them**. To receive Christ Jesus. As Christ Jesus, their seen savior, from me, forever. They have paid me back, as a result,

15 As saying, to me (God). I (the damned) will repay you by hurting you forever, for I (the damned) will never serve you, in your Son, who is called Jesus Christ, forever.

16 And though, I (God) have done this for them, forever, in saying to partake of me (God) in Christ Jesus, forever. They have chose, to recompense me, by refusing correction in life, that is called, to listen to me (God) and receive Christ Jesus, forever.

17 Therefore, I have, spoken, and commanded, them. To repent and be washed in the blood of Jesus Christ,

18 That their, seen before me, true sins. That those true sins, may never appear before me, ever again, and, as forever true.

19 And those Antichrist true nations, they are beastly forever. And they, are found in Satan forever. And in Satan, that image as they have made, as desiring Satan true death, forever. It shall damn them forever.

20 These ungodly true nations. They are antigod and Antichrist, forever. And they are in sin forever, and in death, forever.

21 And they, and them that love Satan, forever. By serving Satan and his (Satan) image, that is called unrepentfulness forever. They (the damned ones) shall be found, in hell fire, as being forever true,

22 Therefore, they are sinful, and they are seen. As being unrepentiful true nations, in death forever. And they are found, in the damningly true image,

23 Of Antichrist and Antichristism, forever. And they are even seen. As being perditious-- sinful-- ungodly. And they, are most surely, Antichrist as forever seen and true.

24 And they are seen, as being, fallen true men, as forever seen. And they are seen, as being, unrepentfully and eternally forever true,

25 As being against me (God), as being forever true, as saith thy God, as being eternally forever seen, and, as forever known.

26 Those, ungodly true nations. As found in the Antichrist true spirit of death, forever. They are considered of me (God), as being spiritually darkened. And, they are, seen by me, as being forever true, as found to me in death, forever.

27 And, all ungodly, true Antichrist, true nations. As they are found by me, forever. As found in Satan true death, as forever true. They are, most surely seen,

28 As being dead unto me forever, as being dead in Satan and with Satan, forever. And, they are, given of themselves, as being forever true, as given unto Satanism, forever. And, they have,

29 And they do, give themselves, willingly, as forever seen. Unto the Antichrist true spirit, as it is found, as true death, as being eternally forever seen.

30 And, they are seen, as before me, as being forever true. As seen as being like unto Satan, as being eternally forever and ever true.

31   All, ungodly, true people, and ungodly true nations. They are made, to be, taken and destroyed, by me, as being eternally forever true. And, that, because,

32   They are of willful forever, true sins, forever. And those seen sins. They are, seen as: "Being antigod and Antichrist," forever.

33   And those seen sins, they are seen, as being eternally forever true, as being, forever seen sins. That are seen sins, in Satan true death, forever.

34   And, those seen sins, forever. They are truthful imaged true sins, that are, imaged in Satan, as being forever true. And, for all, of given, true eternity, and, as forever seen.

35   And, those seen sins, they are seen, as being, "Satanism," as being forever seen. As those seen sins, are seen by me, forever,

36   As they are found by me, forever, in the damned, as being forever seen. As those seen sins, are seen unto me, as faithfully forever and ever true.

37   All unrepentfulness, as it is found by me, forever. As in never desiring to accept Jesus Christ, as this Christ Jesus, being one's true savior, as given of and from me, as being forever true. And to deny Christ Jesus, as savior, forever. It is seen,

38 As being seen. As a damningly forever true life. That shall meet with eternal forever great darkness. That is eternal forever. And, it is seen,

39 As being: "Ever lasting true judgment. And that true judgment, it shall never die in hell, forever. For I the lord of heaven and earth, I shall never die. And I Am eternal, as being forever seen.

40 And, within the damned. As they are found in Satan (Satanism), as being forever true. Then, as they are found, as being eternally forever found, as found in true death, forever,

41 That true death, it is forever seen. And that seen true death, it is truly desired, by the damned, as they are found by me in Satan, as being forever seen. And, they are seen, unto me,

42 As being forever true, in the Antichrist true spirit. As it is found, as being, utter true shame, and, utter true contempt, that is forever seen.

43 And, it is utterly forever seen, and true, as truly found forever. As it is found, in them. That do desire to die unto me, as being forever seen, as seen in sin, forever.

44 All true death, it speaketh unto me, as forever seen. And it is seen, as speaking: "Satanism true death," as forever seen. And, it is a speakinly true image,

45 As it is found as them, that are found in the spiritual true mark. That is called Satan true death, forever.

46 And judgment, it is given unto all Antichrist true nations of death. As those nations, they are found by me, forever. In Satan true death, forever.

47 And, as it is written of me (God), in **Isaiah 24:20-21.** Then is this written, as concerning end time judgment, as concerning judging that true sinful true spirit of sin, forever. As it (sinful true spirit) is found, as being: "True death, in and as Antichrist," forever.

48 Isaiah 24:20: The earth shall reel to and fro like a drunkard, and shall be removed like a cottage: and the transgression thereof shall be heavy upon it: and it shall fall, and not rise again.

49 Isaiah 24:21: And it shall come to pass in that day, that the lord shall punish the host of the high ones that are on high, and the kings of the earth upon the earth.

50 Therefore, all unrepentiful evil transgressors. As found in their fallen, spiritual, unrepentiful true father, who is Satanism, as being forever true, and, as forever seen.

51   They shall die in hell forever. And I shall judge them now, in this world, as being forever seen. As with seen true death, unto them, as forever true. Unless, they repent in Jesus Christ, as being forever seen.

52   And, all of unrepentiful true man, as he liveth in the beastly Satan image of the fallen true earth forever. That imaged true death forever. It is found,

53   In them that are found, as they are found unto me forever. In being against me. As they are found unto me, as being forever true, as death forever.

54   And they, are forever true in Satan true death as forever seen. And, they are, forever seen, in the blasphemous eternal true image of death.

55   That image, is and is of Satan, forever. And is the damned ones, forever. And it is, as Satan true death, as being forever true, as true of the damned, as they are found by me forever, in Satan true life, as it is forever seen, as dead life to me, forever.

56   And they, the Satan ones as they are found, in Satan's true death, as forever seen. Those nations, they shall die unto me, most surely, as being forever true, as true of themselves, forever.

57   And they shall die unto me forever, even in this world, forever. Unless they receive Christ Jesus, as Christ Jesus, being their seen savior,

58   As forever true of themselves, forever. And they without Christ Jesus, forever true. They are already dead unto me forever. And they are found in sin, as being forever true.

59   Unless those nations shall repent of their Antichrist true ways, that are given, from Satan, as being forever true. Then, they will die unto me in hell forever, and in this world, forever.

60   And I shall, even most certainly, as forever true. I shall kill their seed with death, forever. Unless they repent quickly, now in this fallen true earth, as forever seen.

61   Unrepentiful true Man, is of most, certain forever, sinful imaged true death, as forever seen. And that true sinfulness, it keepeth man, away from my (God) great, living, eternal, undying forever, holy true presents. As forever seen.

62   End time judgments, they are most certainly found in today's fallen, against God, true earth, as forever seen. And those true judgment, they are called Christ unto the damned, as God to them, forever.

63   And those Just judgments, they are found functioning in end time judgments, in the earth,

as being forever seen, and felt, as God forever true.

64 And this unrepentiful fallen true earth. It doth reel, to and fro, in end time judgments. That are already applied of me, and are, found of me, as forever true.

65 And those end time last days, true judgments. They are given of me, through Jesus Christ, as being forever seen. And they (judgments) are seen, unto the earth, as forever true, as true of me, forever.

66 And this Christ, he is my (God) eternal, living forever, true Son. And this Christ, he is given of me, unto all nations, even unto all ungodly nations,

67 That those antigod true nations, as they are found forever true, in unrepentfulness forever. That they may ask for Christ Jesus, as he is the Son of God,

68 That they may ask to be accepted in Jesus Christ, forever. By receiving Christly true salvation, as being Christians, as found in faith. That is Christ, as seen in me, forever.

69 And, to go a little further with Isaiah 24:20, is this: Heaviness as found written in Isaiah 24:20. It is in meaning of the days of Noah, that are

found presently, upon this present true earth, as being forever seen.

70   And, through Christ Jesus, being demonstrated by me as my judgment, as it is given against all Antichrist true nations, forever. It is, that those nations, that they shall never rise again, and as being forever true, as to never rise in sin ever again, and truly forever.

71 I (God) Am the righteous holy God and with my holy Son, who is called Christ. We together, do judge the earth, righteously at this time, now of the earth,

72 And that, is end time judgment, forever. And it is seen, as being, ever lastingly, forever true, holy true judgment. And that true judgment, it is called God, as forever seen.

73 And that true judgment, it shall remain, faithfully forever true of me, as it shall remain found in the earth, as forever sure. And it shall remain forever, until Christ has came for the living and the dead. Who are found by me, in this chosen true earth, as forever sure.

74 And we (Christ and God), shall also judge together. In that great white throne judgment. That is most holy, and it is given of me (God). In great recompense, for the unrepentiful true sins. That are found, being demonstrated against me (God), as being forever true.

75 And that great judgment, it is a great, eternal, forever, never dying, Godly true judgment. That judgment, it is eternal just judgment, as being forever seen.

76 That judgment, it is from me (God), for I Am the eternal true God. And that Just Judgment. It is most holy forever seen judgment, as called death.

77 And that true death, it rideth upon the white horse of uttering, true, spoken, inspiringly spoken, speaking true judgment. As being forever seen true judgment, that is called death.

78 And that heavenly true rider, who is named: "Death." He speaketh the word of God, unto all, who claim the spiritual true workings of Satanism, as forever true of themselves, in Satan. forever.

79 And hell is with, and followeth him, that is called the word of death, as forever seen. And he giveth true death unto the beastie eternal true Antichrist true nations called Satan forever.

80 And hell, it receiveth them. That do not desire Christ, as Christ Jesus, being their seen savior, as forever true of themselves in Satan's true death forever.

81 The beastly image, called death. It is a fallen unrepentiful true image of fallen unrepentiful true devils, and unrepentiful fallen true men,

82 As they are being forever seen. In Satan's true works of damnation. That is called death, as being forever seen and judged, by me, forever.

83 This eternal, ungodly, unrepentiful image. That is called the beast. It is seen, as death without God. And death, shall soon appear shortly,

84 As given just recompense. Because of damningly seen true sins. That are found sins, that are found being against me (God). As I Am the creator (God) of heaven and earth, as forever seen.

85 This soon appearing, of just judgment, that is called granted true death, as forever seen. It is for recompense for one being found unto God forever, as they are found in sin forever.

86 Soon, Christ shall receive the dead and the living of the earth, in that great eternal, living forever, true day. That true day, it knows no end, in me (God), forever.

Chapter 36 w/ 73 verses   Great white throne judgment

1   In the great white throne judgment, all devils and unrepentiful true men. They shall all and each, they shall receive their heavenly true rewards,

2   As it is found, given unto themselves, forever. As it is given by me forever, as a given true judgment, that is called death, forever,

3   And that true death, it is forever seen, as true death unto the wicked ones, as they are found by me, in Satanism death, forever.

4   And it is a given true recompense. And, it is forever, truly found, in uttermost, true damnation, that is called granted true death, forever.

5   And that is desired by the damned, as wanton true damnation, that is desired by the damned forever. And it is found from one being seen, as being found in eternal, damning, forever true, sinful true workings, That are called death, forever.

6   Eternal, seen true death, it is found in Satanism, forever. And it is seen, as being true sins, that are found as being eternally forever true, and forever seen,

7   And those seen true sins, they are seen, as being eternally given unto me and being eternally forever true, as being against me, who is the creator of true life, that is called heaven that is God forever.

8   And those seen sins, they are forever seen and forever true. And those seen sins, as they are seen as being eternally forever seen, as being, Satanism forever.

9   They are found by me forever, as I see them through the eyes of Jesus Christ, my eternal true Son, who is called "life in God, forever,"

10   And I do see those eternal damningly true seen sins, forever. And I do see them, as being faithfully found, as found by me, in being faithfully forever found,

11   As those seen sins, they are: "The truly lost ones," forever. And as they (the damned) are found by me, in Satan himself, forever,

12   And those seen sins, in Satanism forever. They are found unto me, as being the damned of the fallen true earth, as being eternally forever true,

13   And those seen sins, that are called true death, forever. Those seen sins, they are found by me forever, in being against my (God) true righteousness,

14 And those seen sins are found, as being eternally forever seen, as being eternally forever true, in true wantonness true death, forever.

15 And, in that great judgment, that is called the white throne judgment. That judgment, it is seen as being eternal just judgment,

16 That is called eternal just judgment, unto the beast, and who is the beast, that is found by me, as forever faithful, as found in eternal, true dead death, forever,

17 And eternal just judgment. It is given faithfully forever true, by me, as being forever seen. And it is,

18 True unto all unrepentiful true beasts of the earth forever. As they are found unto me forever. As being found sinfully forever true. And these shall never desire me, as I Am found in Jesus Christ, forever.

19 And, at that great judgment, even devils shall know that they have received just recompense from me, forever. For they are found unto me forever true, as being against all, that I Am, as I Am God, forever.

20 And that just true judgment, it shall appear in the earth and in heaven forever. And that true judgment, it is granted forever certain, as granted forever unto them,

21 That doth desire Satan's true self, as Satan is found, as being found in seen unrepentfulness, as being forever true.

22 And just judgment, that is called God judging the beast, forever. It is forever true judgment. And it shall be found as God forever, unto all who shall never desire to worship me forever. As I Am their seen creator with eternal true life, as forever true.

23 And though, many shall claim to know me in hell forever, I never really knew them, for they knew only Satan's true self, as they desired Satanism, forever.

24 And they have rejected forever true, all that is me, as I Am God, in Jesus Christ, forever,

25 And, as they, the damned are found unfaithful, unto all that is me, as I Am Christ Jesus, forever. These the damned ones, they shall be found, and they shall be casted alive, away from my holy true presents, that is forever seen.

26 And they shall be casted away into hell fire that burneth with brimstone. And that is called death forever. And, it is, a seen, granted true recompense, for one being found in unrepentfulness, as forever seen, as seen in themselves, as being forever true.

27 And these, the damned ones forever, if they have denied me. As me through Christ Jesus, being their seen savior, forever,

28 Then, they shall die unto me, as being forever true of themselves. Then, they are eternally dead unto me, as being eternally and ever lastingly, found forever, in true death, forever.

29 And, these the damned, in hell fire forever. They should have trusted me, forever. Instead of trusting Satan and Satan's ways of dead death, as it being forever true of themselves.

30 Even these, the damned. They should have not have been ashamed of me and not ashamed of my eternal true words. As they the damned, are seen unto me, as forever true. In eternal seen true sin, forever.

31 If they believe not my faithful true words, as I (God) Am seen, as being the Son of God, with all power, that is called God, as being forever seen.

32 Then I will be greatly ashamed of them, in that great day, that burneth as God forever, unto the wicked forever. And that is forever true, unto all that hate me, as I (God) Am Jesus Christ, forever.

33 And I shall be greatly ashamed of them forever, as they be found forever, as Satanism

forever, in that great judgment, that is to occur shortly in heaven, and, in and upon the earth, as being forever true.

34 And that great judgment, it shall be forever seen, as seen forever upon all ungodly, non Christian nations and upon their true tongues and upon all of their true peoples,

35 And, that great judgment, it is given unto all of the fallen ones, forever. And is given faithfully forever true, as given by me forever,

36 And it is given faithfully forever, to them. Who are found sinful in the fallen true earth,

37 And f they deny me to be in themselves, as me being their true God, forever. Then they have chosen Satan forever, as Satan being their seen savior, who is called eternal true death, and they have received eternal dead death, forever.

38 Therefore, great given true recompense, it is given from me forever, as given by me to them forever. And it is called eternal true death,

39 And it is forever seen true death forever. And that true death, it is seen, as being eternally given by me, as being eternally forever and ever lastingly, eternal from me, forever true.

40   And that true death, it is most holy of me, to the damned forever. And it is forever true, as true in all, that is called God unto the damned,

41   As being in eternal just judgment, that is sent by me to themselves forever. And that judgment, it is found given by me, as being eternally forever true,

42   And it is called God forever. And I will forever, punish them that are unrepentiful to me forever, as given true judgment, forever. And it is given by me, as being eternally forever faithful.

43   And that true judgment, is given by me, unto whom will not ever serve me, as being forever faithful of themselves, forever.

44   And I shall punish them forever with given true punishment, that is called death, and that true death is eternal and ever lastingly correct of me forever,

45   And true death, it shall be found eternally forever, as death that is found in themselves, forever,

46   And I do see their seen sins, forever. And as they are eternally forever true of themselves, as found forever, in their eternal deathly true seen sins, as it is seen unto me, forever.

47 And those seen sins, they are found as a deathly eternal living true damnation unto me forever true, as given of themselves forever, unto me forever.

48 And it is, eternally and forever seen, and it is seen forever. As they chose forever, to not ever serve me faithfully forever true,

49 As forever certain of themselves forever, as they will not serve forever, in Jesus Christ, forever.

50 And, as they do refuse to live forever, in my heaven forever, as in being Christian forever, then,

51 True death, it is seen faithfully forever true, as a granted true death, that is called dead death, and it is a punishing forever true death.

52 And that true death, it is eternal, as a seen true death of punishing, eternal true life. As that life, it is found given of me forever, unto the damned ones, forever,

53 And it is a granted true punishing deathly life, as being forever true. And it shall be forever granted by me, as being eternally forever true, as true to the damned ones, in eternal dead death forever.

54 And, in that great holy true day, that liveth unto me forever, as eternally forever true, as eternal true Judgment. That Judgment, it shall be found,

55 As given of me, faithfully forever through Jesus Christ, forever. And it shall be granted unto all, who are found unto me forever, as found in Satan true death, forever.

56 And that true judgment, it is eternally forever true, unto themselves. As they are seen, as being the damned in Satan forever. And, as they are found by me, as being eternally forever true,

57 As they are found unto me, in the service of serving faithfully forever seen true sin.

58 And, as to, serve unrepentfulness, as being eternally faithfully forever true of themselves, as they are seen as being bestiality, that is called Satanism, forever.

59 But, unto them, that doth receive me and the kingdom of God, as being forever true of themselves to me forever. Then these have accepted my true words, as they are found spoken through Christ Jesus, forever,

60 And I (God in Christ Jesus forever) shall accept them in my body (physically and spiritually), and my (Jesus Christ) blood shall cleanse them forever.

61 And, those who asketh for me to be their seen savior, forever. These shall find me as like unto a great pearl of great endless true value, forever. And I shall open the door of myself (God),

62 Unto all, who sincerely desireth to know the True Father and desireth to know me, as I Am, Jesus Christ, that doth know the Father, in all, that is the True Father, forever.

63 Therefore, as thou asketh, thou shalt receive the father of life, forever, as thou come unto the father forever, through me, the Son of God, forever.

64 And it is my wonderful and true, warming true pleasure, to forever, give you the kingdom of our true father, forever.

65 But, if thou shalt not repent, quickly, and, as forever seen. Then thou shalt perish forever true, and, as forever seen. And thou shalt die and thy seed shall die unto me forever, as saith thy eternal kind God, as being eternally forever seen, and, as forever more.

66 Given true recompense, for unrepentfulness. It is found from desiring damningly true, antigod true sins. That are of most eternal, living forever, true sinfulness, forever,

67 And those who are given of themselves. Unto Satan true death, as being forever seen. They are

found, as being seen, as unrepentiful true one's of the fallen true earth, forever,

68 And they are given unto the sinful true workings that are of eternal living forever true reward, that is found in Hell. And that eternal, true reward,

69 It shall be given to the unrepentiful ones in death forever. For they truly do, enjoy smiting me (God) forever, as with their unrepentfulness,

70 That is called: "I love sin forever. And, at that great white throne judgment. They shall die unto me forever. Therefore, they have their true reward.

71 And, at that great, unending forever true day, that liveth in me (God) forever. That true day, it is life unto the repentful, and it is also seen, as being true death, unto the fallen, that do fall intentionally, to Satan himself, forever.

72 And dead death forever unceasing forever true. It shall be given by me, to themselves forever. For they, truly do not desire Christ Jesus. As Christ Jesus being their seen savior, as given of me, as forever true.

73 And, when one is found, in not desiring to receive Christ Jesus, as being forever true. Then, they shall make their bed in hell forever, and they shall never awake again, to live again, as saith

thy eternal true judge, who is called: "God forever."

Chapter 37 w/ 71 verses   Heavenly true salvation

1   Heavenly true salvation, as found given of me, through Christ Jesus, as being forever seen. It is found of me, in Christ, and is most certainly,

2   Found as being faithfully forever true heavenly true salvation. And it is faithfully given truly of myself (God), as being forever seen and true, as I Am faithful and true, forever.

3   And that salvation, is called granted true life, as found eternal, in me, the father. And it is given unto those repentful true beasts of the earth,

4   That doth love my soon appearing, as appearing soon, in the true earth, forever,

5   And I shall be seen, as Christ Jesus, being spiritually manifested, with all, that is me, as being forever true. And, that is, forever true, as true of me, as forever seen. And it is, forever, as truly seen.

6   And this heavenly true salvation. That is called Christ. It is found in me forever, as being surely seen, as a eternal seen and felt, true, living true, true salvation,

7 As that salivation is forever seen, as I Am seen as being God, forever. And true death, it is found without me, as being forever seen.

8 And true death, as it is given unto the damned ones, as they are found by me, forever, in Satan, forever. It is found, as most surely,

9 As being eternally forever found and true, and it is found without my "heavenly true salvation. And death,

10 That is seen and felt, without salvation, that is called Christ. It shall damn them forever, as to whosoever shall willingly not know Christ,

11 As this Christ Jesus, being their given of me (God), sun of righteousness, that is called: "The Son of God," as being forever true.

12 Eternal, living forever, heavenly true salvation. It is found of me (God). And is in my holy true presents, that is found, of most seen forever and ever, eternal living forever, true life.

13 That life, it is given of me (God), through my (God) Son, who is called Christ Jesus, forever. And, eternal, approved salvation, that is found of me, as being eternally forever faithful, in Christ Jesus. forever,

14 It is, found, given of and by me (God). But those, who are willingly forever, without the

eternal living forever true salvation, that is called Christ.

15 They are found, unto me, as being forever true, without: "My (God) eternal, living forever, true presents," as my presents, is forever seen, and felt as God forever. For I Am that kind God, forever.

16 And, to be found forever faithful, in being seen. As being faithful without Christ, as Christ Jesus, being one's personal, living forever, true savior,

17 Then, they shall die unto me, for all of given true eternity. And they shall never escape hell fire and it's torment. That is called God forever.

18 And, when one is found in unrepentfulness, in never wanting to ever accept, Jesus Christ, as Jesus Christ, being one's true savior, as forever. Then, that is seen,

19 As being against my (God's) true holiness, and it is against, my (God) true, eternal, living forever, true plan. That plan, it is called heavenly forever true salvation.

20 And true salvation, it is found given and sent of me (God), in most certain, forever, true life, forever. And that holy forever and ever true life. It is most forever, eternal true life. That life, it shall never, eternally end forever, and ever true.

21 In that great seen true day, that burneth with eternal seen hell fire and smoke. That is called God in judgment, as being forever seen,

22 All Satanist's (Unrepentiful true men and all unrepentiful true women) shall die unto me as being eternally forever true. And, in that true day, true righteousness,

23 As found in Christ, for repentance, as concerning seen sins, that are seen against me (God) in Hell. That forgiveness, shall never be seen. And my true righteousness, it shall not be found in hell, forever and ever true.

24 Therefore, in Hell, the lost are without a eternal, living forever, true savior, who is called Christ Jesus. And that shall be eternally forever and ever seen.

25 Now, at this time of our earth, I (God) the lord, do punish, all ungodly Antichrist true nations, forever. And I (God) do punish those evil inhabitants of the fallen transgressing earth, as being forever seen.

26 And, I the Lord, who Am seen. As being: "The Eternal Forever True God," as forever seen. I doth punish the ungodly kings of this evil, transgressing, fallen, unrepentiful, true earth, as forever sure.

27 And those Antichrist true nations, they have lifted up themselves in unrepentiful seen sinfulness. That is seen, unto the me (God), "The God of most heaven."

28 And I shall punish those unrepentiful true beasts, with eternal, seen, true death, as forever true. And with, eternal, true destruction. That is from me, forever seen.

29 And that judgment, it is seen. As being forever true and seen. As I Am seen forever. And I Am seen as Jesus Christ, in the earth, forever.

30 And I Am seen as the wrath of the Lamb. For I Am his seen wrath, that demonstrated of myself forever, as against all sinners, forever.

31 And I (God) Am the God of most eternal living forever, true heaven. And I (God) have created all, that is the eternal living true heavens,

32 And them, that doth not desire me. As I Am seen, as being, Jesus Christ. Then, they are seen, unto me forever. As being the blackness of death,

33 That is called Satanism forever, And I shall give them, death, forever true. And my heavenly true salvation, that is called Christ,

34 That salvation, it is not found in the beastly made image of Satan forever. And they, that shall not depart that sinfulness, forever,

35 Then, they shall remain faithfully as forever seen, as seen in the bondage of the image. That is called "The beast," forever,

36 And the imaged true body of Satanism. As found in each of the damned, as to, who are found without heavenly true salvation.

37 Then, as each Satanism true person, that cometh unto me, forever, as seen coming to me, as Christians forever. Then, the body of Satanism, is then, destroyed forever.

38 For, the sinful, true, beastly true body. It is, then being destroyed, through the eternal true preaching, of the heavenly true salvation,

39 That is seen, unto me forever. As to be partaking of the salvation, that is called God. As it is found, in Christ Jesus, forever.

40 Thereby, when one repenteth in Christ Jesus, forever. They have became true beasts of the earth, that are found repentful in Christ Jesus, forever,

41 And they are forgiven by me forever. And they have became, the Sons of God, as forever true. And they are seen unto me forever, as being eternally, the repentful true beasts, of the fallen true earth, forever.

42 But, these who are fallen in unrepentfulness, as being eternally, forever seen. Then, they are found, unto myself, forever. As being, fallen in unrepentfulness, and they are sinfully forever true,

43 As being eternally true, within themselves, as being found against my holy, true, true righteousness, as forever true. And they are found, as being fallen against my true holiness, as forever seen.

44 Yet, these who are fallen truly without me (God) and fallen truly without Christ Jesus, because they purposely chose not Christ Jesus, as Christ Jesus, being their seen personal true savior, from me, forever,

45 Then, they have sinfully exalted themselves, as if they were their own righteous, holy true God. And I shall punish them forever, unless they repent in Christ, as being forever true of themselves, to me, forever.

46 This earth, without heavenly true salvation, that is called God in Christ Jesus, forever. It is, then found unto me, as being forever true.

47 As a fallen, beastly imaged, sinful against God, true earth. And this earth, it is, therefore, seen unto me forever, as being forever seen. As dead unto me, forever,

48 And this true dead death, eternal true earth. It is seen, unto me forever, as being eternally forever, dead in Satan true sinfulness, forever.

49 And the blackness of eternal seen true night. That is called death forever. It is found by me, forever true,

50 As being this unrepentiful beastly imaged true earth, as this blackened in sin, true earth, is filled with the fallen of the earth,

51 As being forever true. And, then fallen true earth, forever. It is most surely seen, as being found unto me forever. In Satan true dead death, as being eternally forever seen, and in Satan, himself, forever.

52 Darkened true death, it is forever seen. As being seen without me (God), the righteous holy God. And is found eternal, without Christ, my eternal, living forever, true Son.

53 And that true Son, he is filled, with most eternal, living forever, heavenly true life. That life, it is called God, as forever seen, and, is truly felt, as forever true.

54 But, righteous in Satan, darkened holy true death, that is called holy sin forever, unto the damned forever. It is seen, as being, a holy, darkened true death,

55 And it is desired by the damned forever. And, it is a truly desired true worship of Satanism. As found within themselves, as they are found unto me,

56 As being forever true. As themselves in worshipping sin. As in desiring unrepentfulness. That is called eternal seen death (sin). In, as being forever true of themselves, unto me, as, forever seen.

57 Righteous darkened true death. It is found, given by me, unto the damned ones, as being eternally forever seen. And it is seen, for desiring to be away from my (God) holy true presents, forever.

58 My eternal, living forever, true presents. It is found, of most eternal, living forever, true life. That true life, it is found, in Jesus Christ, as forever seen, and heard.

59 And it is heard, and it is, forever seen, and seen forever, as I Am seen, as I Am God forever.

60 And Satan himself, is the eternal living true image. That is called "Eternal True Dead Death," And that true image, that is the beast,

61 It is seen, as being unrepentiful true men, and unrepentiful true Satan, and unrepentiful true Satans, and that is forever true.

62 That image, it is forever true, as death, as being forever seen.

63 And that is an true image of Satan, forever. And it is found in most eternal, living forever, true death. And it is seen, as being lifeless true Satan, forever true.

64 And all, unrepentiful true men, forever. They shall serve and worship, Satanism, as forever true of themselves,

65 As they are found unto me forever, in Satan forever. And they are eternally forever seen and felt, as dead death, that is Satan unto me, forever.

66 And, most surely, all that are damned, by me and damned by my Son, who is called, Jesus Christ, forever. They all, without acceptation, forever,

67 They shall worship Satanism, that is called by me, forever, as being seen, as being: unrepentfulness, as it is forever seen.

68 And this, it is without true exception, as being forever true, and, as being eternally forever seen, as seen by me, through Christ Jesus, forever.

69 Therefore, let whosoever will, let him repent unto me, as being forever true,

70   As: "By coming unto me in Christ Jesus, forever." And, as a result, that they may, forever. Receive the heavenly true salvation, that is called, Christ Jesus, as being forever sure.

71   Least, thou die unto me, forever. And upon the earth, and, in hell, as being, eternally forever seen, and, forever true. **SELAH**

Chapter 38 w / 86 verses   Heavenly salvation

1   In this next chapter, my mother, Gladys Wallace was inspired to write this, that is found below, that are these seven verses, with their true heading.

2   And those verses below, they were written in a original letter, without being numbered by her. And she wrote this writing, before 1990 AD. And I have taken that writing,

3   And now, I Am writing it again. And is being written, freshly as the Lord gives me the words, for this writing.

4   At, near the end of this chapter. I have enclosed a copy of a picture, that is of both of my late parents--who are: Marquis Wallace and Gladys Wallace.

5   And I have also taken the true liberty, to include as well, in this chapter. A statement that

is written by Rick Joyner, who had placed it originally,

6 As a true part of a much bigger statement. That he had stated on the web internet site. That is called: "The Elijah list." And he, Rick Joyner,

7 He has given me permission, at Morning Star Fellowship Church. To be able to reprint this peace from him. That is found, in this chapter 38, forever. And this below is from my mother's writing.

Without excuse

8 Millions who have been invited to accept the Lord Jesus Christ, as this Jesus, being their personal seen savior, as being forever true, they insult God, by making excuses.

9 Yes, you make excuse now, but at the great white throne judgment, you will stand before Judge Jesus, and there discover, eternally too late, that you are without excuse (Romans 1:20).

10 You may make excuse for not seeing Jesus as your savior, or you will see him as Judge, but see him, you will.

11 If you choose to make excuse now & not see Jesus as your Personal Savior, then you choose to see him as your Judge at the Great White Throne.

12   And they were judged every man according to their works. And there you will be, without excuse.

13   Why not accept his invitations now as your personal savior, or see him as your Judge at the Great White Throne,

14   Today is the day of Salvation & invitations, see that Jesus pleads for you and me whosoever will come. I will give him, drink water of life.

15   Now, let's go to Mom's original letter, and let's read it, as it is written. I Am not sure when it was written---but I think it was perhaps in 1968 AD.

Testimony about / "Without Excuse"

> **Without Excuse.**
> Millions who have been invited to accept the Lord Jesus as personal Saviour, insult God by making excuse. Yes, you may make excuse now, but at the Great White throne Judgment, you will stand before Judge Jesus and there discover, eternally too late, that you are without excuse (Romans 1:20) you may make excuse for not seeing Jesus as your Saviour, or you will see him as Judge, but see him, you will.
> If you choose to make excuse now & not see Jesus as your personal Saviour, then you choose to see him as your Judge at the Great White Throne. And they were judged every man according to their works. And there you will be, without excuse.
>
> Why not accept his invitations now as your personal Saviour, or see him as your Judge at the Great White Throne
>
> Today is the day of Salvation. invitations, see that Jesus pleads for you and me who'sever will come. I will give him

16   Now, as currently seen, as being freshly written, through God's inspiration, as being, forever true:

17   ***Without excuse***

18   W / 47 verses

19   Millions of people, as found in this world, who have been invited to accept the Lord Jesus

Christ, as this Jesus, being their personal seen savior, as being forever true,

20 They do insult God, by making excuses, not to serve God, as forever true. And yes, you make excuse now, not to repent of thy seen sins, forever.

21 But at the great white throne judgment, you will stand before that eternal true judge, who is seen. As being Jesus Christ.

22 And, it is there, at that great judgment, you shall discover, eternally too late, that thou art, without excuse (Romans 1:20), forever.

23 And, in today's true earth, You may make excuse, for not seeing Jesus as your savior, but you will see him, as thy Judge, as being forever seen. But see me (Jesus Christ), forever, thou shalt.

24 And if thou shalt refuse correction. As found given of me forever. As correction, that is found in this earth. To make thou serve me, as being faithfully forever true.

25 Then thou shalt die unto me forever. And thou shalt remain in thy sinfulness, forever, and your seed, shall die unto me forever.

26 And though, you make and choose, to make excuse, now. To not serve me, in Jesus Christ,

forever. Then thou shalt die unto me forever. And that judgment,

27   It is, given unto all, who shall deny me forever. In not serving me as a Christian, as being forever and ever true. And though, thou shalt not choose Jesus, as your Personal seen savior, as being forever seen.

28   Then you have made a eternal true choice, to see Jesus Christ, as your judge, at the Great White Throne Judgment, forever.

29   And, as it is written "They were judged every man according to their works," And there, at that great eternal, just judgment. That is called God, as forever true,

30   Then, you will be, without excuse. As being forever seen, in thy true sins, as forever sure.

31   And, at this time, why not accept Christ's invitations to serve him (Jesus Christ). As this Christ, being thy personal seen true savior.

32   But, if thou shalt not choose Christ, as Christ Jesus being thy seen savior, forever.

33   Then most certainly, thou shalt see Christ as thy judge, at the Great White Throne Judgment. And that judgment, it is to come to the earth, shortly, as being forever true,

34 And, moreover, today is the day of Salvation and invitations, to repent forever, that one may repent in Christ and be born again, but not according to the flesh, but according to the true spirit of God, as forever true.

35 Therefore, come and see, that this Christ Jesus. That he pleads for you, to be saved forever, Therefore, whosoever will come. I shall give him, the drink. That is called "The water of life."

36 And if thou shalt come to me, I shall forgive thy true sins, forever. And, thou shalt know me, as I Am thy God, who lives, forever true.

37 And I do live forever certain, in all, that is. For all that is, is by hand of life. And that hand, it is seen, unto creation. As being forever sure---as being Jesus Christ forever, saith thy eternal, and most true God, for I Am the only God,

38 And I know of no other God, and there shall never be another true God, forever. And I Am the forever. And I Am forever seen, and I Am forever known--and I Am known, as the life, that is called man, forever.

39 And, I Am the forever, who is without true end, as being forever seen. And I shall love all, as forever true--- who shall love me, in Jesus Christ, forever.

40 Again, at the Great White Throne Judgment. All sinners shall and will, stand before me. For I Am thy great Judge, who is called Jesus Christ. And, it is there, that sinners shall find, eternally:

41 That it is eternally forever too late to repent forever to me. And that great true judgment, that is called life and death, forever.

42 It is, then too late, to then, ask to be saved in that great white throne judgment that is called God in Christ, forever.

43 And, that just judgment. It is granted and given of me through Jesus Christ, as being eternally forever true.

44 And that true judgment, it is given by me, through Christ, forever. And that true judgment, it is forever true. As saith thy eternal God (Romans 1:20), as I Am eternally forever and ever true.

45 And given true judgment. It is, as forever seen and given by me, forever. And is given eternal true judgment, as forever granted unto the damned, as being eternally forever true.

46 And in this world, one may make excuse, for not seeing me as The Christ, as I Am forever true. But, to not choose me as being eternally found.

47 Then that found true sinner, shall die in hell forever. And at that great judgment. Those found sinners who are found eternally without Christ Jesus, forever.

48 They are then found in utter true shame, as being eternally forever true, in sin death, forever. And to be found, in willful, true sin, at that great eternal just Judgment,

49 That is to be found in eternal dead death, forever. And death, it is granted to the lost eternally forever. As a granted true death. For they are seen and found unto me forever, as found in Satanism, forever.

50 And those who are eternally found unto me forever. As being: Known true sinners, forever. They shall then die unto me, as being eternally seen, as being forever true, in Satan dead death, forever.

51 And that true sinner, shall receive, that sentence, that is called eternal true death, forever. As a granted forever true death. That is seen,

52 As being a eternally granted true death, from me. And true death, it is granted by me, through Christ Jesus, because of one's true unrepentfulness, as being eternally forever seen.

53 Therefore, dead Satanism true death. It is eternally forever true, as granted by me through

Jesus Christ, as granted to the shameful forever. At that great white throne judgment, forever.

54 And Satanism true death. It is granted forever sure. And true death, it is granted at that great Judgment, as being eternally seen and felt, as being eternal true night unto the damned, as being eternally forever true, and forever sure.

55 And that is because of their (unrepentiful true sinners) seen and felt, eternal, true rebelliousness. That is forever seen in them that do hate me (God), forever.

56 And they, the damned at that judgment of life, forever. They shall not have the light of true day, that is called Christ Jesus, forever.

57 Therefore, certain true death is most eternal unto them. That doth desire the beastly dead image of sinfulness forever true. And, as a result, they shall die unto me forever, in their seen sin, forever.

58 And true death, it is granted by me forever true. And it is granted by me faithfully forever true. As granted through Christ Jesus, unto them that do enjoy their utter true shame, that is called "To be as dead as Satan is dead unto me, forever."

59 And that granted ness, it is found, given of me, forever true. Unto the damned, who are found at that great judgment, as sin forever.

60 And the damned, they shall most certainly, shall see me (God). As I Am Jesus Christ, as forever true. As seen, at that "Great True Judgment," that is called life, forever.

61 Therefore, one shall see Jesus Christ, forever. As Christ Jesus, being a true Judge, from me (God), forever.

62 And, with all true certainty. All sinners, shall and will, see Christ, as forever true, at that great white throne judgment, forever.

63 Therefore, at the judgment, it shall be: "They were judged every man according to their works." And, those unrepentiful true sinners. They are felt unto me forever true. As granted true death, eternally forever.

64 And at that judgment. I shall reward all men forever. As according to their true Christly righteousness, as it is found in me. And I will most surely, reward the wicked with true, darkened true death, at that great white throne judgment, forever.

65 Therefore, let all unrepentiful true men, everywhere. Refrain from their true sin, or I shall remove those devil ones, in true death, forever.

As saith thy eternal, true God, as I Am eternally forever seen and true forever certain.

66 This picture on the next page. It is my mother and father before they passed away. Both of them are with the Lord.

67   ***Testimony about God's eternal love***

69 W / 9 verses

70 I Roger Dale Wallace, I do say: "That all need to consider our true God in all that is God and is of God, forever." And that we must truly forever, love him.

71 And we must love God forever. And our true God, he will never forsake us and he will always love us, and this is for all of true eternity and forever.

72 And we need to be always, mindful of God's feelings in all that we think, do and say, and that is forever. And we should always lift his holy name, up to all who are in and of the earth, forever.

73 And we should always be willing that none should perish in sin and we should try to help them to understand. That our true God and his eternal kind Son, who is called Jesus Christ,

74 That they are always loving and caring for us. And we should always desire our father God and his Son and always desire to help all men everywhere---as to help them to understand that great love,

75 That is given of God forever, as it is given faithfully from God, forever. As it is given through Jesus Christ, unto all men and unto all women, everywhere, AMEN.

76   And, may God bless, all / As to them, that truly, do desire him (God), eternally forever.

77   I Am, the Lord thy God, forever. And I do say. That these are already, eternally blessed in me (God) through Jesus Christ, forever,

78   And I Am given forever. As given of myself through Jesus my (God) Son, forever. And I (God) Am given unto all, of the earth, forever. As given faithfully, to them that truly do desire me (God), as I (God) Am found in Jesus Christ eternally forever.

79   **Testimony about the kingdom of God**

80 W /   6 verses

81   This that is found here below, in this book. It a statement that is made by Rick Joyner. It will help church of Jesus Christ, to understand. That, at the end of the age, the church shall become all that she is suppose to be, as the church, is found in Jesus Christ, forever,

82   And, also it is seen, in his statement, as noted in Luke 17:20-21. That the kingdom of God, is shown forever, in the church's true mists, forever. For the kingdom of God, is truly found:

83 "As found truly within me (The word me, it means, this: "Our kind eternal true God and Christ Jesus, his Son, forever,") forever, as saith, thy eternal kind God, as being eternally forever and ever true.

84 And, it is most surely found, as being eternally and ever lastingly, eternally forever found within you, as being eternally forever true. For together, the church and us (God and Christ Jesus). We (God and Christ Jesus and the born again true believers in Jesus Christ forever) are one and the same, through Jesus Christ, my Son, forever."

85 This is Rick Joyner's statement:

86 "The greatest sign of the end of the age is going to be the Church becoming all that she is called to be, prepared as a worthy Bride for the King of kings. That is why the Lord, when asked about the signs of the end of the age, responded with the signs that were almost all great troubles. However, He also said in Luke 17:20-21, "The Kingdom of God is not coming with signs to be observed; nor will they say, 'Look, here it is!' or, 'There it is!' For behold, the Kingdom of God is in your midst."

Chapter 39 w/ 109 verses   Living death

1 The Beast, is called sinful true man, and he is a spiritually fallen true beast forever. And he is

seen, as being forever true, as being unrepentiful, and as, being truly forever seen,

2 And the beast, in seen eternal true death, as forever true. He is seen, as being a man of sin, who is called the beast, forever.

3 And the beast, called sinful true man, he is seen, unto me forever true. As being all unrepentiful true men, that are found unto me forever. As being forever true, and, as forever seen, as seen in sin forever.

4 And that wicked, true man of sin, forever. He is seen, as being found, as, all eternal, imaged beastly true men, and, all beastly imaged, true women, as being forever seen, as seen in eternal, dying true death, forever.

5 And that true image, in living true death, as being eternally forever seen. It is called the beast, and who is called the Antichrist, as forever seen. As being seen in dead death forever. And that image, it is, Antichrist,

6 And that image, as Antichrist, it is seen, and it is found, in living true death, as truly forever being seen. And it is heard, as sin forever true, and as, forever seen.

7 And that damningly true image, as made as Satan true death, forever, and is, Satan true death, forever true. It is made in Satan's true likeness,

8 That is called true death, as it is being forever seen. As seen, as being the beast, as forever true.

9 And true death, as it is found by me, forever true. As being the beastly eternal, truly damned. It is found by me, as being forever true. As true in all that Satan is, as death, as being forever seen.

10 And that beast, is found, as a cold in heart true image of Satanism, forever. And it is, also seen, as the earth, as the fallen true earth being as a cold feeling true earth,

11 As the earth is seen by me forever, as being forever true, in coldness of cold love, forever.

12 And that is true, as a hardened stone cold image, as found eternally forever, and ever seen, as truly seen, in dead death, with Satan, and with Satan's kind, who (demons) is called devils (demons), as being forever and ever true.

13 And the beastly image, as found as being the eternal damned, in Satan and Satan true death, forever. It is seen, in earnest and sincere, true death, as forever seen.

14 And the earth, it is utterly fallen, and the earth. Shall never arise unto me again, in sin, as being forever and ever, true again. As to be in sin, again and forever.

15 The fallen true earth, it is seen as being a cold sinful true love, that is made in sin forever. And without Christ Jesus, as savior forever,

16 Then the cold in heart, eternally damned. They shall be forever, truly found, without the warming true love, that is, called Jesus Christ. As this Christ, is found in me, as being, utterly true, utterly forever.

17 And, without Christ, as one's true savior, as forever true. Then all, who are found without Christ, they are found unto me, forever. As being found in unrepentiful true trespasses, and, true unrepentiful true sins, as being forever seen.

18 And the damned, without Christ Jesus, forever. Then they are the fallen true earth, as being forever seen, in sin, forever. And, the fallen true earth, it is seen, in being true, in Satan true death, as being forever true.

19 And the fallen true earth, has became, a fallen unrepentiful, true earth. As it is found unto me, forever. As found unto me, forever true, in unrepentfulness true damnation, as being forever seen. And the earth, it is most surely, seen unto me,

20 As being forever true, in sin forever. As found unto me, in being: "Living true death", in sin, as forever true. And is sin, as being forever seen and heard,

21 And is seen faithful unto me, as being eternally faithfully forever true, as true of the damned, as they are forever certain, as being granted true death, forever.

22 The fallen true earth, it is found, as being, truly being against my true righteousness, forever. And fallen true earth, is even yet, also seen,

23 In being eternally against my true holiness, as being forever true of the damned forever. And the damned are found unto me forever, in true rebelliousness,

24 As being eternally forever seen, as seen as the damned ones, as they are found unto me forever, in Satan true death, forever.

25 And the unrepentiful true image, of this earth, in sin forever. It is, called "The Beast." And that image, that is called the beast.

26 It is a spiritual true image, as it is found in true death, as, being forever seen death. And that death, it is most eternal, as found in the damned ones, forever.

27 And true death, it is seen, as being deathly forever true death, in Satan's true death, as forever seen.

28 And that seen image in Satanism forever. It is truly seen death, as seen in Satan's true death, as forever true. And it is truly seen forever, in the damned of the fallen true earth, forever.

29 And that true image, as found as being beastly eternal true death, as being forever seen. It is all true people, who are seen in loving true sin, forever.

30 And they are seen, as being their true selves, as being unrepentfully forever true to Satan, forever.

31 And they are seen, unto me, as being forever true, in Satan true death, forever. And they are, truly seen, in Satan forever. As being unrepentiful, truly forever true.

32 And they, as the beast, they are, a most sinful true working in Satan true death, as being forever certain, and, as ever lastingly, forever seen, as true death, forever.

33 And they, the damned in Satan forever. They are found, as being cold in the workings of God's true love, forever. And they are seen, as Satan is cold in his love toward me, forever. And Satan shall know the warmth of eternal fire, that is called hell, forever.

34 And to be found in Satan forever. That image in Satan, shall burn in sin forever. For sin shall

consume it's followers forever true, without true end, in hell, forever.

35 And Satan death, it is found by me, forever. As found in earnest and sincere, true death, as forever true, and, as forever seen. And, it is called "Most Living true Death," as being eternally forever and ever true.

36 And living true death, is found in Satan's unrepentfulness. That is seen before my (God's) great, eternal, living forever true presents. As it is found, in "Most Eternal, Living Forever, Unheavenly True life," forever.

37 And Satan's spiritual falleness. It is Satan, as being unrepentfully fallen away from the true righteousness, that is of myself (God), as forever true of Satan, forever,

38 And I Am, eternally forever, and I Am (God), the living God, of both, heaven and earth. And those, who are fallen without Christ Jesus being their seen savior, forever.

39 They are, most surely, given unto the sinful true workings, that are called Satan true death, forever. And it is found, as being eternally, true death as being lifeless, as being fallen forever true.

40 And that true death, in Satan forever. It is seen, as being a ever lasting, eternal, unrepentiful

true sinfulness. As being forever true and forever seen, as seen eternal in the damned, as forever true.

41 And those true workings, in Satan true death, as it is seen, as Satanism forever true. It is found by me, in Satan's true spirit, that is called death, as it is found in unrepentiful true man, forever.

42 And, it is seen, as Satanism forever. And it is found, as being most certainly found, as being eternally forever true, as it is found in being without Christ in themselves,

43 As being eternally forever true, and, as forever seen. And that is true, as true of the damned ones, forever.

44 Damningly true, seen true sins, forever. Those are eternally seen sins, as they are found by me, forever. In Satan true death, that is found unto me forever,

45 As being eternal Satanism, forever. And those seen sins, they are seen by me faithfully forever strong, as eternal dead death forever,

46 And those seen true sins, they are seen and felt, unto me forever. As being, sinful, ungodly, spiritual true sins. And those seen sins, they are eternally forever true, as being true in the damned of the fallen true earth, as forever seen.

47   And, seen sins, in living true death, forever. That shall damn the lost forever, as they are found unto me forever true,

48   As they truly do desire and do love eternally forever, Satan true death, as being eternally forever truly desired in themselves,

49   As that desire is found in wanting in themselves, as I want sin forever. And, they therefore, want in themselves forever, Satan true death, as forever seen,

50   And true death forever, it is found forever seen, as it is forever found forever certain, as in themselves, as their desired true death,

51   And that desire, it is seen in themselves forever, in the eternal true wanting of Satanism, as being forever true of themselves, as they are found in being true to Satan forever. And they shall die unto me forever, and without true end, forever.

52   One's truly discovered true seen sins, forever. Those seen sins, they are found unto me as eternal dead death forever, and those seen sins,

53   They (seen sins) are found unto me forever, as all that is seen and felt unto me forever, as being utterly true, eternal true damnation, that is called "True death," forever

54 Those seen sins, they are considered of me forever. As being forever seen, as seen in one's sinful true death, as being eternally forever true.

55 And to be seen in death forever. It is to be seen as being eternally true unto Satan bestiality forever. And the beast called death, it is seen as being eternal,

56 As in desiring devil like true sinfulness, forever. And the damned of the earth forever. They are seen, as being forever seen,

57 As being ever lastingly seen, in being in true death. As true death, that is seen before me, as being eternally forever true as granted true death, forever.

58 And seen, deathly eternal, true seen sins, as those seen sins, are found as being forever seen, as seen in the damned forever.

59 Then, those true seen sins, shall damn the lost forever. And the damned of the earth forever, they shall be damned forever, as they are found,

60 In Satan's true spirit, forever. And they are found unto me forever, as being eternally, Antichrist, forever.

61 And those chosen and mighty in death, true seen sins. They (seen sins) are found unto me forever, as being Antichrist forever.

62 And those seen true sins forever, they are mighty, in damning the lost unto me, forever. As they the lost, doth enjoy forever, the damningly true cup of unrepentfulness, as it is forever seen.

63 And unrepentfulness forever, it is found, as being a pure cup of damnation, that is called eternal true death, forever. And, that eternal, damningly true drink. It is seen, as being antigod, forever,

64 And it is a everlasting damning true drink in Satan forever. And it shall damn them forever, as to who shall desire that drank, as it being forever seen,

65 As it is seen, of and in themselves, and, as forever made unto themselves forever, and it is truly, forever more.

66 And it is most certainly seen, as being ever lastingly, unrighteous before me, as being forever true. As being true in Satanism true death, as being eternally forever and ever true.

67 And Satan true death, is Satan in and within the damned, forever. And it is seen, as being eternally found, as being unrepentful true man and unrepentful true Satan, together and forever.

68 And that Satan true death forever, in both man and in Satan forever. It is a true, living

deathly true death, as it is forever felt and seen unto me, forever,

69 And that true death, as is given by them, unto me (God). It is most surely, eternal and ever lastingly felt, and it is eternally seen by me,

70 And that true death, forever. It is eternally forever true, as I see them, in their desired true death, as truly forever and ever seen.

71 That true death in Satanism forever. It is found, as being eternally forever true, and it is found forever, as being without me (God), and, it is forever and ever seen, as it is seen unto me forever, as it is the damned ones, forever.

72 And that true death in the damned of the fallen beastie eternal true earth forever. That true death, it is most eternal, forever.

73 And it is forever found, as being eternally forever seen. And it is seen, as being eternally forever seen, as being the eternal truly damned, forever,

74 For the damned ones forever, they are found unto me forever certain, as found unto me in Satan's true likeness, that is called, I (the unrepentiful) desire true death, as being eternally forever true, and as being eternally forever seen.

75 Living true death, it is found by me forever faithful, as being a eternal spiritual true walk. And it is found forever certain, as it is found by me, in the lost, as forever seen.

76 And it is found as being one's personal true falleness. As they are found forever true, as being found unto me in unrepentiful true seen sin that is seen and felt, unto myself, forever,

77 And it is seen and felt, unto me forever. As themselves in their own personal desired true seen sin, as it is forever true in themselves, forever. And it is forever found,

78 As being death forever. And it is found in them, that do eternally forever perish, as they are forever seen. And they are seen unto me forever,

79 As being eternal true death unto me, as being forever and ever true, as death, as forever seen. And, it is a forever seen, true death, as being eternally forever certain, as certain forever, as certain in the damned ones, as forever true.

80 Most eternal, damning forever true life. It is found, in most utter true damnation. That true damnation, it is called true death,

81 As it is seen and felt, unto me forever. And it is forever seen, as seen by me, as being eternally forever true, as being true, in eternal seen dead death, forever.

82 Living true death, as it is eternally found by me, in the sinner. It is found, as being found unto me forever, in Satanism, as being forever seen.

83 And living true death forever. It is seen, as being the beast, as forever true. And the true beast, is unrepentiful true man, as he most surely found unto me forever,

84 As being forever, a eternal: Man of sin, forever. And this is forever true, as forever seen.

85 And those, who are found, in living Satan true death, as being forever true. They shall die forever, unto me forever. Unless they repent and renounce Satan, as eternally forever and ever true.

86 If they, the damned forever, shall not repent, in my servant, who is my living stone, who is called, Jesus Christ, and who (Jesus Christ), is seen and called, the branch,

87 Then, they as the beast, who is called the man of sin. That man (all unrepentiful true men), shall be found in most true death, as forever seen, and, as forever sure,

88 And they, the damned in Satan forever. They shall surely perish, unto me, as being faithfully forever and ever true, in their desired, true death, that is to be as dead as Satan is dead, unto me, forever.

89 And they do perish in Satanism forever, in death forever, in hell forever, in all forever. And they shall sleep the sleep of death, forever.

90 Sinfulness is found in the spiritual true workings of Satan true death, as being forever faithful in the lost unto myself forever.

91 And that Satanism true death, as Satan forever. As found in the damned forever. It is seen, as being forever true. In damningly seen true sin,

92 As being forever true. And they, in Satanism forever, they are found unto me forever. In the name of Satan, forever, and in the mark of sin, called Satan forever.

93 And they the damned, they are found in the complete and whole measure, that is called Satanism forever. And they are measured unto me forever. As measured, in eternal death, forever.

94 And, as they are sealed in Satanism forever. And as they are measured for true judgment, that is called measured true hell fire, forever.

95 Nevertheless, they shall most certainly perish forever true. In their seen, evil true desires, as being forever seen and felt,

96 As they are eternally felt unto me forever, as being eternal true death, as being eternally forever certain, as certain in themselves, forever.

97 And, those seen sins, in the unrepentiful ones, who are called the damned. Those who are lost unto me, as forever true in sin forever. They are seen, as being,

98 As being, truly Antichrist true beasts, forever. And they are sinfully and unrepentfully, found as being forever true, as being eternally found against me, as forever certain.

99 And, I Am, the God of most eternal, true righteousness, and, most true holiness, as being forever seen, and heard. And I Am heard, as my own Son, who is called, Jesus Christ, as forever true.

100 The earth, as it is found, in living true Satan death. It is found, as being dead unto me, as Satan is dead unto me, forever. And the earth, it is found,

101 As being found unto me forever certain, as being truly Satanism forever. And the earth, as being Satan like forever.

102 It is seen, as being a unrepentiful, imaged, sinful, fallen against God, true earth. As the earth, is forever seen, as seen as Satan is seen dead unto me, forever.

103   And this earth, it is not of my holy, true righteousness. That is found, in my eternal, living forever, true Son. Who is called, Jesus Christ,

104   And that true name, as Jesus Christ, forever. It is seen, as being forever true. And, it is forever sought by them, that doth wish, to live forever eternal, unto me, as being forever true.

105   And that holy true name, as it is found, given from and of myself, as being eternally forever, truly seen. It is seen, as being Jesus Christ.

106   And that true name, it is forever. And it is seen and found, unto the repentful true ones, who are found in this fallen true earth, forever.

107   And that name, as being eternally seen, as being: Jesus Christ, forever. It is found, unto the earth and it is found in the earth, forever,

108   And that glorious true name, it liveth in me forever. And it is seen, as being: "Jesus Christ," as forever certain. And it is given from me (God), forever, to the fallen true earth, as being eternally forever true and forever seen.

109   And that true name forever. It is seen, as being, forever seen and felt, as being God. And that is eternally forever and ever true. For I Am God forever, and there shall be no end to that name of Jesus Christ, forever.

Chapter 40 w / 69 verses   My most holy, true name

1   And this Christ, he is my most holy true name, as being forever seen, and heard. And this Christ Jesus, he is eternal, of me, forever.

2   And this eternal Christ, he is heard, as I Am heard. And I Am heard, and I Am forever seen, as seen in being eternally forever true.

3   And that true name, as it is forever seen, as being, Christ Jesus. It is forever seen, and it is forever found, as I Am found. And I Am found, as being and I Am God forever.

4   This Christ Jesus, he is found in me, as being faithfully forever seen, and as being forever seen, and is eternally forever found of me, as forever true.

5   And this Christ Jesus, he is, truly seen, as me forever. And Christ Jesus, is true, as I Am true forever. And that true name (Jesus Christ) , that is found,

6   As being forever true. It is given of myself, into the earth, as being eternally forever true. For I Am true, as I Am forever seen.

7   And my seen true name. It is seen, as being: Most Eternal, Holy Forever, True Truth," And I Am the forever, and I live forever. And in me,

the repentful in Christ Jesus, shall live eternally forever and ever so.

8   And that holy true name, as it is found, as being Jesus Christ, forever. It is most eternal, as it is found most surely, in and as being eternally forever seen, as being, Jesus Christ,

9   And that true name, that is given of me, as being eternally and faithfully forever seen. It is given, from me, as being eternally forever and ever true.

10   And I Am found forever, through my holy true Son, who is called Jesus Christ. And that true name, as it is given faithfully forever true of myself, forever,

11   It is given of me, unto the fallen, unrepentiful, transgressing true earth, as forever true, and, as forever seen.

12   And that true name of Jesus Christ, forever. It is given, that the earth may repent, of it's seen sins, forever. By receiving Christ Jesus,

13   As this Christ Jesus, being one' (sinner one) eternal true savior, as being eternally forever seen.

14   And this Christ Jesus, must be found of me forever, as being eternally, one's personal, living forever, true savior,

15 And he is given faithfully forever sure, as of me and from me (God), as being eternally forever and ever true.

16 And that true name, of Christ Jesus, forever. It is found, of me (God), in heaven above, as forever true and forever heard.

17 And that true name, is a holy forever, never ending true name. And it is a heavenly true name, as it is found given from me, and of me, as being eternally forever true.

18 And, that true name, it is found given faithfully forever true of me, as being forever true, as being true, in being truly forever and ever found,

19 And it is found forever, as being Jesus Christ, my Son. Who is with all, that is called God, as being forever seen. For I Am seen, as God in Christ Jesus. As being forever and ever true.

20 My ever lasting, eternal, living forever, true name. As it is given of myself, forever, as given unto the fallen true world, forever. It is, Jesus Christ.

21 And, that true name, it is most eternal, in me, as being forever seen. And it is seen, as being, faithfully forever true, as being eternally true of me, as forever seen and true. And it is forever sure.

22 And that sure true name. It is, of a royal true priest hood, as being forever seen, as being eternally forever found in me, as being eternally forever true. And it is seen, as being truly given of me,

23 As being given faithfully forever seen. And it is seen, and it is given, as I Am seen, as I Am God forever.

24 And, again, that great, holy, ever lasting, true name. As it is found, in being, Jesus Christ, as being forever seen. It is seen, in most eternal, true truth, forever.

25 And, it is my (God) eternal, living forever, living forever true name. And that true name, it is given of myself (God). And it is placed of myself, as being forever true, as true into the body of Christ Jesus, as being forever seen.

26 Therefore, my great name. It is found, given of me, forever. In most eternal, ever lasting, forever true, heavenly true life, forever.

27 That true life, it is found, given faithfully of me, as being forever true. And it is true, as being Jesus Christ, forever.

28 And it is given of me, unto the repentful true ones. Who are found by me, in the fallen true earth, forever. As they, are found by me, in Jesus Christ, forever.

29 In Jesus Christ, my name, it is most certainly seen. As being, truly forever found, as found unto me, as being forever true. And, my eternal, ever lasting, holy true righteousness, as it is forever seen. It is, therefore, forever seen, as being forever true, and, forever seen.

30 And this righteous, holy true name, that is called Jesus Christ, the Son. It is, given of me, as being forever true, as true in all that I Am, as I Am the love, that is called God, forever,

31 That true name, as being, Jesus Christ. It is my true name, as found given of myself, as being forever seen. And Jesus Christ, is my true righteousness, as being forever seen. As I Am seen, forever.

32 And I (God) Am the eternal living true God, who is "Most heavenly, Forever, Holy True Righteousness." And I (God) Am, "Most Eternal, Living Forever, True Truth."

33 And I Am, "Truth," that is forever seen, and I Am seen, as being, the life, as it forever seen.

34 Therefore, I Am the God of all, and, I Am forever seen as God forever. And I Am most eternal, living forever, true life.

35 And that life, it is me forever. And I Am seen, as being most surely, being eternal, never dying, True Truth," as being forever seen. And, I

live forever, and, "I Am, that I Am," as being forever true.

36 And, in this new day, I shall hiss for thee, O Israel, as being forever true. That thou mayest repent in my shepherd, who is called Jesus Christ, forever.

37 Then, as thou shall accept Jesus Christ, as thy savior, as found in me, as being forever seen. Then, thou shalt find, that my great goodness, it is found unto thee, O Israel, as being forever true, as it is true unto thee, forever.

38 And, great is my beauty, that is found, as being eternally, Jesus Christ, forever. And thy corn, as it is found, as being Jesus Christ. It shall be, new wine, unto thee, forever.

39 For it is not by might, nor power, but it is seen, by my spirit, that is called, Jesus Christ, forever.

40 And, in this new day, arise in me, as Christ Jesus, as being forever true. For great shall be thy peace forever, and, it is a everlasting, true peace, forever,

41 And that peace, it cometh from me, as being forever seen, for the world knoweth it not. For the peace of this sinful true world--it is, seen,

42   Seen as being, anguish and vexation and sorrow of heart--- for being found in Satan true death, as being forever true, in Satanism, as being forever true and forever heard.

43   And it is heard, as sin, as forever true, as saith, the eternal true spirit, that is, called God, as being forever true.

44   And, in these days, all nations. That do, and shall, come against thee forever, O Israel. As they are seen by me, as I seen them, through Christ Jesus, as being forever seen----

45   Their riders (the damned ones forever), they shall come down (come down, it means to fall in death, forever) and die before me, as being eternally forever and ever true.

46   And, I shall smite those Antichrist true ones, with astonishment, and with madness, as being forever and ever seen. And that true punishment,

47   It is seen, and it is given faithfully forever sure by me, forever, as given by my true spirit, forever.

48   And thou o governors of Judah, that art called, the Israeli true people, forever. And I shall deliver thee forever, from the wicked ones, forever.

49 And I shall love thee, forever true, O Israel. And I will be seen, as seen unto all of Israel, as life forever. And I shall even be seen, as forever true,

50 As seen unto all unrepentiful true nations, that are found in Satanism, as forever true. And those seen nations, they do come to fight against thee, O Israel. As to fight thee forever, in valley of Jehoshaphat.

51 And, through Jesus Christ, I shall make thy people, O Israel, as being like a hearth of true fire, as it is found given by me, as being eternally forever true,

52 And, as I have given that true fire, that is called God forever, unto all of the true land, that is called the earth, as being forever seen.

53 And, thou, O Israel, as thou surely, doth accept, Jesus Christ. As Jesus Christ being thy true, seen savior, as being forever seen. Then, thou hath became, of the "House of David," that is called, Jesus Christ,

54 And thou, shalt be found and called, Christians in mine house, as forever seen, as I Am seen. As I Am seen, as being eternally forever, as God forever.

55 And, it is enough, to be as God, but not above God, as saith thy eternal, true and kind God, as being, truly forever and ever true.

56 And thou, O Israel, thou shalt most surely, be seen, as angels of my true spirit, that is called Jesus Christ, as being forever true, and, as forever seen.

57 And, unto you forever, O Israel, I have most surely, poured through Jesus Christ, forever, unto you forever. The true spirit of my true grace,

58 That is seen, and is, as being called, Jesus Christ, as being forever seen, and, it is forever heard, as God forever.

59 And I have also, through Jesus Christ. I have poured upon you forever true, the spirit of true supplication, as it is found, as recorded in the last part of time period of this earth, that is called; "That day,"

60 And, thou shalt look upon Jesus Christ, whom thy forefathers most certainly, did look upon. As they did crucify this Jesus Christ, whom I have raised up, as I have raised him unto me, from that true crucifixion, forever.

61 And this Jesus Christ, he is raised up, from that true death, as onto me forever. As according to the prophesies of old, as I did inspire those prophesies, to be written---And, this holy, true

Son, who is called, Christ Jesus--he is not ashamed of that,

62 Most holy, true crucifixion--but he did lay down his life, that thou couldest have my true life, forever. As it given of myself, unto Christ Jesus and unto thee, forever. As it is found being in Jesus Christ, the Son, as forever seen.

63 And, thy land, O Israel. It shall, indeed and morn for this true Christ Jesus, as thou shalt see him coming in clouds of my present true wrath, that is, called God forever. As it is given true wrath, unto the world, eternally forever.

64 And, as thou, O Israel, shalt be found in Jesus Christ, forever true, and, as being forever seen. Then, then art, unto me, as the pots that have been found in mine house,

65 That are seen unto me forever, like unto the bowls that have been seen before the alter of myself. That alter, it is now, called Jesus Christ, forever.

66 And Jesus Christ, as being forever seen. Then, thou, O Israel, thou art seen in him, as being forever true. And, thou art seen, in Jesus Christ, as being forever faithful.

67 And, thou shalt be found, as being eternally forever found, as being truly forever seen, O Israel. And thou art seen, as being like unto fine

horses, that art seen with bells, that is called "Holiness unto the lord of hosts."

68 And this Christ Jesus, is the holiness of myself forever. And he is forever found, as forever seen, as seen unto all repentful true men,

69 As being eternally forever true, and, as forever seen. And he (Christ Jesus) is seen as God, as being forever true. For I Am God, who is seen in Jesus Christ, as forever certain, and forever more.

Chapter 41 w/101 verses "God's oath with Israel"

1 Now, at this time of the earth (11-1-2007 AD), it would seem to me, Roger Dale Wallace, that our country (USA), maybe being judged of God, in the concern of Israeli land being divided--such as: "Concerning the recent, Jerusalem issue."

2 And, as considering how bad the recent California fires, have been, in California, in this year, of 2007 AD.

3 Then, maybe, we as a nation, we need to consider, that perhaps, we are being cut up by our true God. As concerning, this recent, trying to divide, Israeli land, issue.

4   In other words, are we, the united states and the world. Are we trying to help divide the historic Israeli land oath,

5   That is given of God himself?. If so, we need, to not be trying to change God's eternal, true oath.

6   And, it would seem, to me. That maybe we are being judged, of God. As a disobedient true nation, in regards to the dividing of Israeli true land. But, we do, tend to over look those things of God, as it would seem, to me.

7   And, we do seem, to be looking at those things. As if they are simply a true act of nature, rather than seeing that God is trying to speak to us, as a nation.

8   And, when, we truly, do ignore God. Then, we in turn, we do cause, more punishment, to be able, to perhaps occur from God, to our nation, and, unto the world, forever,

9   And, that punishment. It is, until, we help Israel. To become, all, that Biblical true Israel, is suppose to be. As what, is all reunited true Israeli true land,

10   That is found as being the entire true land called Israel , as God has said, would be as Israeli true land, forever. For that entire true land,

11   It is the Biblically true land of Israel, as it is found under the entire, true oath of God, forever

12   And, that true land of the Bible, it is suppose to be all Biblical true land. That is called Israel forever, and it is to be reunited of God, as all reunited true Israeli Biblical true land, forever.

13   And, to not conform unto all true Biblical true Israel, as it is to be found forever true. As being, all Israeli land, forever,

14   Then, our true and kind God, he will most certainly, hold all of our now leaders, accountable to God himself, forever. For such acts of rebellioness,

15   As they, these leaders, are seen by our true God, as being sinful true leaders and the like. For they chose to not perform the true Israeli land promise of God,

16   Therefore, any Christian leaders and non Christian true leaders, that do demonstrate of themselves, as being publicly against all that is toward God's eternal, Biblical true oath with Israel,

17   Then, that person and or persons, God shall hold that person and or persons, accountable for being found sinfully against God,

18 And, our true world, it is, truly divided over these things, And, there are those, of the world. Who do claim Christianity. But they do not encourage Israel, to be found in all it's seen historic Israeli true land, forever.

19 And, these Christian leaders and the like. That do purposely, do not encourage Israel, to be found in all of it's (Israel) seen true oath, with God,

20 Then, as they perform not God's promise to Israel forever. Then they are performing, against God, true, unlawful true deeds, unto God, forever.

21 And, they are, most surely, seen unto God, forever. As being found in and with, Antichrist true deeds, against God forever.

22 Therefore, those sinful Antichrist true deeds. They are seen unto God, forever. As being, truly rebellious Christian seen leaders and rebellious, true world leaders, and so forth,

23 And those Antichrist true seen sins, they are discovered by our true God, forever. And God shall damn those leaders and such, forever,

24 If they be found in making war against God, by not conforming unto the Israeli land promise of God, forever.

25 And, as they, those sinful true leaders, are seen, unto God forever. They are seen, as being forever true in death before God, as death, forever.

26 As they are found unto God. In their personal true actions, in being not concerned about God's oath. For if they were, concerned. Then they would pursue such things, openly and publicly before God, forever.

27 Therefore, they do refrain from God publicly. And they truly do, perform, personal, unlawful, true deeds, against God, publicly, forever.

28 And, as they do not pursue God, in being on Israel's behalf, publicly, that Israel, maybe reunited with all of her, Biblical true land, forever.

29 Then that action, publicly, in denying God and denying Christ Jesus, to not pursue the oath for Israel, on God's behalf,

30 Then, that is found from a personal, true lack of obedience, unto God and unto Christ Jesus, forever. As that is found in these eternal and most true matters, as their office, calls for these things to be pursued in the world,

31 Therefore, their lack of attention, to the reunification of Israel. Then, that tries to make

God. As God, being a eternal, true liar, in the eyes of the entire true world, forever,

32 For as God hath placed those leaders and so forth, into their public offices, that they may bring forth God's laws, toward all men, forever,

33 Then God hath given those officials and Christian officials of the world, responsibility to conform unto all of the prophesies, that are written concerning God's laws, forever.

34 Therefore, when they refrain from encouraging Israel to seek all of her land, forever. Then these sinful true leaders, they truly are seen,

35 As breaking God's written, true oath, that is the God's true oath with Israel, forever. And that true oath. It is seen, unto the world, forever.

36 And, when they truly do not pursue on God's behalf, that true oath for God. Then they are encouraging God's lawful true oath, as found concerning all Biblical true Israeli land forever, to be null and void, forever.

37 And, those sinful, evil true deeds. They are demonstrated unto God, forever. They are demonstrated unto God, forever. As they truly do perform,

38 Those evil true deeds, before God. As they are seen, as being found toward God, in blasphemous eternal true sin, forever.

39 Therefore, they are Antichrist--truly rebellious unto God, forever, in demonstrating that they think, that they can change God's true oath,

40 By trying to change that oath, by their own seen hands, of mischief. Which is seen, as being Antichrist, forever.

41 And, the church, does need to stress, these Antichrist true things, diligently, unto the body of Christ. And, also, unto all people who effected by this issue, that they may be taught to refrain from their seen, Antichristism, forever.

42 At times, the church world, does seem to focus more on teaching God's love without teaching about God's true wrath, rather than all that is God's love, and God's actions, as concerning what God is prepared to do, to correct this Antichristism issue, forever.

43 Yes, God does forgive, but God does more than just simply forgive us, he is prepared to correct us, if needed, and judge us, if needed.

44 Our God, most certainly, does consider anyone, who resists intentionally, his (God) historic true oath with Israel. As they are found,

45   In and or headed toward being a functional true part the beastly image, that is the beast, that is called fallen true men, forever.

46   And, unto, all nations, if any of those seen leaders and seen judges, and so forth. Are seen in breaking God's eternal true oath with Israel,

47   Then, they, are found wanting unto God forever, as they, be found, in trying to break God's oath. As they are seen, as seen unto God, forever.

48   As they are seen, as being spiritually seen. As they, are found, in being of a true functional part of the anti Christ, true beast, as being forever certain, and, forever true.

49   And that mark of shame, it is written within themselves, as the name of Satan, forever

50   And they are seen, as being of Satan's beastly speaking true ways of speaking blasphemy unto God forever, and that true blasphemy, it is seen and felt,

51   Unto God, as being forever certain and forever seen, by our true God, forever,

52   And, all speaking Satan blasphemous, true leaders and with their already, damned, judges. They are them, that do purposely try to cut up Israel,

53 And those particular, true leaders of the earth and so forth, they are fallen and or headed unto Satanism, forever, and they shall be, most surely, damned forever, in hell forever. Unless they repent in Jesus Christ, quickly, and forever.

54 For at this time of the earth, our true God. He has written concerning these things, already. Therefore, God shall damn all, who shall purposely contend with God, forever,

55 For they purposely try to break God's oath. That is written between, Israel and our true God, forever.

56 Even, as they of the world leaders. Do try to make God break his promise, with Israel. Our true God, shall and does hold each of them, as being held, accountable unto himself (God), forever.

57 Therefore, they are already cursed of God, forever. And God, shall punish them, in this world, and in the world, that is to come.

58 Therefore, these are damned already, therefore, they must repent of their seen sin, quickly. For their seen sins, are already, sinfully, demonstrated, unto God. And our true God, shall judge them, now, and forever.

59 Yea, thou must, come out of the beastly image, whomsoever thou art, or I (God) shall

damn thee, forever, saith thy eternal, true God. As being, forever seen, and, forever true,

60 For if thou repent not. Then thou art found unto me. As thou being like unto Satan's, seen, true rebellioness, forever. Then, thou shalt, most surely, die unto me, as being forever true.

61 *As a note:* From verse 60 to verse 1 of this chapter 41. It was written before today. And today, it is: 1-23-2008 AD. And, from here to below. Is found, a letter that I have written to Mr. Oral Roberts, who is the founder of Oral Roberts University, in Tulsa Oklahoma, USA.

62 That letter, it is written, as it concerning mister Bush, who is the president of the united states (2008 AD) as that true letter, is written in the true regards, of mister Bush, trying to divide, forever---Israel.

63 But first---lets look into these Bible scriptures. That are about the nations of the earth being cut up. As to when they are trying to divide any and all parts of Israeli Biblical national land, that is found under God's oath with Israel.

64 Zechariah 12:1-3

65 1 The burden of the word of the LORD for Israel, saith the LORD, which stretcheth forth the heavens, and layeth the foundation of the earth, and formeth the spirit of man within him.

66   2   Behold, I will make Jerusalem a cup of trembling unto all the people round about, when they shall be in the siege both against Judah and against Jerusalem.

67   3   And in that day will I make Jerusalem a burdensome stone for all people: all that burden themselves with it shall be cut in pieces, though all the people of the earth be gathered together against it.

68   In Zechariah 12:3. It is speaking of end of the days eternal just judgments from God---as it is found given and established of God, forever. And it is given from God forever--as it is given by our true God through Jesus Christ, forever--- For that is found under the words "cut in peaces." As that is found written in 12:3.

69   And those Zechariah 12:3 judgments. They are given from God, through Jesus Christ, unto: Any People, nation, tongue---and, as to whom, may come with unrighteous sinful true burdens against Israel's true land oath, that is made between Israel and our kind God, forever,

70   For Israel's oath is a cup of trembling to all heathen nations, that are found in unrepentiful true seen sin forever. As to when they come to gather in spirit,

71   As before all of Israel and, as before all of Jerusalem. As to do battle against God, forever--

as they are found declaring burdens of sinful true war, against the oath of God--that is established forever---between Israel and God, forever,

72   Therefore, Israel is burdensome stone to all who shall and do declare war against God, forever--as God is seen, as being: Eternal as being eternally forever--Israel forever.

73   And of course--God shall seek to destroy all sinful true nations, who come to do battle against God--for God is Israel and is most surely-- eternal-- as being: "Jerusalem"--and our kind God (God Is the nation called Israel), he lives forever, and he (God) is eternally forever.

74   Below here-- Is a letter, that has been already been written in this eternal, true book, that is called "The God Of Truth."

75   7:07 pm 1-22-2008 AD

76   Dear Oral Roberts,
77   W / 24 verses
78   1   I (Roger Dale Wallace) Am very concerned about our country. Our God is cutting (America's money system is in long term economic trouble) us up (our money, is now clashing, greatly, and without true end, in site, it would appear) in the regards of president Bush trying to divide Israeli land.

79   2   Please pray for him and try to speak to him, to help him understand. Not to do that awful thing, that he is trying to do to all of Israel. And, no doubt, our true God. He will require recompense in this matter. That is, if mister Bush, will not stop,

80   3   Trying to divide the Israeli land oath of God. And, as to what our God shall do, to mister Bush and unto those that help mister Bush to do such evil, I do not know.

81   4   If mister Bush, will not stop trying to divide Israel from having God's written true oath, as it is found forever, in scripture. Then our true, kind God. He shall not hear mister Bush's cries, to him (God).

82   5   And this is because mister Bush is not hearing our true God. As our God has shown him, not to do this attempt in trying to divide all of Israel away from the written true oath of God, that is eternally written between Israel and God, forever.

83   6   One thing is for sure: "Our God is angry with him," For in spirit, mister Bush has gathered himself against Jerusalem, to divide Jerusalem and to divide Israel. And our true God, he will, no doubt:

84   7   He (God) will deal with mister Bush. For mister Bush is being eternally, hard hearted

against all of the Israeli land oath of God, forever. And mister Bush, he is found unto God forever, as in not helping Israel to be found in all Israel's Biblical true land, forever.

85   8   Soon, our true God. He shall leave mister Bush and Satan shall try to obtain mister Bush unto unrepentiful true seen sin, again. For in works, mister Bush has and is blaspheming God by denying to encourage Israel to seek all of her seen Biblical true land forever.

86   9   If mister Bush will not repent, soon. Then remember these scriptures, as they are found as being: "1 Samuel 15:"

87   10   15:22 And Samuel said, Hath the LORD as great delight in burnt offerings and sacrifices, as in obeying the voice of the LORD? Behold, to obey is better than sacrifice, and to hearken than the fat of rams.

88   11   15:23 **For rebellion is as the sin of witchcraft**, and stubbornness is as iniquity and idolatry. Because thou hast rejected the word of the LORD, he hath also rejected thee from being king.

89   12   15:24 And Saul said unto Samuel, I have sinned: for I have transgressed the commandment of the LORD, and thy words: because I feared the people, and obeyed their voice.

90   13   15:25 Now therefore, I pray thee, pardon my sin, and turn again with me, that I may worship the LORD.

91   14   15:26 And Samuel said unto Saul, I will not return with thee: for thou hast rejected the word of the LORD, and the LORD hath rejected thee from being king over Israel.

92   15   15:27 And as Samuel turned about to go away, he laid hold upon the skirt of his mantle, and it rent.

93   16   15:28 And Samuel said unto him, The LORD hath rent the kingdom of Israel from thee this day, and hath given it to a neighbor of thine, that is better than thou.

94   17   Our kind true God, he is not to be taken lightly of. For he is the creator and our true God, he lives forever. And because he (God) lives, we shall live forever. And the choices we make in today's, true world, forever.

95   18   They do and will determine our eternal, true existence, forever. And those eternal true choices, they will, all and each. They shall be found to be making our choice for us to live in heaven or to live in hell with Satan death, forever.

96   19 Many shall die unto God eternally forever. For many shall not repent from their

rebelliousness forever. Therefore, these are damned already. For in deeds and works, as it is given by them, forever, unto our true God, forever,

97   20 They have denied God and do deny God, unto themselves, forever. As to ever accept and believe all, and to fulfill all, that is God's will. As to do all of those eternal, true filling true things, on our true God's behalf, for God, forever.

98   21 And, as those things, are found eternally written to us, forever. As it is already eternally found written from God and by our true God, to us. As those things, are, already, eternally found written, to us, in the Christian Bible, forever.

99   22 Our president needs to seek our true God's favor. As to help Israel to be found forever, in all Biblical true Israeli land forever. Therefore, all sinful unto God, true nations, true kingdoms, true tongues, they do come and go,

100   23 But will those shameful true countries, that are found. As being eternally forever, truly found. As being eternally: anti Israeli land oath, true nations. Will they appear forever in the earth?---no they will not, saith thy God eternally forever, therefore, let all nations, understand, these things eternally forever, least I (God) move

in pain upon them that would desire my hurt, as I (God) Am Israel land, forever.

101   24   Selah

THE JUDGMENT OF THE NATIONS

―――― *The true ark, as given of god, from god, given unto the hands of men, is eternal life, called christ. And is eternally forever found life, called god.*

Therefore, let him that readeth, understand, that this eternal book, that is called "The Judgment Of The Nations".

It is found through the eternal openness, of the ark of myself (god), forever. And it is concerning the testament of myself (god) and of christ, and is eternally forever and ever true.

And, it is true, and that holy true ark, it is, eternally forever unsealed, in these last days, of the fallen, beastly, eternal true earth, forever. ――――

BY ROGER WALLACE

As a note: This entire short version, true book, that is called "The judgment of the nations." It is, chapter 42, as it is found in this book, that is entitled: "The God of truth." This chapter 42, it has, altogether-- 1,129 verses.

Table of contents

Part 1 All nations
Part 2 Pleading with the heathen
Part 3 My hand
Part 4 They that worship the image of the beast
Part 5 Israeli's messiah, forever
Part 6 The dome of the rock
Part 7 The mount of GOD
Part 8 Thy first love
Part 9 Prophet Judge

Introduction

w/ 32 verses

1   As openly unsealed at this time of the fallen earth, forever and ever eternal. As found through a spirit of thus saith the lord of heaven and earth. As given through a spirit of spiritual interpretation. Spoken by God and spoken by Christ. As spoken in eternal out pourings of God's endless eternal true mercies, for all men, everywhere.

2   And is eternally forever eternal, true interpretation, as given from God, in Christ Jesus, forever. And is eternally forever, true interpretation.

3 That interpretation, is called God forever, and is given now, in the earth, forever. And is given from God, through Jesus Christ, eternally forever. And who (Jesus Christ), is the eternal true Son of God.

4 And that interpretation, it is found, as being eternally forever, truly spiritual, Godly true interpretation. As found in spirit, that is given of God's own, eternal, true holy spirit.

5 And is found, in Jesus Christ, forever eternal. And is God eternally forever and ever, true truth eternal. And is a spiritual, uttering, heavenly inspired, interpretation,

6 That proceedeth from our true, and kind God. As being forever eternal, spiritual true interpretation.

7 And, is a spiritual, spoken, uttering inspired, true interpretation, called God in Christ Jesus, forever. And that heavenly, truly spoken, true interpretation,

8 It is from our kind and just, eternal kind God, forever. And it is found, forever eternal. In Christ's eternal true spirit, that is sent from God, eternally forever, unto us, forever.

9 And is a Godly forever and ever, Godly true interpretation. That is of a righteously eternal forever, ever lastingly forever, eternal forever,

Godly forever, true truth eternal, Christly true interpretation.

10 And is a uttering Christly true interpretation. As in being, eternally forever, spiritually spoken, spoken by our kind God, forever.

11 And is faithfully spoken by our the true Father, as being eternally forever spoken unto us, forever. And it is spoken from God forever, through Christ Jesus, forever, as unto the body of Christ. As being eternally forever and ever eternal.

12 And is spoken, as being eternally forever, truly inspired, as spoken as uttering in Christ, as heavenly eternal, unknown eternal, true languages,

13 That are God's languages, that are spoken through us, in us, who are of the body of Christ, as being eternally forever and ever true.

14 And it is found forever eternal of God, as given by our kind God, forever. As given unto all, of the seen true earth, forever. And as being eternally forever eternal.

15 And it is spokenly spoken in God and of God, in Christ Jesus, forever, and is faithfully spoken to the earth forever, as being spoken by our kind and true God, through Christ Jesus, forever. And it is, seen as being, eternally:

16 Heavenly unknown eternal true tongues and heavenly eternal unknown eternal true languages. That are eternally forever found, in the fallen true earth, as being eternally forever true and forever seen.

17 And is found, in being eternally forever spoken. As Godly, spiritual, inspiringly, holy true interpretations. That are most certainly, found as being, heavenly true languages of Godly eternal, heavenly eternal, ever after, eternal true angels, forever.

18 And those, heavenly, unknown, eternal true languages. That are found from God forever. They are found even as like unto the voices of eternal heavenly true angels,

19 That are found spoken of God, in us, as we are seen as being, the body of Christ, as being eternally forever. And those eternal true languages, they are found forever eternal, of and by God, as being eternally forever and ever eternal.

20 And those heavenly eternal angelic tongues and heavenly eternal angelic languages. They shall be inspiringly eternally spoken, forever and ever eternal, in us and from God, forever.

21 And is spoken from God in Christ, as found demonstrated by our kind God forever. And it is found of God forever, as spoken by our true God,

in the body of Christ, as being eternally, faithfully forever spoken by our true God, forever.

22 And is spoken interpretation, that is spoken by our true God, forever. And is spoken as being eternally forever and ever, ever true. As spoken in Jesus Christ, as being eternally forever.

23 And it is spoken forever. As being eternally forever and ever, ever spoken forever. And is spoken, as being from our, precious, kind, eternal true God, as being eternally forever and ever more.

24 And those heavenly unknown eternal true tongues and eternal unknown true languages. That are spoken in us, by the Son called Christ Jesus forever,

25 And is commanded and spoken by our true God's command, in us forever. And it is spoken as being the same heavenly unknown eternal true tongues and eternal, true unknown true languages,

26 That are spoken by heavenly angels, that are seen of our true and kindly, eternal true God, forever.

27 Those, heavenly, unknown, eternal true tongues, and, eternal, unknown true languages.

They have already been speaking in the body of Christ, eternally.

28 And is even now been speaking in the body of Christ, eternally forever. And those seen, heavenly, unknown, eternal true tongues, and, eternal, unknown true languages. They shall remain speaking forever eternal, in the body of Christ, as being eternally forever and ever true.

29 And those seen, heavenly, unknown, eternal true tongues, and, eternal, unknown true languages. They shall always be inspiringly spoken unto us,

30 As being eternally forever and ever eternal, by our kind God, forever, in Christ, eternally forever and ever true. And is inspiringly spoken through the body of Christ, as being eternally forever and ever true.

31 And that eternal truth. Is a true truth, eternal truth. That is a heavenly, ever after, eternal truth of God, that is eternally forever, and is a great, eternal, ever lastingly forever, eternal true truth.

32 "Yea, I Am the AMEN, and I Am the glory called God, for I Am God, and I dwell eternally forever, and ever true, for I shall live eternal of myself, through my (God) eternal true Son, who is called Jesus Christ, forever." SELAH

The judgment of the nations

Part 1 w/ 138 verses   All nations

1 Many people, in the earth, they have desired, to understand, and to know, that which cometh upon the earth, as being forever seen.

2 And, I do say, that most surely, in those seen nations, who hate my great, eternal, true name. As found, as being Jesus Christ, as being, forever true,

3 They are seen, unto me forever. As being forever true, in Satanism forever sure. And, they are seen, as being death unto me forever. And, they are, simply, unrepentfully and unjustly, in unrepentfulness,

4 As being forever truly found, as being faithfully forever true, of themselves, as forever seen. In being against, all that I Am, as I Am God, as forever seen and true.

5 And, those beguiled, true nations. They are seen unto me, as being forever true. As being non Christian nations, forever. And those nations,

6 They shall see vexation of spirit and suffering and great end time famine, and great pestilence, and great war, forever.

7 Yet, they shall see many other things, from their personal, true treasures. That are found in their own, desired, damningly true treasures,

8 That are treasures in death forever. That are called, their desired true death, in Satanism, as being forever seen and forever sought, by the damned ones, forever.

9 And, those beastly true nations, they are found unto me, in death, as being forever seen. And, they are seen, unto me forever. As forever seen, as Satan, forever, and they are seen and felt, unto me,

10 As their desired and most true death, as forever true. And, they are considered of me, forever. To be as dead as Satan is dead, unto me, forever,

11 And, they, the damned in Satan himself, forever. They are seen and found, in utter true shame and utter true contempt, as being forever seen. And they are seen, of eternal living forever, true damnation,

12 And they do worship, as faithfully forever true, within themselves, forever, eternal living forever, true death. As found, given unto themselves, from Satan himself, as being forever true.

13 And, this earth, it is found, fallen in, and, unto Satan himself. As Satan, has became, as a false idol God, unto the damned forever. And it is found, and seen,

14 By the damned, as being forever true, of the damned ones, forever. As they, the damned in Satanism, as being forever seen by me forever.

15 That they do choose Satan, as Satan being their false idol God, as forever true of themselves. As they give of themselves, forever, unto Satan, forever.

16 And this earth, as found, unto Satan himself, as being forever seen in Satan true death, as being forever sure, in death, as being forever true.

17 Then, those non Christian true nations of the earth, as they are seen, as being: "Fallen, unrepentiful, ungodly true nations of the earth."

18 And those nations, they are found by me, in death, as being forever seen. And they shall be perplexed with signs following, For those nations,

19 They are beastly by human fallen nature, forever. And they do refuse, unjustly, as forever true, to ever know me (God), as forever seen, as I Am their true God, forever.

20 And, again, those beastly eternal, damningly true nations, in death forever. As found, unto Satan, as being forever seen. If, they shall refuse, to know my Son, who called Christ, as their savior, forever,

21 And, who (Christ Jesus) is with my heavenly true salvation, that I have created, from my (God) own, eternal, true Love. As being forever seen, in me, as forever true.

22 And that salvation, it is given of me, for all fallen true men, forever. And that salvation, that is called Christ Jesus. It is given, that repentful true men, may arise and cleanse themselves, by calling on the name of God,

23 As that name, is found. As my eternal, living forever, true Son. And, who is called, "Jesus Christ." As being forever seen, of myself, as forever truly seen.

24 If, those non Christian-unrepentiful true nations, who hate me, forever. Shall not repent in Christ Jesus, forever.

25 Then, those beguiled in Satan, true nations. They are called death. And those, beguiled, most true nations, they shall all be clean dissolved, by me forever, or unto they accept and repent, by receiving Christ, forever,

26 As Christ Jesus, being their personal, living forever, true savior. And who is from me (God), as being forever faithfully forever true, with my heavenly true salvation,

27 That is found, given of me (God), as eternally forever and ever true, of me, forever. And it is true, for all of given true eternity, forever.

28 Many Antichrist, true nations, they are found unto me forever. In their own, personal, true choices, found in life and death.

29 And those choices, they are found, unto me, as being forever true, and it is true, by their own, eternal, living forever, true hands,

30 And it is true, that they, either chose Christ Jesus, for the heavenly true salvation, that is given of me (God), as being forever seen.

31 Or they chose not to receive Christ Jesus, forever. And, which is seen, in being forever certain, of themselves, unto me, forever.

32 And those nations, if they shall reject Christ Jesus, forever. Then they shall die unto me forever,

33 Then, my, great, living eternal, given and being given, righteous, holy true judgments. They shall be found of me forever, as given by me forever,

34 As given of me as being forever seen in judgment forever. And it is a fiery given judgment of me (God), that is recompense, that is called granted true death, forever,

35 And that true death, it shall be found given of me, upon and unto those blasphemous eternal true nations, that are called Satan forever,

36 And who are seen. As being, blasphemous eternal true nations of death, forever,

37 And, granted true death, it is found, given of me, as being forever seen. As, given by me forever, unto those Satan nations. As they are found by me forever, in Satan forever. And those nations, they are,

38 Found unto me, forever. As being forever certain, in Satan forever. And they are found, unto me. As being forever true, as being found, as being truly beastly.

39 And, they are seen unto me forever. As being, a anti God, true image, unto me. As being faithfully forever seen, in themselves. As their desired true death, as found in Satan, forever.

40 And, those non Christian nations, as found in their death, as being forever seen true death. As found, as being. A fallen beastly stone image, of given, unrepentiful to receive God, beastly forever, true seen sin,

41 That seen sin, it is found unto me forever. In being unrepentfully forever true, in being against me. As a seen, true sinfulness, as being forever seen, and is seen, in them, that perish unto me in their Satanism, forever.

42 All beastly, eternal, true nations. They are found, unto me forever true. As being anti God and as being anti Christ forever true nations of the earth forever,

43 And those nations, they are found unto me, in Satan. As being forever seen, in granted true death, as forever true.

44 And, they are seen, unto me. As being, found in their desired and most true death. As true death in Satan, is found, working within themselves,

45 As being found, as truly being Satanism, as being forever true of themselves forever, and, that work in Satan that is found themselves, it is forever heard as being a blasphemous eternal image of death forever.

46 And, they, the damned in Satan forever, they are most surely heard, as being eternal true sin, as being forever true, in all that I Am not as God forever.

47 And, they shall die, unto me forever, as being forever true. In their desired, and most true death,

as forever seen. That is working true death, that worketh against me forever.

48 And, they are truly, forever seen, in death forever. And they are seen unto me forever. As being, eternally forever true. As Satan true sin, as being eternally forever true sin, forever.

49 And they are seen by me forever, as death, and they are in agreement with me forever, for that true death and they are in agreement with hell forever, for true death forever.

50 And, in true death, they shall never awake, after that great judgments of eternal just judgments, has occurred, forever. And they shall never awake, again, to live, afterwards (after that great Judgment called life), and forever.

51 In true death, the damned ones of this fallen, true earth, forever. They shall be caste by me, away from me, as being forever true,

52 And they shall be caste into eternal hell fire, that burneth, as being forever seen, as God in judgment, forever. For I Am, God in judgment, as being forever true,

53 And I Am true, unto all of the wicked ones of the earth forever, as I Am forever seen and heard, in Jesus Christ, as being forever seen.

54 And, in hell, is their seen eternal true reward. That is called life, that they have made unto themselves. As being forever seen. As a seen image, called death forever.

55 And that image, as made by the damned ones, as being forever seen, by me forever true. It is called: "Wanted true death, for me (me is the word sinner), in Satan forever,

56 As I (I is the sinner person) Am a found sinner, unto God, as being forever true of myself (myself is the word sinner), forever."

57 And, unto all sinners, who are found unto me, as being forever true, as found in Satan (all true sinners), forever. They shall, be forever seen.

58 And they shall be seen by me, as being faithfully forever seen, In that great eternal, and most mighty and true day. That is called God in judgment, unto Satan, forever,

59 And, those sinners in Satan forever. They all, shall receive their seen true reward. That is called, hell fire, forever. And that reward, it is found,

60 As given of me, unto them, in that great unending true day, that is most forever seen, as being seen, truly forever true. And that day, it is seen. As being most eternal,

61 For I Am most eternal, saith thy God, as being eternally forever and ever true. For I Am eternal, and I live forever. And the forever, it is me (God), forever.

62 In that day, that is glorious in me, forever. The damned, they shall pass back into the earth, in spiritual and physical, true death. As being forever seen, and, as being forever, eternally seen, in death, forever true.

63 Therefore, that passing into eternal forever death. It shall be written by me (God), as being: "They the damned, they are written back into the earth forever, as they truly do desire, Unrepentiful true death, forever."

64 That death, it is desired by the damned ones, forever. And, it is desired by the damned forever. As being, true death, forever. And that true death,

65 It is also seen, as being in Satanism forever. And, it is seen, as being forever seen by me, forever. And it is found, in true death, unto me, forever.

66 That death, it is from being found guilty in unrepentiful true trespasses and unrepentiful true sins, that are unrepentfully forever seen,

67 As being against me (God), as being forever true. For those desired sins, are desired forever,

by the damned, as being forever seen by me, forever.

68 And, they are found unto me forever. As being against receiving my eternal Son, who is called "Christ As Savior, Forever."

69 Eternal death, as found in the damned forever, it seen. As being, unholy and unrighteous, spiritual true works, that is found in Satan's true death, forever.

70 And that death, in the damned forever. It is found, in Satan, as being, forever seen, as true death, as forever true. And it is desired, as being faithfully forever seen, by the lost unto me forever.

71 And that true death, in the damned, it is seen by me forever true. As being forever true, and, forever seen. And that death, it is seen, to be as Satan is dead, forever.

72 And Satanism, seen true works, as found in their desired true death, as being forever seen by me forever. It is called true death, and those works of Satan and of the beast, whom (beast is the word man), is called man, as forever seen.

73 It is forever seen, and, is forever found, in Satan, himself, as granted true death, from me, as being forever true death. And that true death, it is forever seen,

74 As seen in the damned, as being forever true death, forever. And the damned, and, with Satan himself, together, and with Satan's true kind, who (kind is all fallen angels) are called devils, they are all together, as seen and called: "As being the beast," forever.

75 And they are found, unto me, as being forever certain. As being in Satanism unto me, as being forever true of themselves, in the service of their faithful and true worship unto Satan and to Satan's kind, forever.

76 And they are forever seen. And they are seen in death, forever. And, all ungodly, Antichrist, true nations. As they are found by me, as forever sure, as being seen by me, in their, seen sin, forever.

77 And they are found by me, forever. As being forever true, as being seen, in eternal true works, found in death forever. And, it is seen, as heavenly true death. As being forever certain and ever lasting, forever true.

78 And, they the damned and all fallen true nations. They are found unto me forever, as being in Satan forever. And they, are also found unto me forever,

79 In unholy, and, in unrighteous physical true works, that are called, eternal true death, forever.

80 Those unrepentiful true nations in Satan forever. They are even found unto me, as found. In their manifesting, of: "Unrepentiful, true sinful true works." That is called granted true death, forever.

81 And granted true death forever. It is being found forever granted, to them, who are found in Satanism, as being eternally forever true of themselves,

82 As they are found unto me, in the service of Satan. As being forever true of themselves forever.

83 And, if they be found unto me forever, in Satanism, as being eternally forever true of themselves, in Satan's true death, as being forever seen. Then they shall die unto all that is me in Christ Jesus, forever.

84 And, through the judgment of the nations, my eternal just judgments. They are given by me, through Christ Jesus, forever true, unto all nations,

85 who are all non Christian nations of the earth forever. That are seen unto me forever. As being, in Satanism, as being forever true and ever lasting forever, of themselves, forever.

86 And I shall damn them all non Christian nations forever, who are considered by me, as

being, rejectful to me, true nations, forever. And, they shall die unto me, as being forever true of themselves, forever,

87 And, in this judgment of the nations, as being forever seen, upon the unrepentiful forever seen and true, non Christian nations, forever, who are judged,

88 As they will never repent and receive Christ Jesus my eternal true Son, who is with life, that is called God, forever.

89 Then any of those nations, who are found unto me, as being forever certain, as that nation or nations that will never repent and receive Christ forever.

90 Then that nation and or nations, they shall die unto me forever seen, as being forever true. As being forever eternally forever true. And, they are considered by me, as being forever certain,

91 As themselves, in being dead unto me, as forever true, and, as being forever seen, in death, forever true. And, they shall be seen, unto me, as being forever certain, and, true forever, in their sin, as being forever seen.

92 Therefore, end time judgment. It is given of me (God), and is found, of me (God), worthily, unto whom, end time judgments, are forever,

righteously forever due, unto. And that judgment, it is forever truly seen.

93 And all end time judgments, are called life and death, forever. Therefore, let all nations, chose me, or they shall die unto me forever,

94 And that decision, it must be made quickly, saith thy eternal one, who is seen, and is called, the lord thy God, forever.

95 In these true days, forever. All ungodly nations, they shall be judged by me forever. And I will hold them accountable, for the deeds that they do perform,

96 As they do perform those deeds, against me, as being found by me, as being forever true of themselves. As they are found by me, in Satanism forever.

97 And, those, ungodly true deeds, as found, as being true toward me. As they themselves, are seen by me forever true. In that they do perform those deeds, unto me, as being forever true of themselves in Satan forever.

98 And those true deeds, they are seen. As being, in Satan eternally forever true. And those ungodly blasphemous true deeds, they shall be recompense back,

99 Unto themselves, as measured unto themselves, in true punishment, from me, as being forever true, of me forever certain.

100 And, most certainly, measured true punishment, it is given to themselves, from me, as being forever seen true punishment. And that true punishment,

101 It is seen, as being forever true, from me, as being forever and eternally seen, true punishment. That is called God forever,

102 And that true punishment. That is called God forever. It is seen, and is called dead death, as being forever seen, and it is now, found on the earth, and in hell, forever.

103 And that eternal, most true punishment, it is from me forever true. And it is seen, as being true in me forever. And it is, given most surely, unto themselves, as being forever seen, true judgment, forever,

104 And that eternal ever lasting true punishment, it is called eternal dead death forever. And it is from me forever. And I, the lord of heaven and earth, forever,

105 I the lord, I do hold all nations, accountable, for their seen sins. That they, do against all, that is me, as I Am creation, as forever seen.

106 And I, shall damn all non Christian true nations of the earth forever, that will not receive Jesus Christ, forever. And I will send a fire, from me, unto all of them, forever. And I will give death and dissolving and great punishment,

107 Unto those devil nations, as they are found unto me, as being in Satanism forever, as they are seen by me, forever. In their seen true sins, that is called: "I (I is the sinner) desire death, as being forever true,"

108 And, through the judgment of the nations. If these ungodly, true, non Christian nations of the earth, forever, shall not repent and be baptized, in the Son, who is called, Jesus Christ,

109 Then they have most surely, bought upon themselves, and, upon all of their seen children. Death and great eternal, blasting, true destruction, from me, as being forever true of me forever,

110 And I (God) will destroy them with their seen sins, forever. And even those nations, that trust in their false idol Gods, I (God) shall shame those nations, by making those nations, see,

111 That without Christ, they shall die, forever. And that in trusting their idols, that they have bought great dissolving true judgment, from me (God), as being forever true, upon themselves, as being forever seen.

112 And, those Satan true nations in Satanism forever. They shall become greatly angered at their false idols, which hath not life forever. And they shall revolt against their false, seen and hidden idols of falsehood.

113 And those nations which shall not repent, by receiving Jesus Christ, as Christ Jesus, being their savior, as being forever seen. Then, they shall die unto me (God) forever,

114 And their seed shall die unto me (God) forever, unless they repent in Christ Jesus, forever.

115 These false nations, they are not, true nations of life, that is called Christ, unto me (God), forever. And without Christ, in them. They shall die unto me forever.

116 And I will judge them forever, if they destroy not their seen idols, forever. And if they accept not Jesus Christ, as this Jesus being their seen savior, from me, forever,

117 And without Christ Jesus being their seen savior forever. Then they are seen unto me, as being faithfully forever seen, as being seen in Satanism,

118 As being forever true, and they are forever found, unto me forever true. In their desired true death, forever certain.

119 And I, and I shall, trumpet, unto those ungodly, true nations, that are found unto Satan himself, forever, and that are found by me, in their desired true death,

120 As being forever true of themselves. As they are found unto me, in their desired, true, iniquity. That is called sin, forever.

121 And those Satan true nations, they must, therefore, all repent unto me, as being forever true of themselves, forever. Or they shall die unto me, as being forever true.

122 And, they must repent, quickly at this time of the fallen true earth, forever, and turn unto me forever. And I Am seen, as: "The God of truth," forever.

123 And, as I Am truth forever. Those non-Christian, true rebellious, seen nations, as they are found unto me and found by me, in their seen Satanism, forever. They must turn unto me, as being forever true,

124 And, through, my eternal, and most true judgment, that is called: "The judgment of the nations." If they, shall not repent, unto me, as being forever seen,

125 As being quickly seen in repenting to me now, and, as being forever true. Then I shall cause war and or plagues and or famines,

126 To seek out those ungodly true nations. That are nations, that are found unto me, in death, as being forever true, of themselves forever.

127 And I will destroy them forever. And I shall even cause their pleasant true skies, to flee away from them, forever. And I shall stop the rain, unto them, forever,

128 And I shall stop the snow unto them, and I shall cause their crops to die, unto them. And all their animals, shall die, unto me, and I shall fight against those Satanism true ones, as forever seen.

129 And I (God) shall call fire out of the sky to devour them, in all their seen labors. That is found in this Satan true life, forever.

130 And, those ungodly, true, non Christian nations. That are found unto Satanism, forever. They shall cease to exist, in the earth, forever,

131 Unless they repent and receive Jesus Christ, as Christ Jesus, being their seen savior, forever.

132 Therefore, let your false Gods, and let Satan give you life forever. And in his (Satan) hand of life, thou shalt die in his tainted true life, forever, for in sin, thou art already found in Satan himself, forever.

133 And Satan's true hand of life, it isn't Christly true life, as found in me forever, but it is truly found unto me forever, as death forever,

134 And in Satan, thou art already cursed with death and thou shalt die forever, unless thou renounce Satan forever, by accepting Jesus Christ,

135 As by, accepting Jesus Christ, as thy seen, personal, living forever, true savior. As Christ Jesus, is given of me forever, unto the earth, forever.

136 Therefore, let all nations, consider, through the judgment of the nations. That they need to consider, their ways of blasphemous eternal true death, that is forever and ever upon them, forever,

137 And that, they must repent, or I will destroy them, for desiring to be non Christian nations of the earth, forever.

138 And, in me, is the life called man and woman, as forever seen--therefore--repent--or thou shalt die unto me forever, saith thy God, who is thy creator, as forever seen.

Part 2 w / 144 verses Pleading with the heathen

1   Now, as concerning my promise, as it is seen, as it is found in the Christian Bible--in the book of Joel 3:12:

2   **"Let the heathen be awakened, and come up to the valley of Jehoshaphat: for there will I sit to judge all of the heathen round about."**

3   In these days, I (God) do plead with the heathen, for Israel' sake and for my (God) sake. And this pleading, it is for my (God) inheritance, that is found as Jacob, forever.

4   And that, eternal, true inheritance. It is forever seen, and is forever true, and is eternally forever true, as I have declared it to be true, forever.

5   And I (God) Am the true Father, and I (God) Am seen forever true, in Jacob's seed forever. And in my (God) pleading, it is that you all (heathen) may **awake** and consider and understand, whom I (God) Am forever,

6   And that you may understand, as to what is concerning my (God) promises, that are made and found recorded of me (God), with Israel, eternally forever.

7   And I (God) Am seen, in the earth forever. As spoken eternal true truth, that is even spoken

from all unsealed ness and from all unclosed ness, that is given of myself (God) forever true.

8   And that trueness, it is revealed from me (God) eternally forever true, in Christ the Son, forever.

9   End of the days, eternal just judgments. They are given of me (God), in (in means the word through) Christ Jesus, as eternally forever and ever true, of me (God) forever.

10   And those just judgments, they are called life and death, forever, and they are even found of me (God), as found spokenly spoken by me (God),

11   In all of my (God) true voices, that is called The seven true thunders that are seen and felt, as Jesus Christ.

12   Those seven true thunders, they are called God in Christ Jesus forever. And they are found spoken by me (God) in Christ Jesus, in these eternal true days, forever.

13   And they are seen and felt, in the fallen true earth, eternally forever true and forever seen, eternally forever.

14   And those true voices, they are found as heavenly true thunder. And they are, called God forever true in the fallen true earth, forever.

15 And those true voices, they are myself (God) as I (God) Am found thundering eternally forever, in Christ,

16 And as I (God) thunder, I the lord God of heaven and earth, do plead for my (God) heritage, that is called Israel, in these true days of the fallen true earth, forever.

17 And I (God) do plead with all the heathen, who are gathered in spirit, all about (the word about, it means the word around) Israel to destroy Israel,

18 That thou o heathen, thou must repent quickly, now in the earth and forever, for if thou will not repent in Christ my (God) eternal true Son, forever,

19 Then thou and thy seed, shalt perish forever true, from off the land and forever.

20 And that decision, is to be made by you, o heathen. And it shall be, unto you forever, as a valley of decision, found given of me, unto you, forever.

21 That decision, is to be made, by you, now in the earth, forever true. And is, most surely, to be found, now in the earth, forever.

22 And is to be found, in this time period of the earth, that is called "The end of the days," as mentioned in the Christian Bible, forever.

23 And if, thou shalt not repent, and will not encourage Israel to seek her faithful fulfillment of true promise, that is given by me, unto Israel forever,

24 And is seen as Israel found in all of her true Biblical true land forever,

25 Then I (God) shall remove thee in death and great destruction, from of the land of Israel, yea, it is found unto all Biblical true land, forever true, saith God, eternally forever and ever so.

26 Why shall thee seek death, in unrepentfulness that is seen forever true, to not perform the true Israeli land promise unto me (God) forever?

27 I (God) know that thou prayest unto me, without Christ O Ishmael, but I (God) have spoken to thy spirit, to urge thee to consider partaking of the salvation, that is given by me forever, that is called Christ Jesus.

28 But thou preferest instead, to be taught error at the hands of men, rather than to seek the truth, that is called Christ Jesus forever.

29 Many times, have I sent Christians unto thee, to awaken thee out of thy sleep, unto the truth.

And that truth, it is called Christ Jesus. But thou desirest not to be diligent, forever true,

30 In not searching the Christian Bible scriptures, that are found concerning this Christ and thou will not even read and will not even study all that is found concerning this Christ,

31 And that Christ, he is found through my (God) presents, that is called life forever true in me (God) forever.

32 Are you so sure, that these things, aren't so? For if they be true---and they are---Then what wilt thou say unto me (God) in the great day of eternal true judgments, when thou wilt have condemned thy self to hell forever?

33 As you are found fighting against me, O Ishmael, in this life, concerning Christ Jesus. So shall I (God) fight against thee in having eternal life that is called Christ, in that great judgment of judgments,

34 Therefore ye shall not have Christ as thy savior, when thou shalt ask for him during the great judgment of judgments, that is come quickly and forever true, and that great judgment, it will be quickly found in the earth forever and in heaven forever.

35 And, even Abraham thy father, is ashamed of thy sinfulness that is demonstrated against me

(God) and is found demonstrated against Christ Jesus forever,

36 for even now, Abraham is greatly angered at you, for your willful and true, disobedience to not seek the truth, that is called Christ Jesus, forever.

37 And though Abraham loveth thee greatly, he will not accept thee as being unrepentiful unto me (God) forever. For Abraham loveth me (God) and is found in all that Christ Jesus is,

38 And Christ, he is unto the earth forever true. As God forever and ever lasting forever and ever true of me (God), forever. For this Christ Jesus, he is a Son of myself (God), eternally forever and ever true,

39 And I (God) Am found of myself in Christ Jesus forever, for I (God) Am God forever faithful and true forever. And I (God) Am found eternally forever true---as God in Christ, eternally forever faithful and truly forever true.

40 Thou must understand, O Ishmael, that Abraham will not and will never seek another savior for you. But rather, Abraham is ashamed of you,

41 That you have acted so evil towards me (God), as I (God) Am found in Christ, who is my (God) eternal true Son, forever.

42 And Abraham doth not agree with evil tidings towards one and another, but Abraham desirest forever, to be always found in Christ Jesus, who is Christ that is my (God) true Son, forever.

43 Many curses have came upon thy people, o Ishmael, but you shall not obtain my (God) blessings, by hurting and killing others, in the name of myself (God) forever,

44 but if thou, O Ishmael, shalt lay down all thy true evil, then I shall give thee Christ, even as I (God) have given him (Christ Jesus) unto all of the earth forever true.

45 Then thy fore father, Abraham, he shall be pleased with thee, forever certain and forever true.

46 But, if thou, O Ishmael, doth believe that thou can get to heaven by killing thyself as a suicide bomber by taking the lives of the Jews and of those that aren't of Ishmael, then thou art in great error,

47 And if thou shalt continue such Satan behavior, then I shall allow that wickedness to come back unto yourself, as directed against your own people O Ishmael, as a directed granted true recompense, from me forever.

48 And is for thou not making thy governments and thy peoples to not be held accountable, for these hate crimes, that are directed against, both me and are against my Christly eternal true creation forever,

49 Therefore, recompense called death and destruction. It is without true end, unto you forever. And is granted unto you, by me, as forever and ever lasting forever, true unto you, forever true.

50 And is, most truly and surely, eternally forever granted unto you, now and forever true, of me (God) forever. And is granted unto you forever true,

51 Because you have been allowing thy governments and thy peoples and thy tongues, to perform such evil unto my (God) created earth, eternally forever.

52 And it shall remain so, unto you, forever true and forever more. And it shall remain so, to you, and is to remain, until thou O Ishmael, shalt repent and receive Jesus Christ, as Christ Jesus being thy savior, eternally forever true.

53 And if, thou shalt not desire this Christ, who is Jesus Christ. As Christ Jesus being thy savior, forever true. Then thou shalt be dissolved forever true, by me (God) forever.

54 And thou, O Ishmael. Thou shalt be destroyed forever, saith thy God, who is thy eternal, true maker, forever true and forever more.

55 Did I (God) command you, O Ishmael to kill in my name---no I did not command O Ishmael, to kill in my (God) name forever.

56 And I the Lord of heaven and earth, forever. I shall never command O Ishmael without true reason, to seek my created true men and my created true women, to take their lives forever true, from the earth forever.

57 And, when is it approval able, to kill lives ? If thou shalt study and read the Christian Bible, then thou wouldest understand those answers.

58 Your earthly father, Abraham. He has always desired you, O Ishmael, to repent and receive this living true Christ. As this Christ, being thy true savior, who is Jesus Christ, who is my (God) eternal true Son, forever.

59 And that Christ Jesus, he from me (God) and is of me (God), forever true and for all of true eternity and forever.

60 And as you accept this Christ, as thy savior forever. Then thou shalt know the joy of myself (God), in Christ Jesus. As Abraham even doth forever enjoy me (God) in Christ Jesus,

61   And that is spoken, eternally forever and ever true, by me (God), forever.

62   Christ Jesus, is Abraham's true savior and true prophet, and is forever certain in the earth forever true. And this Christ, can be thy savior and thy true prophet, forever, and Abraham doth not desire any other savior, forever.

63   And I (God) do say, therefore, O Ishmael. Take fair warning forever. If thou shalt not stop warring against thy brother, Israel. Then I (God) will most certainly, relieve thee forever from off thy Arab true land.

64   And if thou shalt not stop warring against Israel thy brother. Then I shall most certainly, place upon thee, O Ishmael, all the curses and plagues, that were to destroy Israel, from 70 AD unto 1948 AD,

65   Therefore, the true fire of mouth, that is called Christ Jesus, shall devour you forever, and thou shalt be naked and I (God) shall discover thy shame unto all of the nations, that are of the earth forever, and thou shalt become, only a remnant forever.

66   And, for Abraham's sake, I (God) shall leave most surely, a remnant only of thee forever, instead of wiping all thy seed out forever.

67 And moreover, I (God) shall completely, purge thee because of this unrepentfulness, that is unrepentfulness that is directed against, both me and against Christ, who is Christ that is my (God) Son, forever.

68 And Israel, shall inherit the land of eternal true promise. And this Israel, shall enjoy me (God), in Christ, as eternally forever true and forever more.

69 And I (God) will, most certainly, forever, bless Israel, forever true of me (God), as eternally and ever lastingly, forever true.

70 And, if thou shalt want to remain on any of the Biblical true land of promise, that I have given unto Israel forever, then thou must repent unto me and unto Israel, by receiving Christ as thy true savior, forever.

71 And thou O Ishmael, thou must encourage all Biblical true Israeli land, to be nationalized, to be national Israeli true land, eternally forever true and forever.

72 And I (God) shall remove from each person, that are repentful in Christ Jesus of Ishmael, any of those curses and plagues, when it effects that particular true repenting true person in Christ Jesus of Ishmael,

73 But thou o repentful of Ishmael, by accepting me (God) in Christ Jesus, as Christ Jesus being thy savior. Thou must still abide in all that is commanded by me (God), in (in means through) Christ Jesus.

74 And most certainly, even as I (God) have commanded already, what is concerning the true Biblical Israeli true land, that is concerning the true land of promise, that is promised from me (God), unto Israel eternally forever.

75 That land, it is to most certainly, go back to Israel, eternally forever true. As eternal true promise, forever, and is from me (God), eternally forever true.

76 Know this, O Ishmael, forever. I (God) shall, now bring, O Tyre, and Zidon, and all the coasts of Palestine, down to the valley of Jehoshaphat.

77 And it is, that there, at the valley of Jehoshaphat. That I (God) shall and will, sit to judge, both thee and all thy helping heathen nations,

78 Who shall and do come with thee, to the valley of Jehoshaphat, forever. And it is there, at the valley of Jehoshaphat, that I (God) shall destroy thee and leave only but a sixth part of thee in the earth, forever.

79   And I (God), shall smite thy bow of death, out of thy left hand. And I (God) shall cause thy poisonous arrows of true death, to turn back unto thee forever,

80   Therefore, thy poison arrows of dead death, shall fall out of thy right hand of recompense, that had been formed against me (God) and against Israel, forever.

81   And though thou shalt call upon me without Christ being thy savior, for Israel's defeat at the valley of Jehoshaphat, I will not hear you,

82   And I will not help you at all, O Ishmael. And you do not even read and apply, the Christian Bible, into your lives, forever.

83   But if thou wouldest have read and studied these things, in the Christian Bible. Then thou wouldest not have persecuted Israel, as you have done so, in the earth.

84   Therefore, just as you have forsaken me, as I Am found of myself, as I Am found recorded in the Christian Bible. Then thou hast most surely, bought upon all of thine selves, forever true,

85   Great destruction that is unto you forever. And thou shalt most certainly and forever true. Thou shalt fall upon the mountains and fields of Israel, eternally forever true and forever more.

86   And thy bands, of unrepentiful true heathen nations, they shall fall with thee, also.

87   And the birds shall eat thy bodies, instead of eating Israel. And the beasts of the field, shall eat thee and I (God) will send a fire upon thee, saith thy maker and God, forever true.

88   And when thou shalt fall in Israel, then all of you heathen shall know I (God) Am God forever and that thy life is held in my (God) hand of life forever.

89   And when thou, O Ishmael, shalt fall, even Israel shall understand this Christ Jesus, whom thou shalt most certainly reject, eternally forever true.

90   And I (God) will give thy substance, thy wives and thy children, unto Israel forever. And in their hands, shall thy remnant be blessed in Jesus Christ forever.

91   This judgment, is unto you O Ishmael and is unto thy helping true nations. So that you may decide where you stand in these choices, that I (God) do present unto you, now at this time of the earth, forever true and forever more.

92   Make thy choices wisely, and accept what I (God) command you, least I (God) destroy you for being unrepentiful towards me (God) and towards Israel forever.

93 Therefore, just as I have bought the captivity of Judah and Jerusalem back to the land, that is called Israel, I have created them as Israel, starting in 1948 AD and forever,

94 And Israel, shall in these days, also return onto all Biblical true land, that is recorded as Israel forever. And I (God), shall, now roar out of Zion, against you, eternally forever true.

95 And I do roar against thee O Ishmael, and against thy helping true nations. That are unrepentiful true nations of the earth, that are seen as being unrepentiful in true wickedness, forever. And that wickedness, it is demonstrated against me (God), forever true.

96 And I (God) do, most certainly, therefore, do utter these judgments from my new Jerusalem, as a eternal true shaking against you O Ishmael and against thy helping true nations, forever.

97 Make those decisions, wisely. For the sun and the moon, they are darkened against thee, forever. And they are darkened, as end time judgments, unto you, eternally forever true and forever more.

98 And are darkened by me (God) through Jesus Christ, forever true. And is, until thou shalt repent, in Christ Jesus, eternally forever true and forever seen.

99 In this, new day, arise O Israel and thresh forever, against all that shall come against thee as a thief in the night vision that are them that are called utter true shame,

100 And they are seen as being unrepentiful true ones, who are them that are of the fallen true earth, forever true and forever seen,

101 They do come, to destroy thee, O Israel. But I (God) Am come, that thou mayest, by my hand, that is called Christ Jesus forever. That thou mayest thresh,

102 All of thine true enemies, forever. And thou shalt thresh the heathen, even as wheat is threshed forever.

103 And this Son, who is called Jesus Christ. He (Christ Jesus) shall most surely, grind them to powder. And that is, forever.

104 And thou, O Israel, thou shalt return with Christ, into thy land. As Christ being thy king, eternally forever and ever true, and forever.

105 Therefore, consider all these things, forever, O Israel. For they shall be unto thee, forever true. As thy horn, being made as iron.

106 And I will also make, thy hoofs. As hoofs of brass, that are hoofs that are made in a furnace that burneth with fire.

107 And thou, O Israel. Thy shalt beat in peaces, many unrepentiful true peoples, and unrepentiful true nations, that are ungrateful true nations,

108 That are wicked true nations, that are seen by me (God) and found by me (God). As being wickedly against, both me (God) and against you. And this is eternally forever true.

109 And after, that great end of the age, great battle. Those of Ishmael and of the world, that have survived after being in the battle,

110 If they do desire, to be repentful in their lives, by accepting Jesus Christ. As Christ Jesus, being their personal true savior, forever true.

111 Then they shall be considered unto me forever, as being consecrated unto me (God) forever true. When they have received, Christ Jesus. As Christ Jesus being their personal true savior, forever.

112 And in these last days of the earth forever, I shall be exalted above the hills of Israel forever, and I shall create my mountain of my house forever,

113 And is created unto thee, as Christ Jesus forever and unto the repentful ones of the fallen true earth forever. For I do create new Jerusalem,

114 As Jerusalem rejoicing and with great walls of eternal true joy that is found given of me (God), through Christ Jesus. Unto all of the earth, forever true and forever seen, in the earth, eternally forever true.

115 And at the valley of Jehoshaphat, I do judge Among many peoples, nations, kindred's, and tongues. And it is there, that I shall rebuke for Zion's sake and for my (God) sake,

116 All unrepentiful, true, beastly eternal true nations. With death and great destruction, that is from me (God), eternally forever.

117 And I (God) shall rebuke those peoples, and I (God) shall even give their seen false idols, wormwood that is called God in judgment unto them forever,

118 And it is there, that I (God) shall make those false idols and their priests and their followers, fall in death and great destruction, forever.

119 And their false idols, shall never rise again, to be seen in the fallen true earth, forever true.

120 And through, these end of the days, last true judgments. It is that the heathen may learn to not lift up the sword of war against the true nations of the fallen true earth, forever.

121   And every man shall learn of Christ Jesus and by partaking of the salvation from me (God) as Christ Jesus, that all men may learn war no more and every man shall sit under his own true vine, that he has made as his own true life, forever.

122   These things, they are so, O Israel. And even now, hast thou not understood, that I have assembled thee as Israel again and forever. And thou was once seen,

123   As seen in the earth, as exiled from thy true land, as being halteth of and by me (God), forever. And thou was halted by me, until 1948 AD.

124   And thou hast by my (God) own eternal true power, that is called Christ Jesus. Thou hast returned unto all of Israel forever.

125   Therefore, thou must perform the true oath concerning thy land O Israel, with me (God) forever. And thou must go and obtain all Biblical true land, forever true.

126   For if thou shalt not perform, the oath quickly at this time of the true earth, forever. Then I (God) shall go forth, to bring to pass, that great oath, forever.

127   Therefore, O Israel, is it not better to perform the oath, than for me (God), to perform

it for you, saith thy God, in my (God) Son, who is called Christ Jesus, forever.

128 But know ye this day, that the mouth of the lord of hosts, doth command you, O Israel, to now to perform the true oath, least I (God) move upon thee and upon thy enemies, to make you perform that eternal and most true oath, eternally forever.

129 Yea the mountains of the earth do quake in all that is me (God), as I (God) Am found as Christ Jesus eternally forever. And I (God) shall brandish my (God) great sword,

130 As dipped in the blood of my (God) enemies, who are found as the unrepentiful true nations, who are found in the earth eternally forever,

131 And they, the unrepentiful nations. They shall rise no more and forever, and I (God) Am God, eternally forever true and forever seen.

132 And in the hand of myself forever, is the life called man forever, and I (God) shall repay all, who chose unrepentfulness as eternally forever true of themselves, forever.

133 And the earth is being dissolved of her true seen sins, for the earth, is being burned up in the fire, and in the jealously, that is my (God) own, eternal, true wrath, forever true.

134 And my (God) wrath, it is found, as heavenly true fire. That is from me (God), and is of me (God), forever true and forever seen. In the fallen true earth, forever true.

135 That fire, it is called Christ Jesus, unto the unrepentiful true nations. As eternally forever and forever, eternally forever true.

136 Yea, the world is being burned up, in the wrath of my (God) end time judgments, forever true. And I (God) shall give that true death, unto whom, death is forever, due unto.

137 And in my (God) indignation, is seen my (God) law, that is called Christ Jesus, eternally forever true.

138 And the fierceness of mine own anger, as found given of myself, in these true days. These days, shall therefore, deliver unto me (God) forever, a sweet true odor, that is the earth receiving Christ eternally forever.

139 And I (God) Am true and I (God) Am a true stronghold forever. That stronghold, it is found given of myself through Christ Jesus, against this day of turmoil and trouble, that is seen forever true.

140 And, in me (God), is the life of repentful true men, forever. And that life, it is called God as found in Christ Jesus, eternally forever true.

141 And as a overrunning flood, is end time judgments found in this earth, forever. And now, I (God) shall make a true end, of this fallen true world, that is found in true iniquity, forever.

142 And in my (God) eternal true fury, that fury shall rise in my (God) face, And that face is called Christ Jesus. And I (God) shall deliver the world unto myself (God) forever true, and is delivered unto me (God) for end time judgment,

143 And the world, is delivered unto me (God), forever. And is delivered until this image of beastly eternal true men, has came to a final true close, forever, saith thy eternal one, who is seen and called, God forever and ever true, for I (God) Am God, forever.

144 Now, let's proceed unto the aftermath of that great end of the age--great battle. That is called "The Valley OF Decision."

Part 3 W / 148 verses   **MY hand**

1 O Israel, they (heathen non Christian nations) do come unto thee in this generation, but fear thou not, nor look upon their despair, when I (God) shall destroy them. Pity them not, for they pitied thee not, saith thy true God, as being eternally forever and ever true.

2 Therefore, pity them not, while thou slayeth them by my hand that is called "End of the age,

great just judgment," forever. But have mercy upon them,

3   As to who shall be allowed to escape by my hand, as they escape that great end time great battle. As, to live of themselves again. In Biblical true Israel, as to live forever under thy national direction through me forever.

4   And you shall receive them in all of the national Biblical true Israel, as thy war captives and non Israeli civil captives forever. And do accept all of them unto thy self and teach them all, as it is found. As it is concerning myself, in thee and in Christianity, forever.

5   And, when thou shalt take and be taking all Biblical true land, again. As to be Israel to be found forever, in all of her seen, Biblical true land, forever.

6   Then many of these non Israeli's. They shall flee away from thee and will desire to depart to other countries, as thou are then obtaining all of thy Biblical true land, forever.

7   (As a note-- from here and onward: "It is dealing with non hardest cases and hardest cases," as it is found forever. As concerning the war captives and non Israeli civil captives.)

8   Now, those that can't escape thee, O Israel. Then these are war captives and non Israeli civil

captives unto thee. And thou O Israel, thou shalt only allow those captives of Ishmael, who are found on Biblical true Israeli land,

9 To remain on Israeli Biblical true land forever, as to when those war captives and non Israeli civil captives, have taken the eternal true oath, to me. By speaking that true oath,

10 That they truly do in fact, forever. Do fully accept me and Christianity, fully forever true, and as long as they (captives) renounce (to swear oath publicly to Israel), all that is Islam, openly and publicly, in the eyes of the entire world, publicly forever.

11 Therefore, these that taketh the eternal sworn Godly true oath--They must swear publicly, forever. And each spoken oath, it must be fully heard and seen fully by a panel of 12 Israeli Christly witnesses-- that are from a number of panels of 12 persons each panel.

12 And if they swear not, then thou mayest and shall permanently exile, all non hardest cases from all of Israeli Biblical true land, forever.

13 And, thou shalt place all hardest cases into camp internment, forever. Again, this shall be forever, only to those who are found to be forever: "Hardest true cases of Israeli war captives and hardest true cases of non Israeli civil captives."

14   And, to gain a full release pardon from camp internment, then non hardest case captives. They must perform my eternal oath to me and to you, forever.

15   And they must satisfy thee, as it is concerning their trustworthiness to Israel. But you cannot release any and all hardest cases of war captives and hardest cases of non Israeli civil captives into Israeli Biblical true land, forever.

16   Whosoever is a non hardest case in Israel, and will not ever swear oath to me and to you, Israel. Then they shall fall into exile, forever. And they shall never be allowed to return to Israel, again.

17   And, if it be found, that they are a hardest war captive or a hardest non Israeli civil captive. Then you shall intern to internment camp, that one, forever.

18   Again, as to when hardest cases are found in not taking the true eternal kindly oath, that is to be spoken and preformed to me-- forever, and secondly: As to when these war captives and non Israeli civil one's actions. Do show all of Israel and do show unto all of Israeli land, forever,

19   That these war captives and non Israeli civil captives, are found to be hard hearted against all of Israel, forever. And this is seen to me forever, in their behavior and speech, eternally forever.

20   Then those are hardest cases to me and to you, O Israel. And they shall never be set free, and this shall be forever. For these are found to have chosen to not accept Israel nationality and Israel law, forever.

21   Non hardest cases. If they swear not to me and not to you, O Israel. Then, those non swearing true captives. Each and all of them. Shall be forever,

22   Exiled from Israel forever, and you shall have no pity on them. But before exiling. You will give each war captive and each non Israeli civil captive. A Godly eternal true witness, as to be given as in materials and such, as it is teaching them about Jesus and thy eternal land oath with me, forever.

23   And, that I have recorded these things, in scripture. And that do show that Israel shall be found forever, in all of her true land, forever. Therefore show them Bible teaching, before they gain their freedom, true release.

24   And in so doing, is that they the heathen, may learn to never seek war again and forever. And therefore, a day will come, when many shall convert to Christianity, forever.

25   And exiling is because these heathen ones. They have had no pity on you and they have

desired thy true death and thy true removal from what is Israel and Israel land, to me, forever.

26 And, if any non hardest case war captives or non hardest non Israeli civil captives are found on Biblical true Israeli land, that do willingly and knowingly, perform my oath to me and unto you Israel, and if they have and do prove to Israel-- their loyalty, to Israel, forever.

27 Then, they (non hardest cases) can obtain their freedom to leave Israel and or to have Israeli citizenship by their personal choice. And to obtain Israeli citizenship. Then these heathen war and non Israeli civil captives.

28 They must be made to be swear openly their oath to me and to you. As it is to be found preformed by them to me, as a public true oath to me and to the world, forever.

29 That oath, is eternal to me forever. And they (non hardest cases) must swear to me and to you, Israel. And they must publicly accept Jesus Christ forever. As this Jesus being their national savior, forever.

30 And they (non hardest cases) must become-- Christian--Israeli citizens-- forever. And they must renounce Islam--- publicly forever. And that is to be done to thy expectations and satisfaction--forever.

31 And these must show forth all creditability of themselves. To satisfy their assigned of Israel-- 12 panel Christly judges of Israel, who shall righteously judge these war captives and non Israeli civil captives, forever.

32 Therefore, if a non hardest case, refuse's to take my (God) oath. Then thou shalt not release any of those war captives or non Israeli civil captive escapees from that great end of the age-- great battle, into any of the Israeli true land, forever. But you can exile them, from all of Israel land, forever.

33 Again, without performing eternal true oath unto me forever. Then thou shalt not release any non hardest war captive and no non hardest heathen civil populations person's, as being fully released into any of thy Biblical seen true land, forever.

34 But they that performeth and taketh my seen oath openly and publicly forever. And that do these things to Israeli's satisfaction, forever.

35 Then these non hardest war captives and non hardest civil populations. They can be forever, found forever: On Israeli Biblical true land. And they must be fully educated in their heritage, that is seen as being: "Israeli customs, and education, and the like."

36 And they must receive Israeli education, as it is found as concerning their heritage, as it is found in me through Christ Jesus, forever. For many of these war captives and their captive heathen populations. They are of Abraham thy forefather, forever.

37 And thou must destroy all and each of their Islam synagogues and all that is Islam, forever. Even their Islam books and Islam tapes and Islam computer discs and all that is Islam-- It shall be destroyed and burned and such-- forever.

38 You shall not allow, Islam material to ever be found, whole again, in Israel forever. You shall destroy it most surely, eternally forever, as saith thy eternal, kind God, forever true.

39 And when a released war captive or released non Israeli civil captive. Is found in Israel land, to be religious. They can only hold to Jewish Christianity, forever. But, if they continue to hold unto any other religion (accept Jewish Christianity--forever) such as Islam, in the nation of Israel.

40 Then that crime that is concerning a released war captive or a released non Israeli civil captive. It is shall punishable with life time internment, forever. And thou O Israel. Thou shalt not pity these--who are of Islam death, forever. As saith, thy eternal kind God-- forever.

41   Now, as concerning hardest cases. As they are found in active camp internment. As to when, they accept Jesus Christ, as Jesus being their savior, as being forever true. If they, that is, if any of those hardest cases,

42   Do repent, at any time, in active camp internment, to thy satisfaction. As to renounce their non Jewish Christian religion, such as renouncing Islam, openly forever. Then accept these repentful hardest cases and help them to learn about me--the God of Abraham, forever.

43   Then you shall release and monitor for 3 years or more. Any and all release's, that are a released hardest case. Who is found forever. To be a fully repentful in Jesus Christ, hardest case. And, again, as provided,

44   That they have sworn and proved to thee, forever. That their loyalty to Israel, is sworn and proved by them, as being eternally forever and ever true.

45   But, if after being found as being a released hardest case. That is a released war captive or a released non Israeli civil captive. Who is found to be a released, rehabilitated war captive or rehabilitated non Israeli civil captive,

46   And who is found to be, now returned to their former true sin in being found in non Jewish Christianity (to be a Christian--it is to be Jewish

through being eternally forever--being grafted into Jewish ness--through Jesus Christ being one's savior -- forever), as to be found in another religion, forever, such as Islam.

47   Then, these released hardest case war captives or hardest cases non Israeli civil captives. They shall be punished with life time captivity in camp internment-- again, and forever. And they shall not be ever released again and forever.

48   Therefore, they shall die in internment, forever. Even if they say they have converted once again in and to Jesus Christ. Those cannot be trusted to do right by Israel and right by me, again and forever.

49   They have, wrongfully denied me, forever-- as in to never serving me in Jesus Christ, forever.

50   And they are returned to being religious without me-- as me (God) being not their savior, who is called-- forever-- Jesus Christ. But, as concerning my people, Israel-- who do love me and have not yet accepted Jesus Christ as their savior,

51   They shalt be exempted from this law--while I Am helping Israel--that Israel-- mayest accept and learn about this Jesus Christ, who is Israel's true savior, forever. And truly, Christ Jesus, he is

thy messiah O Israel--- and I have sent him to you, forever.

52 And you may most surely, release the hardest case heathen repentful captives and hardest case repentful non Israeli civil ones. As long as these war captives and war-- non Israeli civil captives---have proven unto thee, forever, O Israel,

53 That they are not in false religion, forever and have sworn oath unto me-- publicly, and as being forever seen, and have accepted Jesus Christ, as this Jesus, being their seen savior, forever. And is Jesus who is given by me, as being eternally faithfully forever and ever true, saith God.

54 And, then, these hardest cases. They are forgiven of their true seen sin. And they shall return free unto and in Biblical true Israel or into any of the world, forever.

55 But if they (hardest cases) shall not renounce Islam. They shall not be released into Israel and they shall not be released into any of the world, forever.

56 And if Israel shalt feel, that any one release---is not righteously in order, for that true release of anyone particular true person, at that time, who is found under thy martial law, at that time of the earth,

57 Then thou shalt not release that particular hardest case true person. But, thou shalt look upon that non repenting hardest case person, as a prisoner unto thee, forever.

58 And thou mayest permanently exile forever-- any non hardest cases, that refuseth to swear my oath -- to Israel and to me (God), forever.

59 Again, O Israel. Thou must not release forever-- any of the hardest war captives and the hardest non Israeli civil captives. As to when they are found unto thee forever,

60 As being eternally found--- to not ever to partake forever--as in not partaking forever-- of my (God) Godly true oath and their behavior and speech is found in being anti Israel forever. Then these, they shall be thy captive war and non Israeli civil captive prisoners-- unto thee-- forever.

61 And those captive war and non Israeli civil captive prisoners-- thou shalt make to perform labors and duties to thee-- forever. That they may be able to be supported finically by thee-- forever.

62 And, as to why these shall perform work, forever. It is because these can never be trusted again, to never make war with Israel and with the world, ever again and forever true.

63 For if these hardest cases were exiled from all of Israel and from all of Biblical true Israel, forever. Then these may try to come to back to Israel, to make war with Israel again, and with the world, again.

64 And if any captive or released captive-- shall kill another person as in knowingly and willfully done. Then they shall give their life for death, forever.

65 And thou O Israel, you shall take that captive one's life in the place of the life that the captive one, killed, as when the captive did that taking as: "Being knowingly and willfully, done by them, forever,"

66 You shall not prolong that life after they have pursued all their reasonable appeals to thee. For the captive's life, shall be given to me in place of the one that the captive, did kill, knowingly and willfully, forever.

67 But in the cases of victim death, that is done accidentally by a captive (whether non hardest case captive or hardest case captive-- while in internment or has been released from internment),

68 That results forever in death to another person. Then any true captive that committeth unwillfully and unknowingly, that true death (wasn't on purpose).

69 Then you shall excuse such persons from that seen mandatory true deathly judgment, that is seen in those issues, forever. And you shall judge those persons, in lesser true circles of judgment,

70 That is if judgment should be needed, forever. And you shall also judge righteously, when a captive has and or is committing crimes against humanity or against Israel, while the captive is still a true captive of Israel or a released true captive of Israel.

71 And in a true case of accidental death done by a captive or by a released captive of Israel. You shall then, not charge criminally. But you may bring forth other lesser circles of judgments, such as an example, in neglect and so forth.

72 If a war captive or a non Israeli civil captive or a released war captive or a released non Israeli civil captive. Has committed willful and true, knowingly true death,

73 Then, if that war captive or non Israeli civil captive or released war captive or released non Israeli civil captive, shall have assets. Then all that is the war captive's or non Israeli civil captive's or released war captive's or released non Israeli civil captive's,

74 It shall now belong to all of Israel, forever. In that Israel may give all of that acquired wealth

unto all of the victims of these war and non Israeli non Israeli civil captives,

75 As to when these war captives or non Israeli civil captives have committed willingly true death-- knowingly forever. And, all collected monies and wealth-- it is for the victims, forever. And that shall be placed all into one general fund for all victims, forever.

76 And mandatory true judgment, for knowingly and willingly true murder. It shall still require, life for life and blood for blood, and assets for victims, forever. And there is no escape from this judgment that is concerning committed willful and true murder, forever.

77 And, just as the war captive, or non Israeli civil captive heathen, has cared not about his or hers victims and their victims families. Therefore, the captive when found guilty in such willful and true murder,

78 Then all of their (captives') public and personal true assets (only what is the captives and not the family own assets -- And you O Israel shall make inventory of family assets and such to make sure what was the captive's is now given to the victims of these captives),

79 Shall fall unto Israel, forever. And nothing shall be left for the captives family. The captives

family shall fend for it's self, without the finical help from the captive, forever.

80 This is because the captive was willing to do the same to Israel, as to when the war captive, or non Israeli civil captive had killed another person,

81 While that true war captive or non Israel civil captive was either: One-- a war captive prisoner to Israel or a released war captive prisoner. And secondly-- was a non Israeli civil true captive prisoner of Israel, or a released non Israeli civil true prisoner of Israel.

82 And in doing these things--it is: That all war captives and non Israeli civil captives-- may learn to not abuse Israel and not to abuse the world--any longer and forever.

83 And, that they may learn to refrain from war-- forever and from their sins-- As thou shalt teach them diligently forever--as to who I Am in thee O Israel. And as to who I Am in Christ Jesus thy savior and who (Christ Jesus) their savior, forever.

84 And thou shalt teach them Christ Jesus and Jewish heritage forever. And I will at that time, I will have already placed together--A program for these war captives and non Israeli civil captives-- so that thou wilt know. As to who shall be

released and not released into Israel land and not released into the world.

85 Thy prisoners shall not be mistreated by thee--forever. But you shall work to diligently--to reverse their lack of proper knowledge in knowing me in Christ Jesus thy savior O Israel.

86 And you shall teach them Jewish heritage forever and my customs. And you shall teach them, all that is me--as I Am found in your Christian torah Bible-- O Israel.

87 Now--as concerning these war captives and non Israeli civil captives having children while in thy camp education centers and the like.

88 If, both of the parents of a said child--Are found to be placed by Israel law-- forever--in internment. Because both of those parents have been found as a ruled and found guilty-- Israeli legal "hardest true case,"

89 As for being found to be forever--as being found guilty Among--- hardest cases. That are found, in being against: "Israel having their land oath with me, as Israel's right to exist as a nation, by me forever."

90 Then, if both captive parents. Whether, war captives or non Israeli civil captives-- If they shall have children or do have then children, while being a captive--

91 Then if they have any, said child or children--while under serving their lifetime true internment, because of being found guilty and being placed to serve in internment forever.

92 Then thou shalt, separate forever. These children from their war captive parents or non Israeli civil captive parents. And Israel and the world, shall help to fully educate these children forever.

93 And when-- these children-- Who have become legally: "Parentless in my eyes—forever." Israel shall take them for Israeli citizens and teach them me--and about their Christian and Jewish heritage. And those children-- thou shalt arrange their adoption to Israeli citizenship--forever.

94 But any child, that is legally deemed forever, by Israeli law. To be found to be a wanting anti Israeli citizen, forever. Then you shall treat such child, as if that child, was an adult war captive or a non Israeli civil captive.

95 And they shall fall under the same terms as being judged, as if they were an actual, adult, forever. This is begins at the age of 12-- and forever.

96 And if only one parent is found to serve for life, because they are found guilty in being a true hardest issue true case, forever. Then thou shalt

release the said child and or children of said parents, unto the released one--who is a war captive parent or a non Israeli civil parent, forever.

97 If both parents are serving internment (whether life or not). Israel shall educate these children fully in Israeli customs and heritage and the like.

98 And you, O Israel. You shall not discriminate between an Israeli child and the captive parent child (remember, many of these captive children. They are of Abraham thy fore father, forever).

99 Again, as each captive is released from internment. Then thou mayest reunite these children with their released captive parent or released captive parents.

100 And Israel shall be legally responsible for these children. Then Israel must forever: "Teach these children-- torah and Israeli customs and such, forever.

101 And in the hardest true cases. As to when both captive true parents are found guilty against all of Israel land existence forever,

102 Then their children. You shall make them, forever. True citizens of Israel. As to when they have proved. That they are eternally found worthy of Israeli citizenship, forever.

103 In these days O Israel. Thou O Israel, must also teach thy seed (refugees to Israel from other lands of the earth) that shall seek to be Israeli citizens during that great war. That they must upon entering Israel, forever.

104 That they must perform and swore the same oath of loyalty to me as the war captive and non Israeli civil captives do swear to me in that day for entrance into Israeli citizenship-- forever.

105 And Israel, ye shall diligently teach the war captives and non Israeli civil captives, as they are found in Biblical true Israel,

106 As to why I do these things to the captives, forever. And it is because the heathen has bought my judgment upon themselves forever, and it is not on Israel, forever.

107 And ye shall show that this end of the age great end time battle was foretold to occur by me forever. And that as I have promised my righteousness in all the earth forever, so then have I now been completing the promise as I have made it to my servant David as an example.

108 And, if thou, O Israel, shalt not do all of these things, that I speak unto you forever true, as being righteousness forever,

109 Then, I (God) shall correct you as a non repenting true nation, forever, and it shall remain

upon thee forever. Until thou repenteth unto me, for being cruel unto the heathen. For thou must set an true example of myself, unto the world, forever, as through Christ Jesus. forever.

110   Therefore work with the repentful war captives and repentful non Israeli civil captives of Ishmael. And deliver the unholy Ishmael hardest cases. That are found eternally forever,

111   As they are found, in being eternally forever. As being against Israel to exist forever, and deliver those war and non Israeli civil captives to thy camp internments, forever.

112 And that shall happen. If internment shall be found to be needed in any one or more, particular true cases.

113   And thou shalt, show and diligently teach, these Ishmael heathen. Who are seen, as being: "War captives and non Israeli civil captives of Israel," Biblical true scripture, forever,

114   Therefore, teach in thy internments, mandatory true Biblical true scripture. That the heathen, may truly depart forever, the image of the beast, as the beast is unrepentiful true men, as they are found in Satan death, forever.

115 And thou shalt release the repenting worthy ones into the Israeli land forever, if they shall

take the oath and have proved satisfactory to thy pleasing, that they are worthy of my release.

116 And anyone (war captive and non Israeli civil captive), who taketh life, purposely in Israel, after their release from internment. They shall give their life, as life for life. And thou shalt not pity them, for they pitied thee not, nor did they have pity on the land, that is called Israel.

117 And in during all of these things, thou shalt have put away from thy selves, as being forever true. True evil, that had been formed against thee, as being forever true.

118 All Christian nations shall help thee fully in these matters, least I place judgment upon them, that forsaketh thee. Therefore, anyone, particular true Christian nation, that shall not be helpful, fully unto thee, forever,

119 Then I shall deal fully with that Christian true nation. Till that true Christian nation, shall conform unto this law. That I do give unto you, forever. And that I do give unto the world, as being forever true of myself, forever.

120 Thou shalt appoint panels of 12 people each panel, as being seen, Christly filled judges, per panel. As they judge forever, the war captive and non Israeli civil captive internees. That I may help thee to know, who is truly, rehabilitated,

121   Therefore, when a war captive or a non Israeli civil captive detainee. Shall pass that 12 judge Christly panel board, by a 10 or more true vote, then thou shall release such said person into the thy land, as being truly free.

122   But, in being free, thou mayest yet, for a period of three years, keep such released person under true martial probation.

123   Then, as being free. The same laws shall also apply to all of those once war captives and non Israeli civil captives. As to when they had been placed into camp internment.

124   And to when, if these war captives or non Israeli civil captives. As having had been released from camp internment. Have then: "Committed willful and knowingly true death to an Israeli citizen or Israeli citizens.

125   The same willful and knowingly death requirement. It shall apply to acquirements. For war captives and non Israeli civil captives, to be remain released as a probationary war captive or a probationary non Israeli civil captive of Israel.

126   But, thou, O Israel: "Thou shalt not release any war captive or non Israeli civil captive person after their serving that three years," if it be seen, that said person has not fully, within reason. Done unto thy expected true expectation, to be released fully into Israel land, forever.

127 These that are to be released on the tree year probationary term. These must, perform my oath unto me, in being thy faithful true brother, forever,

128 And in performing oath to me and to Israel, forever. Then that war captive or non Israeli civil captive. That one, must say publicly in the eyes of the world. That they will accept you, forever. As they are seen before my seeing true presents, that is called life, forever.

129 And they must publicly and openly conform to be Israeli citizenship forever. As to when that person is found, to be found released by Israel forever--upon any land, that is seen as being Israel, Biblically forever.

130 And they must record with Israel-- their spoken and written true oath that is to Israel. And it is to be found, forever. In their own true hand writing, to Israel, forever.

131 And this to be written and to be a spoken true oath to me and to Israel. And it must be witnessed by the 12 Christly judges panel, that are fully assigned to their case, for their personal release from camp internment, forever.

132 And You shall not prolong any release from camp internment. As to when it is reasonable to occur by the hand of Israel.

133 And the Christian world and Christian nations. They are to help you (Israel) do these things. That the world, may truly, beat their plowshares of eternal seen hope to me, forever.

134 As it being a beated hope into Godly true swords of Godly true Christly true righteousness, that is called God forever.

135 And that hope, it is given eternally forever true. As it is given faithfully by me, forever. As it is found, even now given of me forever. As it is found through Jesus Christ, my Son, forever.

136 And, as it is now given, of me, forever. As even being a end of the days-- eternal seen, true salvation. That salvation, it is given of me through Jesus the Son, forever.

137 And that true salvation. It is for all men, everywhere. And it is given, faithfully of me, forever. As it is given, unto all of the people of the earth, forever, as saith, thy eternal, kind and loving true God, as being eternally and righteously-- as forever said, and seen by me, forever.

138 And if any war captive or non Israeli civil captive-- hardest case. Shall receive Jesus Christ. As this Jesus being their savior, forever. And has proven satisfactory to thy pleasing, O Israel, forever that they are truly changed unto thee forever and unto me forever.

139 And if they have also preformed my oath and etc. Then you shall give a full pardon to that repented one forever. And they shall be set free from their active camp internment center, forever. Even into Biblical true Israel, forever.

140 And if Israel has taken wealth from a war or civil captive. Then thou shalt restore that wealth reasonably unto them, forever. As long that wealth, that they had,

141 Wasn't gained to them, by them hurting Israeli property and or killing people in Israel. Same holds true-- if it was done by them, anywhere else in the world, also.

142 But those to be released, war captives and non Israeli civil captives. You may monitor them each, for a period of three years or more, as thou shalt determine righteously, in that true issue, through me. As it is found, then through my 12 Christly panel Judges, who are of the panels of Israeli law judges, forever.

143 But if the released one from internment-- shall kill again and or damage Israeli true property, to keep Israel from being a nation again. Then, that full pardon will not cover-- then committed true murder and or purposed damage to destroy Israel from being a nation, again and forever.

144 Israel shall not keep these internees alive when they have committed true murder. And you shall not exchange any seen true terrorists for thy Israeli people, in a unfair exchange of people for people. And hardest cases shall never be allowed by me to be exchanged forever.

145 Now, concerning the child or children of the hardest cases. When it is seen that the once legal parent or once legal parents is being released by Israel.

146 If the child or children has already been adopted out to be Israeli citizen, forever. Then these children shall remain Israeli adoptees of Israel, forever.

147 And those children shall not return, as a legal child, to the once captive parent or captive parents, at all and forever.

148 And that is because I shall not place these children back into non Israeli status, forever. They are apart of Israel land and it's seen true heritage, in me, forever.

Part 4 w 171 verses   They that worship the image of the beast

1 This entire part 4. It is seen, as being newly written, prophetic true works of true spirit. And those works, they are seen from God and are of God, eternally forever true.

2   And those works, that are from God, through Christ Jesus. They are concerning the repentful of the earth. And are concerning them, who are found in the beastly eternal image, that is the beast, called unrepentiful man, forever.

3   The fallen number of sinful man, is the fallen number of himself, as he is seen as the unrepentiful true beast. As he is found in eternal true death, as being eternally forever true and forever more.

4   My (God) prophetic, most true, unsealed and unclosed, true works. They are of myself (God), as I Am God forever true and forever seen. And they are seen, as found occurring of myself (God), in Christ Jesus, eternally forever true.

5   And those works, they are called God forever. And they are found of myself (God), through Christ Jesus, in the earth, eternally forever seen and forever felt, as forever true and forever more.

6   And those works, they are found, according as I have written, as concerning them to occur, in the earth, as forever true, and are forever unsealed Biblical true scriptures, that are found of my (God) word and of my (God) unwritten true words, forever.

7   And those words and word, they are called God. And they are found, in both, the Bible and found in my seven true thunders that wasn't

written by me, but had been sealed by me, in Christ Jesus, eternally forever,

8   Those things are in these days of the earth, unsealed and unclosed forever. And the church and the world it's self, are all witnesses unto that most eternal, true fact, forever.

9   And because of the unsealed ness and unclosed ness forever, the beast shall come to knowledge, that the beast will perish forever, unless, they the beast, shall repent and receive Christ Jesus, as it's eternal lord and true savior, forever.

10 For in today's world, these things of unsealed ness and unclosed ness, they are being written of myself, and demonstrated of myself (God), unto them of the earth, forever.

11 And are unsealed and unclosed forever, and they are concerning the true world, and they are now seen and are being seen by today's generation, that is, the entire, true world, forever true,

12 And is seen as unsealed scriptures that are seen by today's true earth forever, and it is shown, that through unsealed spiritual interpretation of scriptures,

13 Is that, our true world, is learning desired true righteousness, that is from our true God, forever.

And is found, as given unto us, forever, through Jesus Christ, as eternally forever true.

14 Those prophetic, unsealed, true works. They are seen, as unsealed true works of God, in Christ forever true. And those works, they are found to Israel forever, and unto the whole earth, forever,

15 And as these works, are demonstrated of God, in the earth, through Jesus Christ, our lord and savior. It is, that the beast shall come to understand, that they must not partake of the beastly eternal true damnation,

16 That is called "The worship of eternal, true, unrepentiful true death, forever," For they, the unrepentiful, that do desire unrepentfully,

17 That damningly true image, of earnest and sincere, true death forever. They shall most certainly perish, in hell, eternally forever and ever true, forever.

18 Moreover, in these days, all newly unsealed prophetic written true works. They are most certainly, being newly prophetically written. In our today's, true earth, forever.

19 And they are being truly written by the spirit of God, as found in his eternal true Son, forever. His Son, he is called, Jesus Christ, forever and ever true.

20   And as to why these unsealed prophetic scriptures are being prophetically written in our today's true world. It is found through spiritual interpretation of unsealed scriptures. As according to happen as found in our King James, everyday, true Bible.

21   These are newly unsealed written true works, of the spirit of God, as found in Christ forever. And they were prophesied of God, to occur, in the end of the days, timeframe of the earth, eternally forever true.

22   And they are seen, as unsealed newly written prophetic true works. That are found, given by our precious and true God, from the ark of his true Testament,

23   As found from heaven above, and is found of God, as given of God, into the hearts of repentful true men, through Christ Jesus, eternally forever and ever true of God, "The Father," forever.

24   But unto they, that worship the true image of the dragon, that is called Satanism forever. They shall most surely die unto me forever, and in hell, their name and mark of Satan, shall not help them in hell forever.

25   But as concerning these writings, that are from the unsealed ness and unclosed ness, that is sent from myself (God), forever. They were prophesied of myself (God), to occur in today's

earth and generation, forever true and forever more.

26 And is noted in Biblical scriptures, of long ago. That unsealed ness and unclosed ness, they were to occur in this present time, of our fallen true earth, forever sure and forever more, as unsealed and unclosed by me, in Christ, eternally forever sure and forever true.

27 And it is, that these newly written prophetic true works. They were and are, to be seen by the whole world, in this true generation. And in this generation, it is called "the end of the days" timeframe, of the earth, eternally forever true.

28 We, who are the body of Christ, we shall see our true Christ, as he is seen in our true day, as declaring through the openness of the temple in heaven.

29 These newly written and being written, true prophetic true works. That are given of God, through Christ Jesus, eternally forever, and is given unto the body of Christ, and unto the whole world, without true measure, eternally forever and ever true.

30 And it is, also, that Biblical true knowledge, shall be increased through out, the entire true earth, forever seen. And many shall run to and fro,

31 In Biblical true knowledge. Because of the open little book, that is found and seen, in the angel's hand, as found recorded of our true and kind God, in Revelation 10:2.

32 And that, open little true book. It is now, found eternally forever true, as opened and being opened in our time of days, according to The Book of Revelation.

33 And that true openness, it is seen and is from the temple of God, And is from, God himself, in Christ Jesus, eternally forever and ever true and forever more.

34 And is found opened of our true and kind one, who is called "OUR GOD FOREVER." And is opened unto us forever true and forever more.

35 That open true book, is now to be to be prophesied again, before many peoples, and before many true nations, and before many true tongues, and before many true kings, forever.

36 And the beast, shall be prophesied unto forever, concerning God's wrath, that is demonstrated through Christ Jesus, unto the damned, eternally forever true and forever seen and felt from God forever,

37 And is felt as eternal just judgment, that shall not be quenched on the earth and shall not be quenched in hell forever.

38 Therefore, the only true escape, shall be and is, accepting Christ in this world, as one's eternal, true savior, eternally forever true.

39 And without Christ, as Christ being one's true savior from God forever. Then death, it is eternally forever seen, as granted true death, forever granted,

40 And true death, it is granted unto them, as they the unrepentiful of the fallen true earth forever,

41 Are found of themselves worshipping the false beastly image of eternal life (their eternal life---is not God's eternal life called Christ Jesus forever),

42 That is found of both, themselves and of the false prophet, who is the false prophet of eternal true lies, forever true.

43 And granted true death, it is given unto them of the beastly eternal true image of beastly eternal true death forever, and is granted most surely,

44 As a granted true death, that is death that is granted as eternally forever true, from me. As forever truly granted of me (God), forever.

45 For these do enjoy their sinfully desired, unrepentfulness, that is found in them, forever certain and forever more.

46 And they are found in their true worship of eternal, seen true death. That death, it is eternally forever true and forever more. As found in themselves, for all of given true eternity, and is, forever true and forever more.

47 And these are seen as themselves, as they are seen as the Antichrist true beast, who are eternally forever true of themselves, as dead death, forever.

48 For these Antichrist true beasts, they do love, to serve the true worship of Satanism, that is forever true and forever more, in them that shall die unto God forever. And they are them, the damned, forever,

49 And they the damned, they are forever seen, as the rejected of God and rejected of Christ Jesus, eternally forever rejected. And they are rejected, for all of given true eternity,

50 And they are forever seen, as dead unto God, and dead unto Christ, eternally forever true and forever more, And they shall be caste out, away

from me (God), eternally forever true, saith thy God, eternally forever and ever true, of me, heavenly forever true.

51 Again, these newly prophetic written works, they are concerning their relationship to Biblical prophecy, and they are now being newly written of God, in the earth, forever. And is found demonstrated through Christ Jesus, eternally forever true.

52 And those works, are through Christ Jesus, as being newly prophetically written. As concerning their relationship, to Biblical scriptures of old, that were to occur and are occurring in the earth, eternally forever true and forever more.

53 And these unsealed newly prophetic written works, they were mentioned of old, to occur in our generation, through Christ, having prevailed in the unsealing them, eternally forever.

54 And they were found, to have occurred, as recorded of our true God and by his dear eternal true Son, forever. And his Son, he is called Christ Jesus,

55 And this Jesus, he is seen as according to the scriptures, as "the lion of the tribe of Judah," the root of David. And this is forever true.

56 Our Christ, is actively declaring (spoken and written utterance) through the openness of the temple in heaven, in our present time of days,

57 These unsealed newly written, true prophetic, thundering, uttered, spiritual and physical, true works. That are from and of God, eternally forever true and forever more.

58 And that declaring, it is seen as the seven true voices of God, as thundering in and through Christ Jesus, eternally forever true.

59 And they are seen and felt, as the pearls of Godly true thunder. And they are, heavenly true pearls, of thundering eternal, unsealed ness and unclosed ness, eternally forever true.

60 And what is declared, by our true God, in Christ Jesus forever. It is seen and felt, as uttered, unsealed, newly written, and being newly written,

61 As prophetic true works, that are from God, in Christ, eternally forever true and forever more. And shall always be, seen in and of God, eternally forever true.

62 And are, most surely, from God himself, in Christ Jesus. As eternally forever and ever true, and are forever more. And are seen, even as: "EVER LASTINGLY TRUE" forever.

63 Heavenly true thunder, that is from God in Christ Jesus, forever true. It is lightning seen, as being openly declared by the shaking of Christ's hand, in the earth.

64 And that shaking, it is found in our true generation, given by the spirit of God, through Christ Jesus. As eternally forever true and forever more.

65 This declaring, of God's eternal, true judgments forever. They are declared by the prophetic lightening true voices, that are the anointed fiery pillars, of God forever,

66 And they are the body of Christ, and they are the church. And the church is found uttering of God, these found, seven true voices of God, that are called, Christ Jesus, forever.

67 And through Christ Jesus, the church shall, prophetically quake the entire world, through the holy spirit, that is found in Christ Jesus, eternally forever.

68 And this quaking, it is found without true measure in openness forever. For Christ Jesus, he shall speak all, that was sealed and was closed, eternally forever.

69 And those, that do utter of God through Christ Jesus, in a true spirit of: "Thus saith the lord," eternally forever. These have no seen true

measure of personal seen sins, within themselves, eternally forever true.

70 And they, shall, most certainly, prophesy in a true spirit of "Thus saith the lord of heaven and earth," eternally forever.

71 And they shall even preach in a prophesying true spirit of God through Christ, as time shall be no longer found in the fallen true earth, forever.

72 And they shall, even preach, Christ Jesus and Christ Jesus crucified, and they shall even preach, eternal end time judgment,

73 And this is eternally forever true of themselves, from me (God), in Christ Jesus, forever. For these are seen and found, as my (God) anointed true chariots, who are of my (God) own, eternal true glory, forever true and forever more.

74 And they are seen, as chosen in Christ. And they are given wholly over to the complete and whole measure, that is me (God) forever.

75 And I, as Lord and Savior, I Am declaring, those opened hail stones of prophetic newly written and being written, true workings. Through the body of Christ, eternally forever true and forever seen, heavenly forever true.

76 And these pillars, of my (God) true fire. They are seen fiery of me, as Christ's spiritual feet. That are found spiritually standing upon the physical sea and upon the physical land, and are them that are seen prophesying unto the earth, forever.

77 And through the body of Christ, my (God) Son called Christ, he (Christ) is performing the Hallowed true oath: "That there should be time no longer," in the earth forever.

78 Therefore, the body of Christ is preaching these prophesying, great hail stones of the heavenly true prophetic true fire, that is found from the altar of myself (God), eternally forever.

79 Those are, most surely, my (God) great given truths, that are concerning my unsealed holy words of scripture, that is given to my (God), today's world.

80 And it is given of me (God), as being eternally forever true. As it is true unto them of the fallen true earth, forever. And it is seen and heard, unto the fallen true beast, in all that I Am, as I Am given of myself, unto Christ Jesus, eternally forever true.

81 And is that the beastly eternal true earth, may repent and be washed in the blood of Christ. For Christ is my (God) Son, who is of me (God), for I (God) Am, the living true God, forever true.

82 And this, only begotten Son, who is of me (God), the living true God, forever. He is called Christ Jesus. And this Christ is full of my (God) eternal true righteousness, forever sure and forever true.

83 But the rejected of me forever, they do love to be sinful in unrepentfulness forever true. And they do follow the false miracles of heavenly true fire,

84 That seemeth to promise eternal true life without the presents of God, but is not eternal true life of God forever. And they that do follow such beguiling. That is given from the hand of the beast and from the hand of the dragon, who is the dragon that is seen as the false prophet of death.

85 They shall die in their sin forever true, and unto me as heavenly forever true. And I will not hear them in hell forever, when they shall ask in hell, for Christ Jesus to be their personal true savior, forever.

86 For in this life, they do reject me (God), as I Am Jesus Christ, forever. And that rejection, it is called wanted true death, forever.

87 And it is seen by me (God), from their own free will, that they do reject me (God), as being eternally forever true, of themselves. As they are

found by me, as being truly found in Satan, forever.

88 Christ Jesus, he is my eternal, true Son. Who is found, as Godly true righteousness, that is eternally forever true. And this Christ, he is given by my (God) own true hand, as given by me,

89 Unto all, precious, righteous, true souls, who are found repenting unto me forever true, in my eternal and most true alter, that is my given eternal true presents, that is called Christ forever.

90 And most surely, they are found in and of Christ Jesus, as faithfully forever true, of themselves, in Christ Jesus, forever.

91 And they have most surely, have been set free, from their personal seen sins. That are seen sins that are against my (God)great nature, eternally forever true.

92 And through the common salvation, that is found of myself (God), in Christ Jesus forever. These chosen in Christ, do bare my (God) own eternal, holy spirit, forever.

93 And these have been set free from the sinful true prison, that is this present eternal true life. That is found in eternal true corruption, forever true and forever more.

94 And most certainly forever true, thy life in this world, is corruption. When one is not found in Christ's eternal, true spirit, forever.

95 And sin, doth bring forth, eternal true death, forever. But the gift, of my (God) living eternal true life. It is found in Christ, eternally forever and ever true, of myself, as God forever.

96 This Christ, he is the heavenly true gift, that is given from myself, forever (God) true. And this Christ, is most eternal, in me forever.

97 And Christ Jesus, he is given of me (God), unto the fallen true earth, forever true, even as God forever. For I (God) Am forever and I (God) Am found of myself (God), as God in Christ, eternally forever true and forever more.

98 And this Christ, he (Christ Jesus) is with eternal life, that is seen, as forever true, of me (God), forever certain and forever sure.

99 And that true life, it is most certainty found, of myself (God). In the now, and in the tomorrow, that is to come from me (God), eternally forever and ever true,

100 For I (God) Am God, who is forever seen and forever felt. As truly forever true, and forever seen. As thy life, forever certain and forever true.

101 This part of part 4, it is called: "The beastly image"

102 These who desire Satan and Satan's ways of evil forever, they are found unto me and unto Christ Jesus, as forever true, in the true image, that is seen as "The beastly Image." That is them in Satanism, forever,

103 These do enjoy death forever, for they seek me not as their creator in Christ Jesus forever. Therefore, I shall find these rebellious ones and I will give them dissolving true judgment, forever.

104 Therefore take fair warning, thou who is and shall always be as Satan forever, when thou choseth not Christ in me, as Christ being thy savior, as being eternally forever and ever true of the damned, forever.

105 But I do plead with thee O earth, that that needest to convert unto me, or thou shalt most surely depart this life into hell forever,

106 For I shall dissolve thee in this world forever, for even now, end time judgments of me, forever true. They are seeking them out forever, who loveth Satanism, instead loving me and desiring me in Christ Jesus forever,

107 And in hell, is found no end of hell forever. For I Am without true end forever, as thy

punisher forever, for that art found unto me, when found in hell,

108 As having been found in this life, as being rebellious against me forever true of thy self, as death forever certain and forever true.

109 For in this life, thou hast chose to be found unto me, as death as found true beastly, eternal true death forever, and that was chose by thee,

110 As chosen unrepentfully desired true death, that is chosen to be like unto Satan is dead unto me forever true, in being rebellious against me, forever and ever true,

111 And is true of the dead without Christ forever, saith God, eternally forever true, unto the unrepentiful truly lost, who are found as forever true and ever true,

112 In found eternal true unrepentfulness, that is forever sure and forever seen, of themselves forever. As true death forever true, unto them forever sure and forever true.

113 And they are eternally forever and ever true, in their desired, true sins. That are true seen sins of earnest and sincere, true dead death, forever sure.

114 The unrepentfully, they are found, as eternally lost unto me, in unrepentiful true sin

forever. For they do chose, to desire to be eternally forever true,

115 As desiring to be forever faithful, unto themselves, as being in the image of unrepentiful desired true unrepentiful true sin forever.

116 And they, do hold that eternal true image, that is the image found in earnest and sincere true death forever, For these do enjoy their false prophet of lies,

117 Who hath promised the unrepentiful true life, but hath deceived them forever, for he hath given them, instead, eternal dying true death forever, and is found as dead death, in hell forever.

118 For they, of the beastly eternal true image of Satan and unrepentiful true man forever, they do desire to be away from me, eternally forever and ever true, of themselves, as granted true death forever.

119 And that death, it is most surely, given unto beastly eternal true men and beastly eternal true women, who desireth the eternal power, of death, that is called Satanism forever.

120 For Satan hath given his power, that is called "Eternal dying true death," unto the man (man is mankind) forever. For it is given unto

blasphemous eternal true beastly men and blasphemous eternal true beastly women,

121 That is given unto their beastly image, that is a beastly stone image of sincere and true death, forever. And is given unto themselves in death, forever true.

122 That is given unto themselves forever, that the image may both, speak blasphemy, against God eternally forever and ever true, and to give dead death unto themselves, forever certain and forever,

123 And is given unto themselves, who are found to desire Satanism, forever true of themselves. As desiring Satan, as truly forever and ever true of themselves,

124 And they do desire the image called Satan, and they do forever, speak with the imaged true voice, that is found unto me (God) and is of themselves,

125 As a speaking true imaged true voice, that is found speaking true imaged, true blasphemy. That is blasphemous eternal true image, as found in earnest and sincere, true death, forever true,

126 And that speaking blasphemous true death, it is the eternal true image, of their seen and their desired, true blasphemous desired unrepentfulness.

127 That unrepentfulness, it is seen in them, as to not ever want Christ Jesus, as their savior, forever true and forever certain and forever.

128 It is desired in them, the unrepentiful of the fallen true earth. That image, may both, speak and condemn me, as I Am found as God forever true.

129 For they wish that they may live without me. And they desire to not believe me, that I Am God forever, for they wish to not believe all these things, forever, that I do speak.

130 That image shall most surely be put to unrest forever, for they shall die and be no more and this is forever. And they shall find, unto themselves forever, hell forever.

131 He that speaketh unto me, as the blasphemous eternal true image of death, in utter blasphemy forever. That person shall not find me forever but shall live in true death forever, in hell forever.

132 For if in this life, they seek me not in Christ Jesus, as Christ Jesus being their savior. Then they, who are damned. They are then already damned by me, forever and for all of given true eternity.

133 Satan doth desire the beastly image, that the image may both live as lifelessness forever and

speak blasphemously eternally forever true. And Satan desired to destroy all that is created in my eternal true image called life forever.

134 And they whose name isn't recorded in the Lamb's book of life, then that life is already found as blasphemous unto me forever,

135 And if, they who are of the damned imaged of lost souls, shall repent unto me in Christ, as Christ Jesus being their true savior, then their name shall be found unto me, as recorded in Christ Jesus. forever.

136 Let not the name of unrepentfulness, that is called Satanism. Ever be found within in thee, least I move upon thee, to kill thee and thy seed, forever, O unrepentiful one of the fallen true earth, forever.

137 Give not thy life unto the image of unrepentiful true sins. For those seen sins, they are seen forever and found faithful, in the unrepentiful truly dying,

138 Who are found as the dying true beast, that is dead forever. And the beastly true image, is found unto me forever faithful as death forever.

139 It is seen as the true image, that is true voice of death forever. And I shall not allow that image to remain as this earth, forever,

140   And, even now, end time judgments are riding through out the earth, to seek that which is lost in unrepentiful true seen sin, that the earth may repent in Christ Jesus,

141   For without Christ Jesus as one's true savior, forever. Then that unrepentiful true life, it shall depart this world, as forever true and forever without true end, as being eternally forever true.

142   In this world, many do believe in the false miracles of what appears to be eternal life, in unending sin forever. But it isn't eternal life of me forever, but is dead death forever. And they that desire dead death, they shall depart from this world forever.

143   And again, false miracles of heavenly true fire that appeareth to come down out of heaven, to give unending eternal life to be beastly eternal true image of earnest and sincere true death forever,

144   That is a false image of life, and they who desire that image, they must depart that image, by calling upon the name of Jesus Christ for my forgiveness, that is forever true and forever,

145   But if thou shalt not chose me in Christ, as Christ Jesus being thy eternal true savior, forever. Then thou shalt most surely, depart from his world forever. And thou shalt not appear with

Christ Jesus, in my (God) eternal true glory, forever.

146 And in thy dragon rebellioness, thy dragon true voice, it shall not save thee by speaking blasphemously unto me, in thy Satanism. And that is true forever and ever sure,

147 Therefore depart from thy dragoness iniquity, least I move upon thee, o unrepentiful one, who is found in the voice of this transgressing, departing away from me, true world.

148 That world is found as "Eternal true corruption," forever. And this world and heaven, they shall both, depart from before me, forever certain and forever true.

149 And this fallen true world, it shall depart from before me forever, and is now departing away from me, without true end. And is found departing without true end, unto them that desireth not Christ, as Christ being their true savior, forever.

150 For they, shall depart unto hell forever, and I shall not send them another savior, while they be found in hell forever, saith God unto the beast and unto it's true image,

151 That true image, is the image of the damned forever, and who are seen unto me forever true,

as sincere, true death, that is eternally forever true, as found forever, in unrepentfulness, eternally forever.

152 Unrepentfulness towards me forever, is this fallen, beastie, eternal true earth. And all of the unrepentiful true earth, is seen by me, as eternally forever and ever true of themselves, as dead death, eternally forever true.

153 For these Satan like eternal ones, are found in eternal rebellion ness. And are by choice, without both, Christ and without Christianity, forever and ever true of myself (God).

154 Eternal, true, unrepentiful true sins. They are found of uttermost, given true death. That death is eternally forever true and forever faithful, and is found faithfully in the damned forever true themselves forever,

155 For these do desire to be more like Satan and Satanism, as eternally forever and ever true of themselves, as the voice of the beast forever.

156 And these are eternally forever true, in being completely against me saith God, unto the beastly true, who are seen as the damned forever faithful, of themselves forever. As found in their seen, earnest and sincere, true death, eternally forever true.

157 And these, they do sport themselves, against me, forever true, saith God. For these are all against me. And I Am truth, that is found in Christ Jesus. And that is forever and ever true, of the damned, who are without true hope, in hell, forever.

158 These do desire to be like Satan, forever. And they do desire, the true damning eternal worship that they perform of themselves unto the beastly image of fallen true men and fallen true women and fallen true devils, forever.

159 The beastly, eternal, damningly true, eternal true image of unrepentiful true sin. It is found forever faithful, in the anti Christ ones of dead death forever,

160 For they are of the true voice of the Antichrist true beast of Satanism and Satan forever. And they are found, as given of themselves unto, eternal true unrepentfulness forever true,

161 And they are in dragon's true voice of spoken true death forever, and as a result of that blasphemy, they are given by their own choice, unto uttermost, perditious, true eternal dying true death, forever.

162 That is a blasphemous eternal true image, that is found as dragon true death, that is forever

true and forever. And is found, as a most holy, in their own true site, true death.

163 That death is most eternal in them in the beast's body forever. And is a eternal forever, as a true eternal, dying true image of the dragon, who is the dragon called Satan and Satanism forever.

164 That image of the beast, is Antichrist and is anti-God, forever. And is found eternally forever true, in the damned. And is within themselves, forever and ever true, without true end, forever.

165 And there is no true end, forever unto themselves, as death forever. And this is because, they the beast. They desire forever, to not receive me, in Christ Jesus. As Christ Jesus, being their personal, true savior, forever.

166 Therefore, because they desire not me and desire not the Son called Christ, who is Christ Jesus. Then they are for all of given true eternity, unto me forever,

167 As eternal, seen in and as, a damning true damnation, that is called eternal dying true death. And as a result of those things, they are seen forever faithful,

168 As being seen and found faithful, unto their personally desired, and true, unrepentfulness, forever. As a faithfully seen unrepentfulness, that

is found and seen within them, as death forever true,

169 And is in them and seen in them, as a living, true damnation. That is called, unrepentiful true death, forever.

170 That damnation, it is found as uttering true death. And that death, it shall be given unto them. That are found in unrepentfulness, forever.

171 Therefore, they shall be allowed, granted true death, forever true. And they shall receive hell forever, as dead death eternally forever true and forever.

Part 5 w / 157 verses. "Israel's messiah, forever"

1 In this part 5, this whole written true part. It will show Christ Jesus' relationship to Israel, as being Israel's messiah, forever.

2 Therefore, let us began in this eternal true book, that is called, Zephaniah. That I (God) may show forth that understanding to Israel and to the world, forever.

3 **Zephaniah 1:11-14 and Joel 1:18**

4 **Verse 11: Howl, ye inhabitants of Maktesh, for all the merchant people are cut down; all they that bear silver are cut off.**

5   Verse 12: And it shall come to pass at that time, that I will search Jerusalem with candles, and punish the men that are settled on their lees: that say in their heart, The LORD will not do good, neither will he do evil.

6   Verse 13: Therefore their goods shall become a booty, and their a houses desolation: they shall also build houses, but not inhabit them; and they shall plant vineyards, but not drink the wine thereof.

7   Verse 14: The great day of the LORD is near, it is near, and hasteth greatly, even the voice of the day of the LORD: the mighty man shall cry there bitterly.

8   And Joel 1:18: How do the beasts groan! The herds of cattle are perplexed, because they have no pasture; yea, the flocks of sheep are made desolate.

9   In Zephaniah 1:11, Israel is going to be exiled for sinfulness, idol worship, and rejecting Christ as their savior.

10   And the word merchant in Zephaniah 1:11. It is Israel, and this is the starting of the Day of the Lord as noted in Joel 1:15-18.

11   The word beast as found recorded by me (God) in the book of Joel 1:18, it is Israel.

12   And the words, "Is not the meat cut off," as found recorded in Joel 1:16, is the old ways to me (God) forever. They are changed unto Christ Jesus, is the only way to me (God), forever.

13   For I (God) have torn the veil, as recorded in the Christian new Testament, and this is forever, For now, through Christ Jesus, thou mayest approach me, freely forever, as I (God) Am thy true Father, as I (God) Am found in thy repentful true spirit, forever.

14   And, again, in Zephaniah 1:11, the words: "Bear silver." They mean the old ways of worship me (God) before the birth of Christ Jesus, was stopped forever.

15   And that is since the birth of Christ Jesus, and now the only way to me, who (God) is the God, who (God) is called and seen, as being: "The Eternal One of Life." Is to come to me (God) in Jesus Christ forever.

16   And, again, bear silver, also is seen in meaning that Israel's people, shall not handle the things of myself any longer in their past sinful unrepentiful shape before Christ's birth.

17   And, again, in Zephaniah 1:12 the word candles. It is the workings of Christianity. And the words "settled on their lees." It is in meaning of Israel thinking in their heart, that I (God) would not put Israel to being exiled for their lack

of concern about the sinfulness in my (God) country that is called Israel, forever.

18 And, in Zephaniah 1:13 is to show that Israel will be exiled prior to 1948.

19 And, in Zephaniah 1:14 is Christianity to happen. And the word sun is judgment that is also found recorded by me (God), in Joel 2:31.

20 And also, in Zephaniah 1:14. That verse is to show anointing in Christ Jesus in relationship to the word "bitterly." And this is the word of God being preached thru Christians during the timeline frame of the earth, that is called "The Day of Lord." This is in relationship to Acts 6:8-15 and Acts 7:1-60 and Christ preaching the gospel.

21 This in Acts is in regards of giving Israel trumpet and alarm concerning Israel's timeline period of wrath desolation and vengeance desolation that is pronounced of myself (God) upon Israel, that will take place if Israel should reject Christ as their savior.

22 That wrathful true period, it started when Apostle Paul began preaching to the gentiles, that was about the salvation of Israel, as it was given unto the gentiles, that is called Jesus Christ, forever--and that wrathful true period, it ran to 1948 AD. And it shall never return to Israel, forever.

23 Now, I Roger, I do say to remember what Stephen had said in Christian book of acts 6:8-15, that Jesus of Nazareth shall **destroy this place.** This understanding is taken from the knowledge of Acts 6:8-15, as concerning the statements of the false witnesses found against Stephen.

24 After reading those verses in acts 6:8-15. it would suggest that Stephen was saying that Christ shall destroy Israel, by exiling Israel from its own true land, if Israel shall reject Christ as their savior.

25 And, no doubt one of the things that Stephen was saying. It was in trying to get Israel's council. To understand what God had said in Deuteronomy 18:15-19.

26 Israel's council, as noted in Acts 6:12. They did not understand what Stephen was saying. So they thought Stephen was blasphemous toward Moses and toward me (God),

27 And I Roger, I do say that they judged Stephen according to Acts 7:57-58, which is Stephen being stoned to death. And this was because of Israel's council's great error, in understanding the scriptures, as in regards to their savior, who is called Jesus Christ.

28 To give further insight to this event with Stephen, Is to read this in Acts below, these two

chapters, they fully explain Stephen's witness as found concerning his true Christ, and who is our true Christ.

29 Stephen's statement, as found in the new Testament, in the king James version of the Holy Bible. He was according to the Bible, a man of faith and power, as found in God, through Jesus Christ forever. And Stephen did great wonders and great miracles, Among the Jewish nation of Israel, before 70 AD.

30 This the wording that Stephen did great wonders and miracles is in meaning that Christ Jesus did the these things through Stephen,

31 for Stephen is only a vessel of God in whom Christ manifested his spiritual presents in doing all of these things that are called wonders and miracles.

32 I (God) will, now begin Stephen's story as it is found recorded by me (God) in the book of Acts 6:8-15, then also Stephens' story, as it is found in Acts 7:1-60.

33 Acts 6:8-15 From here to end of part 4--it has an extra 102 Bible verses included in part 4.

6:8: And Stephen, full of faith and power, did great wonders and miracles Among the people.

6:9 Then there arose certain of the synagogue, which is called the synagogue of the Libertines, and Cyrenians, and Alexandrians, and of them of Cilicia and of Asia, disputing with Stephen.

6:10 And they were not able to resist the wisdom and the spirit by which he spake.

6:11 Then they suborned men, which said, We have heard him speak blasphemous words against Moses, and against God.

6:12 And they stirred up the people, and the elders, and the scribes, and came upon him, and caught him, and brought him to the council,

6:13 And set up false witnesses, which said, This man ceaseth not to speak blasphemous words against this holy place, and the law:

6:14 For we have heard him say, that this Jesus of Nazareth shall destroy this place, and shall change the customs which Moses delivered us.

6:15 And all that sat in the council, looking stedfastly on him, saw his face as it had been the face of an angel.

Acts Chapter 7:1-60

7:1 Then said the high priest, Are these things so?

7:2   And he said, Men, brethren, and fathers, hearken; The God of glory appeared unto our father Abraham, when he was in Mesopotamia, before he dwelt in Charran,

7:3   And said unto him, Get thee out of thy country, and from thy kindred, and come into the land which I shall shew thee.

7:4   Then came he out of the land of the Chaldaeans, and dwelt in Charran: and from thence, when his father was dead, he removed him into this land, wherein ye now dwell.

7:5   And he gave him none inheritance in it, no, not so much as to set his foot on: yet he promised that he would give it to him for a possession, and to his seed after him, when as yet he had no child.

7:6   And God spake on this wise, That his seed should sojourn in a strange land; and that they should bring them into bondage, and entreat them evil four hundred years.

7:7   And the nation to whom they shall be in bondage will I judge, said God: and after that shall they come forth, and serve me in this place.

7:8   And he gave him the covenant of circumcision: and so Abraham begat Isaac, and circumcised him the eighth day; and Isaac begat Jacob; and Jacob begat the twelve patriarchs.

7:9 And the patriarchs, moved with envy, sold Joseph into Egypt: but God was with him,

7:10 And delivered him out of all his afflictions, and gave him favour and wisdom in the sight of Pharaoh king of Egypt; and he made him governor over Egypt and all his house.

7:11 Now there came a dearth over all the land of Egypt and Canaan, and great affliction: and our fathers found no sustenance.

7:12 But when Jacob heard that there was corn in Egypt, he sent out our fathers first.

7:13 And at the second time Joseph was made known to his brethren; and Joseph's kindred was made known unto Pharaoh.

7:14 Then sent Joseph, and called his father Jacob to him, and all his kindred, threescore and fifteen souls.

7:15 So Jacob went down into Egypt, and died, he, and our fathers.

7:16 And were carried over into Sychem, and laid in the sepulcher that Abraham bought for a sum of money of the Sons of Emmor the father of Sychem.

7:17 But when the time of the promise drew nigh, which God had sworn to Abraham, the people grew and multiplied in Egypt,

7:18 Till another king arose, which knew not Joseph.

7:19 The same dealt subtly with our kindred, and evil entreated our fathers, so that they cast out their young children, to the end they might not live.

7:20 In which time Moses was born, and was exceeding fair, and nourished up in his father's house three months:

7:21 And when he was cast out, Pharaoh's daughter took him up, and nourished him for her own Son.

7:22 And Moses was learned in all the wisdom of the Egyptians, and was mighty in words and in deeds.

7:23 And when he was full forty years old, it came into his heart to visit his brethren the children of Israel.

7:24 And seeing one of them suffer wrong, he defended him, and avenged him that was oppressed, and smote the Egyptian:

7:25 For he supposed his brethren would have understood how that God by his hand would deliver them: but they understood not.

7:26 And the next day he shewed himself unto them as they strove, and would have set them at one again, saying, Sirs, ye are brethren; why do ye wrong one to another?

7:27 But he that did his neighbour wrong thrust him away, saying, Who made thee a ruler and a judge over us?

7:28 Wilt thou kill me, as thou didest the Egyptian yesterday?

7:29 Then fled Moses at this saying, and was a stranger in the land of Madian, where he begat two Sons.

7:30 And when forty years were expired, there appeared to him in the wilderness of Mount Sinai an angel of the Lord in a flame of fire in a bush.

7:31 When Moses saw it, he wondered at the sight: and as he drew near to behold it, the voice of the LORD came unto him,

7:32 Saying, I Am the God of thy fathers, the God of Abraham, and the God of Isaac, and the God of Jacob. Then Moses trembled, and durst not behold.

7:33 Then said the Lord to him, Put off thy shoes from thy feet: for the place where thou standest is holy ground.

7:34 I have seen, I have seen the affliction of my people which is in Egypt, and I have heard their groaning, and Am come down to deliver them. And now come, I will send thee into Egypt.

7:35 This Moses whom they refused, saying, Who made thee a ruler and a judge? The same did God send to be a ruler and a deliverer by the hand of the angel which appeared to him in the bush.

7:36 He brought them out, after that he had shewed wonders and signs in the land of Egypt, and in the Red sea, and in the wilderness forty years.

7:37 This is that Moses, which said unto the children of Israel, A prophet shall the Lord your God raise up unto you of your brethren, like unto me; him shall ye hear.

7:38 This is he, that was in the church in the wilderness with the angel which spake to him in the mount Sinai, and with our fathers: who received the lively oracles to give unto us:

7:39 To whom our fathers would not obey, but thrust him from them, and in their hearts turned back again into Egypt,

7:40 Saying unto Aaron, Make us Gods to go before us: for as for this Moses, which brought us out of the land of Egypt, we Wot not what is become of him.

7:41 And they made a calf in those days, and offered sacrifice unto the idol, and rejoiced in the works of their own hands.

7:42 Then God turned, and gave them up to worship the host of heaven; as it is written in the book of the prophets, O ye house of Israel, have ye offered to me slain beasts and sacrifices by the space of forty years in the wilderness?

7:43 Yea, ye took up the tabernacle of Moloch, and the star of your god Remphan, figures which ye made to worship them: and I will carry you away beyond Babylon.

7:44 Our fathers had the tabernacle of witness in the wilderness, as he had appointed, speaking unto Moses, that he should make it according to the fashion that he had seen.

7:45 Which also our fathers that came after brought in with Jesus into the possession of the Gentiles, whom God drave out before the face of our fathers, unto the days of David;

7:46 Who found favour before God, and desired to find a tabernacle for the God of Jacob.

7:47 But Solomon built him an house.

7:48 Howbeit the most High dwelleth not in temples made with hands; as saith the prophet,

7:49 Heaven is my throne, and earth is my footstool: what house will ye build me? saith the Lord: or what is the place of my rest?

7:50 Hath not my hand made all these things?

7:51 Ye stiff necked and uncircumcised in heart and ears, ye do always resist the Holy Ghost: as your fathers did, so do ye.

7:52 Which of the prophets have not your fathers persecuted? and they have slain them which shewed before of the coming of the Just One; of whom ye have been now the betrayers and murderers:

7:53 Who have received the law by the disposition of angels, and have not kept it.

7:54 When they heard these things, they were cut to the heart, and they gnashed on him with their teeth.

7:55 But he, being full of the Holy Ghost, looked up stedfastly into heaven, and saw the glory of God, and Jesus standing on the right hand of God,

7:56   And said, Behold, I see the heavens opened, and the Son of man standing on the right hand of God.

7:57   Then they cried out with a loud voice, and stopped their ears, and ran upon him with one accord,

7:58   And cast him out of the city, and stoned him: and the witnesses laid down their clothes at a young man's feet, whose name was Saul.

7:59   And they stoned Stephen, calling upon God, and saying, Lord Jesus, receive my spirit.

7:60   And he kneeled down, and cried with a loud voice, Lord, lay not this sin to their charge. And when he had said this, he fell

34 **Now,** to go even further to show the messiah of Israel, forever. As to who is seen as being, Jesus Christ, forever. Let us now go on to what Apostle Paul wrote, in Acts 13

35   But first, as concerning Stephen, that above story, it speaks for its true self, forever true,

36 The reason those things happen to Stephen, is because the Jews were so hard in not believing that Jesus, is their chosen true savior,

37 And that this is part of the reason why Jesus was sent unto the gentiles. Then a statement of apostle Paul, as recorded in acts 13:15 thru 49,

38 It will show that the savior of Israel, was sent unto the gentiles because of their unbelief. And this action of the Jews, this allowed the gentiles to receive the chosen true salvation of myself (God), for their seen sins, which is seen as bringing prophesy to pass, in Isaiah 53:11.

Acts 13:15-49

15:15 And after the reading of the law and the prophets the rulers of the synagogue sent unto them, saying, Ye men and brethren, if ye have any word of exhortation for the people, say on.

15:16 Then Paul stood up, and beckoning with his hand said, Men of Israel, and ye that fear God, give audience.

15:17 The God of this people of Israel chose our fathers, and exalted the people when they dwelt as strangers in the land of Egypt, and with an high arm brought he them out of it.

15:18 And about the time of forty years suffered he their manners in the wilderness.

15:19 And when he had destroyed seven nations in the land of Canaan, he divided their land to them by lot.

15:20 And after that he gave unto them judges about the space of four hundred and fifty years, until Samuel the prophet.

15:21 And afterward they desired a king: and God gave unto them Saul the Son of Cis, a man of the tribe of Benjamin, by the space of forty years.

15:22 And when he had removed him, he raised up unto them David to be their king; to whom also he gave their testimony, and said, I have found David the Son of Jesse, a man after mine own heart, which shall fulfil all my will.

15:23 Of this man's seed hath God according to his promise raised unto Israel a Saviour, Jesus:

15:24 When John had first preached before his coming the baptism of repentance to all the people of Israel.

15:25 And as John fulfilled his course, he said, Whom think ye that I Am? I Am not he. But, behold, there cometh one after me, whose shoes of his feet I Am not worthy to loose.

15:26 Men and brethren, children of the stock of Abraham, and whosoever Among you feareth God, to you is the word of this salvation sent.

15:27 For they that dwell at Jerusalem, and their rulers, because they knew him not, nor yet the voices of the prophets which are read every Sabbath day, they have fulfilled them in condemning him.

15:28 And though they found no cause of death in him, yet desired they Pilate that he should be slain.

15:29 And when they had fulfilled all that was written of him, they took him down from the tree, and laid him in a sepulcher.

15:30 But God raised him from the dead:

15:31 And he was seen many days of them which came up with him from Galilee to Jerusalem, who are his witnesses unto the people.

15:32 And we declare unto you glad tidings, how that the promise which was made unto the fathers,

15:33 God hath fulfilled the same unto us their children, in that he hat raised up Jesus again; as it is also written in the second psalm, Thou art my Son, this day have I begotten thee.

15:34 And as concerning that he raised him up from the dead, now no more to return to corruption, he said on this wise, I will give you the sure mercies of David.

15:35 Wherefore he saith also in another psalm, Thou shalt not suffer thine Holy One to see corruption.

15:36 For David, after he had served his own generation by the will of God, fell on sleep, and was laid unto his fathers, and saw corruption:

15:37 But he, whom God raised again, saw no corruption.

15:38 Be it known unto you therefore, men and brethren, that through this man is preached unto you the forgiveness of sins:

15:39 And by him all that believe are justified from all things, from which ye could not be justified by the law of Moses.

15:40 Beware therefore, lest that come upon you, which is spoken of in the prophets;

15:41 Behold, ye despisers, and wonder, and perish: for I work a work in your days, a work which ye shall in no wise believe, though a man declare it unto you.

15:42 And when the Jews were gone out of the synagogue, the Gentiles besought that these words might be preached to them the next Sabbath.

15:43 Now when the congregation was broken up, many of the Jews and religious proselytes followed Paul and Barnabas: who, speaking to them, persuaded them to continue in the grace of God.

15:44 And the next Sabbath day came almost the whole city together to hear the word of God.

15:45 But when the Jews saw the multitudes, they were filled with envy, and spake against those things which were spoken by Paul, contradicting and blaspheming.

15:46 Then Paul and Barnabas waxed bold, and said, It was necessary that the word of God should first have been spoken to you: but seeing ye put it from you, and judge yourselves unworthy of everlasting life, lo, we turn to the Gentiles.

15:47 For so hath the Lord commanded us, saying, I have set thee to be a light of the Gentiles, that thou shouldest be for salvation unto the ends of the earth.

15:48 And when the Gentiles heard this, they were glad, and glorified the word of the Lord: and as many as were ordained to eternal life believed.

15:49 And the word of the Lord was published throughout all the region.

39 The above statements, is self explaining, as to why Jesus was sent unto the gentiles. And it was so, because of Israel's unbelief in Jesus Christ, as him being their chosen messiah, forever.

40 But wasn't it foretold O Israel, to occur that way? Yea it was, therefore, search out diligently and I will teach thee and show you the way to me, as it is found through your messiah, who is Jesus Christ, who is thy eternal true king, as he is given of me, unto you, and unto the world, forever.

41 And because of those things, as concerning your messiah, who is of the seed of king David, forever. The whole world has a chance for salvation,

42 And yet, Israel still can receive that chosen true salvation, as it is found as being eternally forever so, as being eternally, forever seen, as being, Jesus Christ, forever true.

43 And I have always desired, that all of Israel, would accept this chosen true Christ Jesus, who is Israel's eternal true hope, and eternal true salvation, forever.

44 Now, concerning Zephaniah 1:16.

45 This is seen as speaking concerning the day of trumpet and alarm is found recorded by me forever, in Zephaniah 1:16,

46 And is in the same timeframe period mentioned and named as "The Day of The Lord."

47 This trumpet and alarm time period. It is found from the birth of Christ, as the very beginning of The Day of The lord, and it remains throughout the entire time, that is called the Day of The Lord.

48 To give more light concerning the book of Zephaniah 1:16-18. The words fenced cities and high towers, they are in meaning of the entire nation of Israel, before 1948 AD.

49 And, In Zephaniah 1:17. Israel shall walk like blind (grope) men, because of no spiritual light, that is found outside of Christ Jesus, who (Jesus Christ) is the "LIGHT OF GOD."

50 And the words poured out are in meaning of darkness upon Israel. That is called judgments of God.

51 And in Zephaniah 1:18. Is The Day of Wrath which is judgment noted in Zephaniah 1:17, as to be given to Israel, in which Israel shall be exiled prior to 1948 AD.

52 And the words, as written as being, whole land. It is in meaning of the land of Israel.

53 And the words, Speedy riddance of all them. It is in meaning of Israel's people, being exiled, before 1948 AD.

54 In this part of this holy book. It is about my (God) servant, who is called "The Branch." And this true section, is it is also about the book of Nahum.

55 Zechariah 3:8-10

56 3:8 Hear now, O Joshua the high priest, thou, and thy fellows that   sit before thee: for they are men wondered at: for, behold, I will bring forth my servant the BRANCH.

57 3:9 For behold the stone that I have laid before Joshua; upon one stone shall be seven eyes: behold, I will engrave the graving thereof, saith the LORD of hosts, and I will remove the iniquity of that land in one day.

58 3:10 In that day, saith the LORD of hosts, shall ye call every man his neighbor under the vine and under the fig tree.

59 In Zechariah 3:8--- I means God, and Christ Jesus, is the word servant and Christ Jesus is also the man called the branch.

60 In 9 is that Christ Jesus is the one stone that has the seven eyes which are the seven spirits of

God. The word remove and this is in reference to the death, burial,

61 And the resurrection of Jesus Christ. One Day, it also refers to the very moment the veil of the temple would be tore in two (Of course this happened with the resurrection of Jesus Christ).

62 And this also is about Christ Jesus Paying our sin debt unto God, that we could be redeemed thru the blood of Jesus Christ Jesus, forever.

63 In 3:10--- the words "In that day." It is in meaning that during the entire timeline frame of the earth, that is called "The Day of the Lord."

64 That all true people, who accept Jesus Christ, as this Jesus being their personal seen savior, forever. They shall all be brothers and sisters in Christianity, forever.

65 In other words: For us to be Christians, we shall call fellow Christians, our neighbor. And this Christ Jesus, he is the vine, and he is also seen as being the fig tree, forever.

66 As Christians, we are the neighbor branches that are made clean bare white from having been forgiven of our true sinfulness, forever.

67 Yet, in this, Israel is made clean bare white thru their acceptance of Christ Jesus, as receiving this Jesus, as one being eternally forever

forgiven, as forgiven from one's seen sins, forever,

68 And, the gentiles are even, forgiven through Christ Jesus, forever. And we are therefore, grafted into Israel, spiritually. As found thru accepting Jesus Christ, as this Jesus, being ones true savior, forever.

69 Grafted means the gentiles become thru the blood of Christ Jesus, clean bare white branches of Christ spiritually. And Christ Jesus, is the fig tree and the vine.

70 To understand more of who this Christ is to Israel. Is to read some in Nahum--- chapters 1, 2, and 3.

Nahum chapters 1, 2, and 3.

71 In Nahum 1:5: It is talking about Jesus Christ being judgment unto the world, as being end time, last days judgment. And that is seen, in other words, as being: "End of the days judgment." That is given from God, to the wicked true earth, forever.

72 In Nahum 1:6 is Jesus Christ as word written as being "his."

73 In Nahum 1:8 is Jesus Christ as the word written as being "he."

74 In Nahum 1:15: The word him is talking about Jesus Christ.

75 In Nahum 2:1, Christ Jesus is the words: "he that dasheth in peaces." And the words before thy face. It is Israel before Israel went into exile before 1948 AD.

76 And the word keep, is in meaning as: Christians, remain strong in God's true spirit. For God will abase Israel with Israel's exile, before 1948 AD.

77 In Nahum 2:2: The words turned away, it is: God is changing Israel's old way of worship prior to the birth of Christ, for Christ is born, and Christ is preaching the kingdom of God, and in which this is Christ publishing the gospel of the kingdom of God.

78 And the excellency of Jacob. Is that the old ways of worship in Israel, is changed with the birth of Christ, unto the worship of God, is then found forever through Jesus Christ. For Christ Jesus, is the resurrection,

79 And this Christ Jesus, he is the life, which is has become the excellency of Israel, that is considered Christianity, forever.

80 And the word emptiers, is Christians. And the emptiers are preaching the gospel, and souls are

being saved (marred is the word saved) in Israel, forever. The word vine, is the nation of Israel.

81 In Nahum 2:3-- is the word shield, and it is the anointed preaching of Christ as it is found in and of God, forever.

82 And the words--Mighty men. This is Christians preaching. The word red is the blood of Christ is already applied to Christians that are preaching.

83 And the words Valiant men, is Christians who have Christ in their heart, forever.

84 And the word chariots are Christians preaching the good news of the kingdom of God, in the anointing which is referred to, as being flaming torches. And the word preparation is the resurrection.

85 And the words--Fir trees. This is Israel's people, when Christ is resurrected. "Of course the resurrection hadn't occurred yet, when this anointed true scripture, was written forever."

86 In Nahum 2:4--- Chariots are Christians preaching the gospel, in which shall jostle the minds and hearts, to render these to the promise of the eternal true hope,

87   That is found in Christ, to one living his or her's own true life, as a anointed true Christian of heavenly anointed cleansing true fire,

88   That bringeth the true salvation of God's great and wonderful, true presents of love, and is of God's own true consideration,

89   For them that love God forever. For God loveth them and giveth them, salvation unto whomsoever, that shall and do love him (GOD). and unto them that shall also love God's own true Son, who is called, Jesus Christ, forever.

90   The words--Torches are Christians, and lightnings. Those words are the anointing of God, as found in Christ, unto the true salvation of God, that liveth forever.

91   In Nahum 2:5, it is starting to tell of exiling of Israel, before 1948 AD, for Israel's true sinfulness and worship of idols. The word haste, it also means Israel is heading into exile, in around, 70 AD.

92   The word wall, it means: "Headed to the temple of God to pray for deliverance from exiling around 70 AD."

93   In Nahum 2:6 the word opened. It means Israel will be exiled around 70 AD. And Israel is dissolved, until 1948 AD.

94 In Nahum 2:8, the word Nineveh. It means Israel's nation, since it's (of old) beginning.

95 In Nahum 2:10, it is Israel and this sinful perverse corrupt Israel. It is physically to be removed by God, through the warring gentiles. Who shall exile all of Israel, from their (Israel) nation's true land and it's true country.

96 And the word faces, it is Israel's people of Israeli heritage. And the word blackness, it is spiritual and physical true judgments, to be applied upon Israel.

97 And the word gather, it means empowered judgment from God, as to be occurring to Israel, and occurring in Israel's nation of true heritage.

98 In Nahum 2:12, this is the corruption of Israel and the gentile nations, as one together. In the mind and spirit, with the tangible true fruits, together.

99 In Nahum 2:13, is the word against, it is God that is against the corrupted true nation of Israel that God had formed and fashioned. But Israel, had corrupted her true self, and went a whoring from her (Israel) husband, who is called God.

100 The word chariots, is in found meaning of Israel's people and the word smoke, it is the active timeframe of day of wrath desolation,

101 And it is the same timeframe, as the day vengeance desolation judgment, that is from start unto finish, of the timeframe that is called the day of wrath desolation.

102 The word sword is wrath, and that is judgments of God upon Israel, till 1948 AD. And the words, young lions. It means Israel's people shall always perish with only a remnant to survive until 1948 AD. This is one way the scripture speaks of this,

103 I (God) will purge the rebels, "from Israel before 1948 AD. In other words." The words messengers, it is the corrupted true people of Israel, with all of their corruption, that is found being eternally against God, forever.

104 This about purge, it is found in a different location in the Bible.

105 The word heard, it means the old ways of Israel shall be no (heard) more and forever. For God has done a new thing in the earth for it is called Christianity. This is found in Isaiah 43:19, about a new thing.

106 In Nahum 3:1, is the bloody city, it is referring to Israel.

107 In Nahum 3:7--- Nineveh is in meaning to say, the nation of Israel is desolate because of

applied judgment that is to come from God around 70 AD.

108 In Nahum 3:10, the word she is showing Israel, that Israel is already considered of God, As Israel is to be exiled. And of course, that exiling will happen around 70 AD.

109 In 3:12 the word eater is the warring gentiles actually taking the land, and the belongings of Israel's people, during the siege that is to come against Israel, around 70 AD.

110 In Nahum 3:16, the word merchant. It is Israel's people of corruptness, teaching their damnable ways against God, to Israel's people, and teaching corruption, to the world during Israel's existence before the fall of Israel, around 70 AD.

111 Israel was suppose to set the example of applied, living righteousness of God, as to be applied to one's ways before God, and to be seen unto the world, forever.

112 In Nahum 3:18, is the words "O king of Assyria." And this Is Israel in meaning of Assyria, therefore, it can be said like this:

113 "O king of Israel" thy Shepard's of the flocks of God do slumber in their personal responsibilities to the flocks of God and perdition that maketh desolate doth and maketh haste unto

them that shall dwell in the dust, and no man shall desire the Israeli people before 1948 AD, who are not in Christ as Christians.

114   In Nahum 3:19--- before 1948 AD Israel had a spiritual bruise that is sinfulness with no way to cure her self (Israel), for Israel is corrupt in their sin offerings before the face of God, and Israel has went a whoring away from their true God of righteousness, before 1948 AD.

115   The word wound is the effect of sin already found in Israel, and it is grievous before God. And, because of that. God has a grievance against Israel, before 1948 AD,

116   For Israel has broken the Hallowed true Oath before 1948 AD, in not performing true righteousness of God, unto all of Israel, and unto all of the world, forever.

117   Moreover, all of this corrupted history concerning Israel, has bought applied judgments of God before 1948 AD upon Israel, and those judgments has lifted away and from off of Israel, since 1948 AD. For Israel, is now blessed of God,

118   Instead of being cursed of God, while Israel was under previous exiling judgment of God as found in eternal true curses, when God had pushed Israel into all the corners of the earth, prior to 1948 AD.

119 *Now* let us go onto Zephaniah 3:1-20. This will show some on the history of Israel, as in regards to Israel's chosen true messiah, as being found as salvation to Israel and to the fallen true world.

120   Zephaniah 3:1-20

121   In Zephaniah 3:1--the words: :The oppressing city," it is Israel before Israel was exiled before 1948 AD.

122 In Zephaniah 3:2---the word she, it is Israel. And the word voice is God sending his word to Israel to repent.

123 In Zephaniah 3:3---Her is Israel.

124   In Zephaniah 3:4---Her is Israel. In this verse--Israel hath committed the abomination of desolation, that maketh all of Israel, most desolate before 70 AD.

125 In Zephaniah 3:5--the lord is in the midst of Israel and God is showing Israel their sin before 70 AD, everyday. That Israel may repent.

126 In Zephaniah 3:6---is effects of the gentiles having been helping Israel to sin, while Israel is still a nation before 70 AD, that that issue will stop when Israel exiled in 70 AD.

127   Therefore, Israel's streets and cities are going into exile in 70 AD, and all Israeli streets and cities, shall no more have Israel citizens on them, forever, until 1948 AD.

128   In Zephaniah 3:7--- fear means Israel to receive instruction. And dwelling means Israel. And I is God. And the word they, it is Israel before 1948 AD. And the word their, it is in meaning of Israel before 1948 AD.

129   In Zephaniah 3:8--- the words-- wait. It means for Israel's faithfulness unto God, to understand that Israel shall be punished,

130   But Israel shall return in 1948 AD to their land, and, that God will rise up to the gentiles, in judgment, that is called "End of the days judgments" forever,

131   And this is about the wrath of the Lamb, and is also known also as end time judgments upon the whole earth, that all men may repent of their sins, by receiving Jesus Christ, as one's savior, forever true.

132   The word wait, it means to wait on God in seeing God rise to the non Christians nations, in end time judgments, in our true day of this earth, forever

133   Therefore, the words: "day that I rise." It means the time of end time judgments occurring

during the day of the lord and that Israel shall be a nation again in 1948 AD and forever.

134 Again, in Zephaniah 3:8--the word determination. It means God is planning end time judgments, upon the entire earth,

135 To make the entire true earth repent of it's seen sins, and, God shall gather all of the nations, in the end time judgment,

136 To make them all repent or be dissolved by me (God), And when these nations shall repent unto me (God) forever, this brings Israel, honor, praise, and glory through them accepting Christ as one's savior.

137 The word devoured. It means the true effects of end time judgments upon them (sinners), that do dwell upon the earth.

138 In Zephaniah 3:9---the words---a pure language. Those words are speaking about speaking in other tongues as the spirit gives utterance.

139 And speaking in other tongues, it is for whosoever will, let him come and receive this pure heavenly language (this is forever),

140 And this is also found in Joel 3:9. And it is in referral to the day of Pentecost, as noted in the

book of Joel. And it is also found, in the book of Acts.

141 In Zephaniah 3:9--the word consent-- it is in referral of serving God through Christ, as a Christian. And that as a Christian, we all are as one in God, forever.

142 In Zephaniah 3:10--the word daughter. It is Christianity that gives the offerings of praises and worship unto the God of Israel.

143 In Zephaniah 3:11--the words—"my holy mountain." It is Christ and Christianity, and this is offered from God unto Israel, during the complete timeframe of the day of the lord.

144 In Zephaniah 3:12. It is about Christianity is the afflicted and poor people and they are found during the entire timeframe of the day of the lord.

145 In Zephaniah 3:13-- the word remnant. It is Israel is a nation again, starting in 1948 AD, and forever.

146 And, that as a Christian, the true Israeli seen people, they shall walk as Christ like, unto God, forever.

147 And they shall desire to walk righteously before God, and not want to sin forever. As they shall walk faithfully in Jesus Christ, unto the "True Father" forever certain.

148 In Zephaniah 3:14--- This is present day Israel, in that Israel should rejoice now, as being Christian forever, because of the blessings of God are now found concerning Israel, forever. This started in 1948 AD and forever.

149 In Zephaniah 3:15-- the words "the king of Israel." They are found in meaning of that when Israel became a nation, in 1948 AD.

150 And that the old ways of the Israeli people serving evil kings without the voice of the Israeli people ruling and governing the Israeli nation before 1948 AD, would be stopped forever.

151 Therefore, corrupt evil kings having idols and etc in Israel. It is stopped forever, starting in 1948 AD.

152 In Zephaniah 3:16, is that Israel is a nation again, starting in 1948 AD and forever. And this 3:16 is also referring to today's world and forever.

153 In Zephaniah 3:17, the word save. It means that God shall bring back all the people of Israeli heritage to the nation of Israel, starting in 1948 AD and forever, and Israel being Christian as well.

154 In Zephaniah 3:18, is that Israel is a nation again, starting in 1948 AD and forever.

155 In Zephaniah 3:19, is that Israel is a nation again, starting in 1948 AD and forever. And the word get, is in meaning of being carried out by God, as noted in Haggai 2.

156 And also, 3:19, it also means, that Israel shall be protected and never cease to be a nation, again and forever.

157 In Zephaniah 3:20, the words "turned back your captivity." It is in meaning of Israel being a nation again, starting in 1948 AD and forever. And that is found also in the book of Haggai-- chapter 2.

1 Part 6 w / 118 verses   The dome of the rock

2 The dome of the rock building and all of it's seen foundation and all of it's foundation, seen land. That is used for the dome of the rock building, that the building sitteth on,

3 Thou shalt remove that presents, physically, away from my seeing presents, that is called Christ Jesus, forever,

4 And you, O Israel, you may keep the rock of importance, that is found in the center of that dome, for historical true sake,

5 But thou, shalt remove that dome temple, and it's seen foundation land, away from me, forever.

Therefore, take a sufficient Amount of it's land that the dome building sitteth on, and all of it's seen temple dome building, away from me (God), forever.

6 And, thou shalt replenish that area foundation land space, with new land, that is to be found from within Israel's true borders, forever. And, all historical true evidence, as it maybe found, in being found from that foundation area, that shall be dug up,

7 Then, thou mayest truly keep it forever. But what is found concerning both: The dome of the rock building itself and secondly: It's dome building foundation land area, where the building sitteth on,

8 Thou mayest truly not keep those things. forever. But what ever else is found in that true dig, then thou mayest truly keep it for historical true sake---

9 But nothing shall be kept of the dome of the rock building it's self, and nothing shall be kept of it's seen foundation land, where the dome building sitteth on, that is concerning the dome building itself,

10 And, as to why--- I (God) shall not be insulted by those, who may desire to come to that site wholeheartedly, for other reasons. Rather than to seek me, who (God) is the God of truth,

11 For, they may try to come only to seek the remains of the fallen dome, rather than me, forever. Therefore, I shall not be insulted by them, who accept not, Christ Jesus, as Christ Jesus being their seen savior, forever,

12 And, all of the remains of that dome temple building, it shall be, fully within reason, crushed and given to the wind. And is to be given to wind, over the ocean, forever.

13 Then, the foundation land area that the dome of the rock building, had sat on. It shall be burned with great fire. And that burned true land, it shall be given to the sea, forever.

14 And that burned land, it is to kept away from Israel and away from the world, forever. For I chose to cleanse this land with fire.

15 For I wish to restore this land, as to what it was, prior to 70 AD, before the gentiles had taken procession of it, at that time.

16 And whatever dome of the rock building material burnables are found in that temple, then thou mayest truly burn it and scatter it, over the ocean, as well,

17 And I, truly, do desire nothing to be left of that then burned true foundation land area and dome building. For I desire that spot that is my land, to be made once again forever, to be made

pure unto me. For I do chose, to rebuild another temple,

18 On that, then restored to me, pure true land. And I want to rebuild that new temple, on that, then restored true land. As that then restored true land, had appeared, originally to me (God), before 70 AD.

19 And while, thou shalt do all of those things. Then do them separately, away from each other (The dome building and it's building foundation land area), forever.

20 And, keep nothing at all. That is found, from both, the dome of the rock building and keep nothing of what had been, once, it's seen building foundation land,

21 But diligently, remove both; "That dome temple building and all of it's seen and unseen, dome building foundation sufficient land area, away from the land of Israel. As being removed eternally forever and ever, removed forever."

22 And I (God) shall grant, a new, and a pure, true temple. To now be built, unto me, by Israel, and by grafted true Israel, forever.

23 And, it is, to be built by me (Israel and grafted true Israel, shall build this for me [God]), as being forever true, of me, forever.

24 And that new temple, it is to be rebuilt, now, at this time of the true earth, forever, as saith thy eternal, true God, as being, eternally forever and ever true. For I Am true, forever.

25 Again, all of the dome of the rock building, and all of it's dome building foundation land area, Ye shall, therefore, take all of the that dome temple mount area and the building dome,

26 And burn that land dome area. And then, that burned land and burned dome. It shall be removed, physically, now, away from mount Moriah, at this time, forever, and do not forget to crush the dome building entirely forever

27 And, all of this must be done, now. For all of that dome land area, is to now be given back fully unto Israel, as being forever true, and now to be finished, unto me,

28 (no one shall have complete control and have complete authority over all of that complete true land of mount Moriah, accept Israel only and forever. And that is to be found unto me, forever true, and without true end. And that is seen, as being eternally forever and ever true),

29 As all of that particular land, that is called mount Moriah. Is already forever, a part of true Israel, as being eternally forever seen.

30 And, I have already given all of that temple mount land and it's seen dome, and all of mount Moriah, unto Israel, already and forever.

31 And the glory of this latter house (My new temple and it's new buildings) shall be greater than the former house, and in this house,

32 That I shall build now in the earth, I shall grant my peace forever true, and I shall fill mine own true house, with mine, true glory, forever, for Christ Jesus, he is found in this home (the new temple), forever.

33 And this new temple, is my new home, forever, and thy new home, spiritually forever. And it is our true home, and our true mansion, unto whomsoever,

34 Thou art, unto me. As thou art found unto me, spiritually forever, in Jesus Christ, forever. And as thou art found eternally forever true, unto me, as thou art found unto me, as being eternally forever true, in Jesus Christ, as being eternally forever true and forever more.

35 And I shall grant that true peace forever and ever true, and thou shalt see, the desire of the nations, that do come to mine house and is our true house, and is our true mansion, forever,

36 And I shall receive them in Christ my glory forever, and greater things, than my Son Christ,

hath did. Shall these in Christ Jesus, do forever true, in me. As being eternally forever and ever true, and, forever more.

37 And this is because Christ Jesus hath came to me in mine eternal true glory, forever. And I do, in these days, also, render eternal seen vengeance, to mine seen true adversaries, forever,

38 And I shall also be merciful to Israel and unto the land of Israel, forever. And in these true days, thou O Israel. Thou shalt build me mine true temple and it's once seen buildings, again, and, forever,

39 And, that I may appear personally, forever. As mine own eternal true self, as being forever true, within that true temple, that is, called God forever sure. And is, called Christ Jesus, forever,

40 And thou O Israel, happy art thou, o my people, who are saved unto me, forever true, through Jesus Christ. And what people of the earth, O Israel. Are like unto thee forever, when thou art found unto me forever, in Jesus Christ, forever.

41 Yea, it is them, who are redeemed unto me, through Jesus Christ, forever. For they are my glory, that is called eternal life, forever. And, I Am thy shield, O Israel, and as the shield of thine own true help, forever. And I Am thy sword of

thine own true excellency, as it is found as being: "Jesus Christ," forever.

42 And thou, O Israel, as being in Christ Jesus, forever. Thou shalt tread upon all of thine true enemies, forever. And this is, as being eternally forever and ever true, in me, forever.

43 And thou, art even my own chosen true chariot of light, that is called Jesus Christ, forever, O Israel. And thou shalt dwell, in safety alone.

44 And that Christly true safety, it is called Israel dwelling eternally forever, as one in and with me (God), through Jesus Christ, as being eternally forever and ever seen, and that is seen unto me forever.

45 And, I have opened unto you, forever, O Israel and unto the world, The fountain of Jacob, that is called Jesus Christ, unto you, as being eternally forever true, O Israel. And thou, O Israel, thou art, unto me, as being eternally forever true,

46 As being, Israel, eternally forever seen and true. And, as being, forever truly seen, as being: A eternal and most true people, who are called "A eternal true Land of corn and wine, forever."

47 And the gentiles of the entire true earth, they do come to gather with thee, of this risen one

(Jesus Christ), who (Jesus Christ) is thy corn and wine, forever, O Israel,

48 And thou O Israel, art my little one, as thou art found unto me in Jesus Christ, forever. And there are unto thee (Israel) forever, gentiles of the gentile nations of the earth, forever. That truly do desire,

49 To come, to Israel and seek Christly Godliness, forever. Even though, one can find this eternal true Christ, who is me forever,

50 Through a simple true prayer of repentance unto me, forever. Even, no matter where that true person unto me, maybe found in all of the true earth, as being forever seen. And that is forever true, and, is forever, eternally seen.

51 And when, this Christ Jesus, shall sit upon his and my throne, many shall come to worship me, in Jerusalem, freely, and forever. And he (Christ Jesus) shall be,

52 Most surely, seated physically upon my throne, that thou shalt build for me now, in Jerusalem, in these eternal true days, forever, and is seen as being my new temple and my new buildings. And thou, shalt, most certainly,

53 Through Jesus Christ, destroy all of my enemies and thy enemies, together and forever.

And the new temple, it is to be finished, through Jesus Christ, forever.

54 And I do show mercy unto thousands, who do chose Christ Jesus, forever. As they, truly, do chose this Christ Jesus, as Christ Jesus, being their seen savior, as being forever true, from me, forever,

55 And these, in Jesus Christ, forever. They do, chose to do those loving eternal true things, such as: accepting Jesus Christ, as this eternal one (Jesus Christ),

56 Being their seen savior, as being forever true and forever seen. And that true desire, as it is demonstrated, unto me, through Christ Jesus, forever.

57 And that true desire in the repentful true ones of the earth, forever. For, to have Christ Jesus, forever. It is, found, unto me, as being forever true, from their fleshly true heart, as being eternally forever and ever true,

58 And these, in Christ Jesus, forever. They are, most surely seen, as being, desirethsome. To always want, and, to always, chose to love me,

59 As being openly and freely, forever true, of themselves to me in Christ Jesus forever. And, they do keep my eternal, true commandments, as

being forever and ever true, of themselves, toward me, forever.

60 Therefore, in all of these things, that I tell you today, rejoice O Israel and the world. And quickly, reunite all of this mount Moriah area true land, back unto Israel, as Israel, forever.

61 And you, O Israel, you may keep the rock of importance, that is found in the center of the dome, for historical true sake. But remember, all of the dome of the rock building, and all of the dome building land foundation area. It must be fully destroyed and no remains, to remain of it, forever.

62 And ye O Israel, ye shall remove all presents of the gentile non Jewish faith, away from mount moriah, forever. And ye shall remove it away from all of Israel and away from all of Biblical true Israel, forever.

63 This removing, it is forever. And this removing, it shall be done in like manner, as thou shalt deal with the dome building and with it's foundation land area.

64 And when Israel is found forever, within all Biblical true Israeli land forever. Then thou O Israel, thou shalt eternally forever, remove forever:

65 All religious presents of non Jewish Israeli religious sites from all Israel and Biblical true Israel, forever (Christian faith is considered by me forever, as being a true functional part of Jewish religion, that is me forever. And I Am "The God of truth," forever),

66 Those non Jewish non Christian religious sites. They are to never appear again and forever, in Israel, forever. As saith thy eternal kind God, forever.

67 And I do, most certainly, do command another Godly true temple, as I had once there in Israel, before 70 AD. For it to be, now rebuilt, again and forever. And this, new Godly true temple,

68 It is, to now, be fully built, by Israel and by grafted true Israel, unto myself (God), as being eternally forever true, on mount Moriah, forever.

69 ALL Christian nations, are to help Israel, in these eternal true matters. And if any of the Christian true world, shall not encourage Israel and will not help Israel, in these regards,

70 Then truly, those particular true Christian nations, they as each, they shall be, quickly punished by me, forever. And they shall be punished,

71 Until they conform unto my (God) word, as it is found in this book and in these days, as my servant Roger Dale Wallace, doth write and is writing in these days, for me, through Jesus Christ, forever,

72 And, if any of those Christian nations and any of the world nations, shall not help Israel, with any of these true things. Then I will, most surely. Render fire and rebuke, unto all of those seen nations, who will not help Israel, in these eternal true matters, forever.

73 And that most eternal, true punishment. It shall remain until those nations, fully comply, with my (God) great word, as concerning this issue, forever.

74 And, also, all the books that I do write through my servant, Roger. They shall, all appear, forever, in my (God) new temple, that is, to be now built,

75 Now on mount Moriah, and that true temple, it is, most surely, to be rebuilt, only by, Israel and by grafted true Israel (Christians), forever.

76 No unclean hands, shall approach the temple, while it is being built, for all hands that aren't either Christian or Jewish hands, they are unto me, as being unclean, forever.

77 And, if any unclean one does come near me, while I (God and Christ Jesus, they are the temple) Am being built on mount Moriah, I will deal with that particular true one, myself (God), forever.

78 After that true temple, is finished being built. Then only Christians, shall enter into the most holy true sites, as those true sites, are found in the temple, forever,

79 For the unclean (not being a Christian is considered unclean), shall not approach unto me, as I Am the most holy true sites, that are found in the temple. Least I break forth upon whosoever is found, in not being a Christian unto me, forever,

80 Therefore, I will break forth upon anyone, who will purposely approach unto me, as being firmly seen, as being seen unto me forever, as a non Christian, forever.

81 Only holy Christly true hands, shall appear before me forever, in my most holy true sites, as they be found in the rebuilt true temple, forever.

82 Therefore, appoint Levites, to appear, who are Christian, unto me, forever. As they shall handle the Christian true duties of the temple, forever.

83 And the Greek orthodox church in Jerusalem, shall administer this duty before me, with the

Levites, forever. And they shall be care takers of this rebuilt true temple, as well, and forever.

84 Make sure, that whosoever shall appear in the holiest parts of the temple, as being caretakers, that they, surely be cleansed in Jesus Christ, forever,

85 Therefore, let each person, examine himself forever, before entering this forever, unending true duty. As it is found in the most holy true parts, of the temple, forever.

86 The unclean may appear in the temple, for teaching and the like, but the unclean, they shall not appear before me, in the most holiest true parts of the temple,

87 Least I move upon them, who are found unto me forever, as being wickedly, as they be found unto me, as being, mischievous unto me, forever.

88 I Am a holy God, therefore, come before me in Christ Jesus, forever, least I break forth upon thou, who doth not chose Christ Jesus, forever,

89 For if thou chose not, this Christ Jesus, as this Christ Jesus being thy seen savior, forever. Then, I shall, destroy thee, most surely, forever.

90 Moreover, and again, that, to be rebuilt true temple. It shall not and it is, to never be

constructed to handle again, animal sacrifices, as being forever true.

91 For Christ Jesus, he (Jesus Christ) has given of his blood, forever. That thou mayest approach me, freely, in the temple, as being forever seen.

92 And, you shall design this new temple, by taking in a new design, that bests suites all Christian pure faiths, as they are found, given by me, as being forever true,

93 As they are found unto me, throughout all of the true world, forever. And, you shall sing and teach and learn in my true temple, forever.

94 And my anointed and true gospel, it shall be preached and taught in my new temple, and this new temple, it is to be found as part of my new Jerusalem, that I doth, create, forever.

95 And that new, to be built, true temple. It is, even to be called Jesus Christ, forever. And, spiritually, my new Jerusalem, it isn't made with hands, and it doth come down out of heaven, from me forever, unto all men, forever,

96 And, that true temple, it is to be found in Israel, forever, and unto all of the earth, forever. And, you shall most surely, design this true temple, to represent me,

97 As I Am found, as I Am found as being all Christly true churches, that are already found, throughout all of the earth, as being forever true.

98 Therefore, take in, those true designs of all of the true world Christly true churches, in these days, and model also, according to my old temple, as well. But do not design my temple, for animal scarifies, at all and forever.

99 And, again, all of these books, that my servant, Roger Dale Wallace doth write, as I have command him through Christ Jesus, to write, forever:

100 All of those seen books, they shall each appear, forever, as a prophesying true testimony, unto Israel, and unto the world, as being forever true, and that is forever true of me (God), and is forever seen.

101 Ye shall also take the Christian Bible, which is my torah. And you shall place it, as well, into that new temple, as a living true testimony, as I shall show it, also, unto all of the world, forever.

102 Therefore, thus saith thy God, eternally forever. Conform thou, unto all, that is commanded of thee, O Israel and commanded of the, O world,

103 And, as I do and have given unto thee, as being eternally forever true, O Israel. And, I shall

send Christ unto thee, soon. And though, no man, knows the day nor hour of Christ's true return, for the living and the dead, of this earth, forever,

104 ye can know, that it is found, in this eternal true generation of signs, that doth, truly follow the faithful true Son, who is called, Jesus Christ,

105 And those, true in God, eternal true signs. They are me and from me, as being eternally forever seen, in me, and are, eternally forever. And those, true signs. They truly,

106 Do follow, this eternal, true Christ Jesus. As this Christ Jesus, is found, eternal in me, as being eternally forever seen,

107 And this Christ Jesus, he is eternally forever seen, as I Am seen, even as I Am God forever. And this, true Christ Jesus. He is forever, and he is faithfully forever seen, and true,

108 And he (Jesus Christ), is found in me, as my (Christ Jesus) true Son, who is given from me (God), unto all the Sons of men, forever. And he (Jesus Christ), is eternally forever seen, as I (God) Am seen,

109 And this same, Christ Jesus. He is, even seen, as being eternally forever true, as my true breath, as being eternally forever seen. And that true breath, it is, called God, eternally forever.

110   And this eternal one, he is, most surely, called Christ Jesus, forever. And he is most surely, eternally forever true, and, forever seen. As seen, as being: Jesus Christ, the Son, who is called God, forever.

111   And this same Jesus, he hath spoken unto thee, forever, O Israel, and, unto the, O true world. And this same, Jesus Christ, he hast spoken unto thee (all people of the earth forever), forever, as concerning the kingdom of God, forever,

112   And the kingdom of God, forever. It is mentioned by this eternal Christ, forever. And as he has even mentioned it, as it is found recorded, by me, in the eternal true book of Luke, as it found, recorded in chapter 21:31.

113   And, this, my new, given true command, to build, now, my new and most true, rebuilt true temple, forever. It is found, given of me (God), faithfully unto you, O Israel and unto you, O earth, forever.

114   And, that new command, it is found, given of me, most surely, unto both of thee, O Israel and unto thee, O true world. As it shall be, and is found, unto both of thee, forever. And it is, now, commanded to occur, in this true day and true hour, as being eternally forever true.

115 And, that in doing so, that I (God), may, quickly, do all, that I (God) have said, that I (God) would do, as being eternally forever true, and, forever more. And, I Am, forever more.

116 Moreover, again: "As concerning the dig." It means to remove and not keep anything that is a part of the dome building--that is found as the building dome itself and secondly:

117 To remove and not keep what ever is found of the dome building itself, that is found in the dome foundation land, that is found under the dome building. Anything else, that is found in that true dig, at the dome and etc. That maybe kept for historical true sake, forever.

118 And I, do truly, love thee, forever, O Israel. And I Am sincerely forever and ever true, of myself, forever, O great Israel. And thou (Israel), shalt be found, forever, in Jesus Christ, forever.

Part 7 w/ 113 verses   The mount of GOD

1 My fellow brother, in Jesus Christ our true Lord and savior, as being eternally forever true: Dear Brother Irineos 1st:

2 Our God, he has entrusted you personally, with all of these written true works. Therefore, you must exercise extreme care and caution, for many Christian people through out all of the earth,

3   May be exalted in themselves, in puffing true knowledge, and have taught that puffly true knowledge error, as it is found and seen by our true God, forever.

4   As it is found concerning these puffy ones forever, as concerning their false views of Biblical true end time prophecy,

5   And, as concerning, how deep, that great error has ran throughout the entire true earth, as concerning that true fact. Many, throughout all of the true earth, forever.

6   They may try to resist God's true words, as you have now, been entrusted of God to perform on God's behalf, which are all of these unsealed and unclosed, true wonders of God, forever.

7   And, it is a great thundering eternal quaking true responsibility, therefore, let no man come between you and these new scriptures, that I have and Am delivering to you, on our true God's behalf, as being forever seen.

8   For "Our True Father," he hast most surely, entrusted you personally, with these new thundering true works. Therefore, seek his favor and guidance,

9   That you may know, as to how to proceed on God's behalf, with these new *evening light* true

things of God. This is because, of all of these new books,

10   That are found from our eternal true God, forever. That are being and going to be seen forever, as being: "New holy scriptures,"

11   And now, these new things and the Christian Bible. They are now, one together, forever. For they are God and they are Christ Jesus, forever.

12   And these new lightning true works, they are most surely, hailing unto the earth forever, as great hail stones of truth, that is called God in Jesus Christ, forever.

13   And those hail stones, they are found, in being given of God, forever, and from God, eternally forever. And that is eternally forever true, as given from our kind God, forever.

14   And they are, eternally forever and ever true, and that is most surely, eternally related as being forever seen, as concerning the work of the two witnesses, as it is found recorded in the book of The Revelation of Jesus Christ.

15   Again, I strongly caution you, to be most careful, when seeking advice from end time prophecy teachers, and the like.

16   For some are wolves in sheep's clothing, and some are exalted, as if they are God in all things,

and of course, some are Christ like, and they will help thee and encourage thee,

17 And they will not hinder these new works, for they will understand what is happening in the spirit of God, as Jesus Christ has opened the seals in The Book of Revelation,

18 As that true opening, is now being seen, as it is given unto us forever, by Jesus Christ in the True Father, forever. And true opening, it is called unsealed truth,

19 And it is now being seen in our true generation, as being eternally forever true. And, it is my wish, that you follow your heart, in all of these things, forever.

20 And, no doubt, you will have to reasonably, share these eternal true truths with the public, at this time. And many, shall desire my personal true harm and personal true hurt, forever.

21 But my life, it is not mine to live. For it is Christ, who liveth his life in this body of death, forever. Therefore, Christ in the True Father, forever. He (Jesus Christ) shall in that great day, change this deathly eternal true body, in a twinkling of an eye, forever.

22 And, in these days, much confusion has been taught concerning the man of sin issue (taught against scripture). And the man of sin issue, it is

found recorded in the new Testament. For this confusion, that is and has been taught.

23 It is concerning the true temple in Jerusalem, being rebuilt, and the church world teaching that a Antichrist one will be sitting as God himself, in that new, rebuilt true temple in Jerusalem, and that a peace pack shall also be made at the same time, for 3 and half years.

24 But, in reality, those actual new Testament, true Bible scriptures, as found concerning forever, the man of sin. They are only symbolic in meaning, for true interpretation of scripture. And, in no wise, shall this ever be seen, as a physical interpretation of scripture. And that is forever.

25 And these new Testament scriptures, they are found only forever, to be symbolic in nature to be interpreted. In other words: Those new Testament verses, they are only concerning forever, spiritual true matters,

26 As it is found concerning all of the earth's, true men of sin, everywhere. For to be a sinner, is to already be found unto God forever, as being found in perdition, forever.

27 And, again, this man of sin issue, it is only symbolic, and it is found to be forever, as all exalted Noah's type days sinners, who desire Satanism forever,

28 As it is found according to the new Testament, in where these are found unto God forever, as perdition. Which means utter true final true perdition, forever.

29 And some of these people, they are Noah's type true people, who are seen unto God forever. As being eternally forever true, as being lukewarm true Christians, who are seen unto God forever,

30 As being eternally forever found, as being chaff and tares, in Jesus Christ. And they have been found exalting themselves, as if they were God, forever. And these heady minded ones, in the loftiness of Satan, forever.

31 They do purposely, not conform unto all that is and is called God. And as it is found concerning our true God in Jesus Christ, who (Jesus Christ) is God's own eternal true Son, forever.

32 And these, they have as a result, forever. They have sinfully exalted themselves, forever. As if, they are God, for all of true eternity. And they are seen by our God, forever. As being unrepentiful true sin, forever.

33 And, as a result, of desiring Satanism forever. These have been seen unto God forever, as sin forever. And they shall most surely shall die unto God forever,

34 And they shall never be forgiven, for they truly do not ever desire true forgiveness, from God forever.

35 And these, they are seen. As being lukewarm ones (unfaithful to God true Christians), forever. And they are seen, as even found sitting spiritually in temple of God, that is called Jesus Christ, forever.

36 And they have lifted themselves up forever, as if they are God, forever. And these, they are seen, unto God forever. As being eternally forever, as being eternal true Sons and eternal true daughters of eternal true perdition, forever,

37 And they are seen by our true God, forever. As they are seen unto God forever, as being Antichrist and antigod, forever. For these purposely, they truly do chose, to never want to learn, all that is and is called God, forever.

38 For they truly have gone the way, spiritually back to Baal, as they truly do desire, Satanism, forever.

39 Therefore, there are those in Christ Jesus, forever. Who are spewed of God forever and spewed of Jesus Christ, forever. And they are truly reprobate unto all that is God and is called God, forever.

40 And that new rebuilt true temple, it shall be, now built on the mount, at Jerusalem. And no antichrist nor devil, shall ever physically sit in that new rebuilt true temple, forever.

41 And to believe, that an antichrist one will physically sit in that new rebuilt true temple, in Jerusalem, when it is built. It is to believe, that Satan's true lie, forever.

42 For to believe such a great lie, it is to believe great error against the written true scriptures, as they are found recorded in the new Testament, forever.

43 For those new Testament verses, they are only to be spiritually interpreted, about man's true falleness forever, as he is seen in our true day forever. As being like unto what was Noah's true days of the earth, forever.

44 Therefore, again, what the new Testament, is saying. It is saying, that mankind in our true day, would become sinful unto God, forever. As like unto the men,

45 Who were found by our true God, in the past, who are seen as being Noah's true days. And because of all these things, as it is found forever, as concerning our present true earth, forever,

46 Then, our true God, would have to judge the entire true earth, because of our true earth's present exalted true sinfulness, forever.

47 And, that in being found like unto Noah's true days, forever, in our true time of this earth, forever. That is found, in being against our kind, eternal true God, forever.

48 And those current true days, they are found forever, on our current true earth, now and forever true. For the judgments of God, they are currently found in all of the earth, now and forever. And those true judgments. They do show this Noah issue, forever.

49 And I have explained these things, quite some time ago, already to the church world. But many, still hold to the false teaching,

50 That a Antichrist one, shall physically sit in the temple in Jerusalem, when that true temple, has been rebuilt, forever.

51 And Satan hath apparently tried to teach that great error to the church world, and many have followed it faithfully of themselves,

52 As that great error, it is found by our true God, in their self exaltedness, as they truly do desire to be as God in temple of God, that is called Jesus Christ,

53 And many lukewarm Christians (teachers and the like), they are found unto God forever. As being lifted in the pride of this world, for many have turned,

54 From the natural true course of natural God given true life. That they may truly seek, unnatural true desires and unnatural true lusts, forever.

55 And some of this unnaturalness forever. It (unnaturalness forever) is most surely, eternally found even in some sinful true people,

56 Who are faithful of themselves, forever, as being eternally lost unto God, forever. As they truly do seek forever, same sex marriages, forever.

57 And to appease, that true, unnatural true lust, as it is seen eternally forever true, in the shameful unto God, forever. They are therefore seen unto God forever,

58 As being eternally forever true, as being against God, forever. And they shall even continue forever, to speak that eternal seen blasphemy, against God, forever.

59 And it is true of themselves unto God forever. And it is seen by our true God, as it is faithfully forever true of themselves, as they truly

do desire the wicked one forever, who is called Satan, forever.

60 And these, they are damned, forever. That is, if they shall not repent of all their seen before God true sins,

61 That they truly do desire in themselves, as being eternally forever seen, as being, eternally: "Satanism, forever."

62 And many, have even left the natural true course of this God given natural true life, as it is found concerning forever, the birthing of their seen, natural true children, forever (talking about abortion--forever).

63 And many, shall and do seek sinful true abortion, when the matters of life and death, aren't even a Godly eternal true factor, as it is to be made in those decisions, forever.

64 And in these days, many do those eternal seen true blasphemes, openly before God and openly before Jesus Christ, forever. And our true God, he shall require life for life, forever. And as it found concerning those sinful true choices, that they, the shameful, do make, forever.

65 And sinful true choices, forever. They are found forever, as it is found, as concerning those eternal true choices, as they the damned forever, do truly do desire Satan and Satanism, forever.

66 Therefore, to be unrepentfully sinful to God, forever. It is to run the risk, of eternal seen true death, forever. And that is why, many, shall never make it to their great elderly old age, in this fallen true world, forever,

67 And that is why, some are sickly in their body, even to the point of true death, forever. And they shall die unto God forever and unto Jesus Christ, forever.

68 But, in the true course of natural true life forever. Some eternal true sicknesses. They are not always pronounced from God forever, as judgment forever.

69 Therefore, let each person examine them self, forever. As to see, if that true person, is found in unrepentiful true seen sin, forever, and that, that true person, may repent forever, and not die unto God, forever.

70 And, all of these, eternal, true eternal true writings. That I (Roger) Am writing from our true God, as they are being found written through Jesus Christ, who (Jesus Christ) is our eternal, true savior, forever.

71 They are all and each, as found, currently as being eternally demonstrated from God, through Jesus Christ the Son, forever. And those thunderous eternal true writings,

72 They are thunderly given from Christ Jesus, and from our thundering true God, as being eternally forever seen and certain, forever.

73 And, as a result, those eternal, true, thunderous true writings. They are given from God forever, unto the body of Christ, eternally forever and ever seen, and felt, as being found from God, eternally forever and ever true.

74 And, all these earth quaking true writings. They do thunderly reveal, what is term; "The man of sin," forever. And, which is the revealing the spiritual sinful true state of sinful Satan mankind. That is called "The days of Noah."

75 And which is this generation of the earth, as being eternally forever seen. And this seen true revealing, as given unto us forever, as concerning of the man (men) of sin and of the daughter (daughters) of sin,

76 This is, to now be seen and understood, from our true God and from his true Son, who (Jesus Christ) is called Jesus Christ, forever, and as it is now given unto the body of Christ, forever. And this eternal true understanding,

77 It is given now and forever, from God to the earth, as to understand that issue concerning perdition, forever. And it is to be understood in these eternal true days, forever.

78 And it is found, as concerning the new Testament true scriptures, that are found, as speaking about the man of sin.

79 And from the time of Adam, all men are perditious unto God forever, when they are found forever, by our true God, forever. As being a true sinner, forever.

80 Therefore, as a Noah's day type true sinner, forever. These have became, utterly perditious, and compete, and seen, as eternal dead death, forever. And they are seen, as being eternally found,

81 As being forever, as final seen true ruin. As that seen perdition. Is seen before God, as being eternally forever true and forever more.

82 And these Noah type sinners, which include all chaff and all tares in Christ Jesus, forever. They are those, that Christ Jesus is revealing,

83 As they are found forever true. In their true wickedness, that wicked true men truly do desire forever, as being Satanism forever.

84 For sinful true man, has lifted himself up forever, as being eternally seen in his true sins, as those seen sins, are seen forever before God, as being a eternal damningly true abomination,

85 For these, true daughters of sin and these true men of sin, people. They are seen before me (God), forever. In their truly desired true Satanness, that is called true death, forever.

86 And, as a result, man has bought himself, now into the dust of death, forever. That is, if sinful true man, shall in these days, never repent unto God, forever.

87 And this is because, they will not ever desire to repent and receive Jesus Christ, as this eternal Jesus, being one's true seen savior, forever.

88 And, again, we are in those Noah type true days. That are currently found in all of the earth, as being forever true. And this Christ, and the "True Father," they are revealing this sinful exalted true state of man's sinfulness, forever.

89 And it is being revealed by them (God and Christ Jesus), as it is found by them (God and Christ Jesus) forever, as they truly do reveal sinful true man forever,

90 In these, my eternal true writings. That are given from our true God, himself, forever. And which are found through Jesus Christ, who is God's own, eternal true Son, forever.

91 And it is being recorded in these eternal true days, as God hast said it would occur in our true

days, as it is most surely, found mentioned of God through Jesus Christ, in the new Testament.

92 And it is being found, as being revealed through me, as Christ Jesus, giveth this inspiration to me forever, as being eternally seen from our "True Father God," forever. And it is, currently and presently,

93 Being eternally seen, as it is found recorded in these eternal true writings, that our true Father, doth write through me, in these true, thundering true days, of this eternal true earth, forever.

94 For Christ, he is the Godly true thunder, as he (Christ Jesus) is eternally found, in and of God, forever. And he is found, most surely, eternally forever true, and faithful from God, as eternal, forever.

95 And this Christ Jesus, he is found in these eternal true days, forever. And this Jesus Christ, he is seen, as thundering eternally forever true, in all that is God, forever.

96 And Christ Jesus, is the heavenly true thundering, that is given unto us forever, as a given true thundering true gem of God, forever.

97 And we, in Jesus Christ, forever. We are seen, as eternally thundering through this eternal true Son, who is called Jesus Christ, forever,

98 And we, through Jesus Christ, forever. We most surely do, as we are found mightily, in and through God, forever. We do prophetically thunder, eternally forever true,

99 As thundering forever, as: "FOREVER OF AND BY OUR TRUE KIND GOD, FOREVER." And this same eternal one, he is called Jesus Christ. And he is, the faithful true Son of God himself, forever.

100 And this faithful one is Christ Jesus, and he is a eternal true gem of God, as being eternally forever true, and as being with all that is called God, as God is found forever, in Jesus Christ, his own true Son, forever.

101 And this Christ Jesus, he is now, performing the end time true oath of preaching the everlasting true end time gospel, as it is to now be preached to them, that do dwell in our true earth, forever,

102 And that is concerning, that time shall be no more and forever. Therefore, the gospel is being preached as everlasting true judgment, that is called "The end of the days, great judgments, forever."

103 And those end time judgments, they are given from God "The Father," forever. And those just judgments, they are called life and death, forever.

104   And they are most surely seen as eternal just judgment, forever, and are eternal true judgment, that is called God forever, and it is given unto us, forever,

105   For our true days of this fallen true earth forever. They are like unto Noah's true days, forever. And that issue, it is concerning our true time of this fallen true earth, forever. And that issue, it is now being preached unto all nations, kindred's and tongues, forever.

106   And the voice of that true commandment. It is seen and given from God through Jesus Christ, forever.

107   And it is seen, as being: "Fear God forever and give glory to God, forever, for the hour of our true God's eternal just judgments, they have arrived in this utterly fallen, true earth, forever."

108   "And those just judgments, they are called God forever. And they are now, being seen, as now and forever, as they are found, now as they are given from God, forever.

109   And those just judgments, they are called God, eternally forever. As they are given of God, to this fallen true earth, forever. And they are given unto us, from our true God, forever. And they are seen, as being eternal just judgment, as forever true,

110 And that just judgment, it is found, now and forever, in this fallen true earth, as being eternally forever and ever true," from God, forever.

111 And that is a righteously true given true judgment, as it is found forever, as it is given of God unto the earth, forever. And it is given unto us, through Jesus Christ, the Son of God himself (God), forever.

112 And I, Roger, I have most surely, have already written, as it is concerning the man of sin true situation, as it is already found written by me forever, to the church forever. But, there are those, who still hold fast to the false reality of a physical occurrence,

113 Of an actual physical true man of sin or a physical true Antichrist true devil, setting physically in temple at Jerusalem, and showing himself, as if he were God, forever. (continued over and into part 8)

Part 8 w / 71 verses   Thy first love

1 *And*, how great an error, as it is found demonstrated against the holy truth of scripture. As these in exaltedness (found in part 7:112), forever.

2 As they have deceived many with their false teachings, that are found demonstrated against

the truth. That is the truth, that is called "God in Christ Jesus," forever.

3 And many, shall never return to their first love. That is being repentful in God forever and loving God with a complete and sincere, true spirit, as it should always be found, in the eyes of God, forever.

4 And when, the new temple, is rebuilt in Jerusalem. Neither a devil (Satan and Satan's kind called demons forever) nor a true sinner, shall ever sit in the throne of God, in Jerusalem, forever, and as to deceive men,

5 As if, any of them (Satan and Satan's kind and all unrepentiful found as mankind forever), were God forever, as by sitting physically in the temple of God, as that new temple, shall be found forever, on Mount Moriah, forever.

6 And to believe, that any of that false teaching, can physically happen to the soon to be rebuilt true temple in Jerusalem, that is to be rebuilt and seen before God, forever.

7 Then, this false belief, it shall damn all, that shall preach that false belief. As if it were truly, forever eternally approved of God, forever, as they speak it, as if, it were truly, an approved gospel true truth, forever.

8   And our true "Father God." He has not taught such false beliefs. Only willful true unrepentiful true sin, can teach such false beliefs. As it is found in being against God, eternally forever,

9   And, even now, our true and kind, eternal true God. He himself, is now, presently and actively, occupying all of the true temple mount area, forever. And this is most holy to him (God), forever.

10   And our true God, will occupy it, forever. And Christ Jesus, he (Jesus Christ) shall soon, occupy it physically himself, with God the Father, forever. And, through "God The Father."

11   Christ Jesus, he shall physically forever, occupy the true throne of God, forever. For this Christ Jesus, he is the rightful true king of Israel, as being eternally forever true, and, as forever seen,

12   And this seen, Christ Jesus. He (Jesus Christ) is seen, as he is given and sent by our eternal true God, as being all that is and is called God, forever.

13   And this true Christ Jesus, he shall be seen forever true, and he is seen forever, as being eternally, the true Son of God, forever.

14   And this Christ Jesus, he shall, as eternally forever true and forever seen. He (Jesus Christ)

shall be physically seated on king David's true throne, forever.

15 And, even now, our true God himself, he shall now begin to chase unclean hands, away from the true temple mount area, forever. And the angels of our precious true God, forever. They shall,

16 Now appear, at times in the true temple mount area, forever. As in full view concerning themselves, unto our true God and who (God) is their true God, forever,

17 And those seen true angels, they shall be seen forever, in full view, with the sword of God, as it is now drawn forever. And that viewing,

18 It shall be seen, faithfully forever true from God, at times, as to be seen forever, on the mount of God, forever. For that true mount, it is called and is: "All of mount Mariah," as it is forever seen and forever true.

19 And those Godly true angels, in "God The True Father," forever. They shall, now show by their own personal true appearance. The actual true location of the old temple, as to how it was, in the days of old.

20 And the true sword of God, it is now, thunderly drawn upon and unto the unclean ones, forever. And that great and mighty true voice,

that is the true, quaking true sword of God forever,

21 It is, most eternal. For it is our thunderly, hailing true God, forever true and forever seen.

22 And that true, quickening true, hailing true sword. It is most surely seen, and it is forever, called God. And those, drawn, true kindly, eternal true swords,

23 They are seen, as being eternally: "The seven true thundering eternal true voices of God," And they are God, forever."

24 And those seven true voices. They are Godly true thunder. And they shall, in these days, thunderly and quakinly. They shall speak, all that is given to them, from our true, kind God, forever,

25 And those seven thunderous true voices, that are called God forever. They shall speak forever, as it is given, to those eternal and most true angels (Christians), to speak in Christ Jesus forever,

26 And those kindly eternal true voices. That are called God forever. They are found eternally forever eternal, as they are found from the eternal one, who is seen and called God forever, and who is our true God, forever sure.

27 And those speaking true angelic ones. They are most surely, eternal in "God The Father," forever. And these eternal, true Christly eternal true angels,

28 They are, most surely, eternal of and from God, forever. For our true kind God and his eternal true Son, who is called Jesus Christ,

29 They do dwell forever, in these eternal thundering true angels (Christians), as being eternally forever true of themselves (God and Christ Jesus, forever), as being our true kind God and his dear eternal true Son, who (Jesus Christ) is called Jesus Christ,

30 They are called the true life, that is called God, forever. For that life, it is found from God forever, in Jesus Christ, forever. And the life, as it is found from God forever, in Christ Jesus forever. It is called God in Jesus Christ forever.

31 And our true God, he shall forever, speak through those thunderous true angels (Christians forever), that are of himself (God) forever, in Jesus Christ forever.

32 And these true Christly true angels, they shall thunderly speak our true God's eternal seen hailing true wrath and hailing true mercy, forever.

33 And those prophetic, angelic true swords. They are now, thunderly drawn upon and unto the unclean ones, forever.

34 And these prophesying true swords. They are eternally forever eternally seen from our true Christ and his true Father God, forever.

35 And these, thunderous, true hailing, true angelic prophesying true angels, in Jesus Christ, forever.

36 They shall be seen hailing our God's eternal seen truth, as it shall and is, given from God, through Jesus Christ, forever, and it is given of Christ in (in means the word by) "The True Father," forever,

37 And that true truth, it is called Jesus Christ in the True Father, forever, and it is spoken through themselves (angelic spoken utterances found through Christians forever), forever,

38 As it is most surely, eternally spoken by our true God, through those angelic angel true hosts, forever, as it is now, being spoken forever, at the holy true mount, that is called mount Moriah, at Jerusalem, forever,

39 And through our true God's eternal true direction, forever. These Christly anointed true Christian angels, they shall, most surely, eternally forever,

40 They shall even point the way, to the actual true temple mount, old sanctuary area, and this is to be forever seen, from me (God), forever.

41 And I Roger, I do say, that our thundering, earth quaking, true God, who is most kind forever. He shall even begin to now, to thunderly chase, the unrepentiful true gentiles, away from the mount of God, as being eternally forever and ever seen.

42 And many, unclean ones, at the true temple mount area. They shall die, as a result of their defiance to leave the temple mount, forever.

43 For these, may try to hinder all of Israel. As Israel is commanded in these days, as commanded in regards of Israel's true responsibility to the God of Abraham, forever. As it is found concerning the true temple mount issue, forever.

44 And to not be Christian, it is to be unclean forever. And to be not Jewish, it is considered as well, as being unclean unto God forever.

45 Therefore, to enter the temple mount, one must be either truly Jewish, and if not truly Jewish, then Christian forever.

46 And if a unclean one, does enters the temple mount area forever. Then if they be found before God forever. As to be firmly set forever, unto

Satan forever. Then the eternal just judgment, from God,

47 It shall fall upon those unclean ones forever, who are seen on the temple mount true area, forever. And that true judgment. It shall seek them out forever,

48 And that true judgment, as it is a given true death, from God, forever. And it is seen, as being eternally forever, as given from God, as being eternally forever true and forever seen of God, forever.

49 And it is to be given from God forever, as because God himself, he is seen, as being eternally forever true, without true end, as he is now, found forever, at the true mount of holiness (temple mount on Moriah), that is called God, forever

50 And God, he is most surely, forever. As to be seen forever, at the mount of his true throne, forever. As it is called mount Moriah, forever. And God's eternal true presents,

51 On that holy true mount of Moriah, forever. It is to now be made manifest and known throughout all of the earth, as God is now on the mount, as being eternally forever and ever true.

52 And his (God) eternal true presents, on the mount of justice (mount Moriah), forever. It is

eternally forever, as to be seen, as being: **"Holy"** -- as being forever true.

53 And God shall dwell on mount Moriah forever, for God shall in these eternal true days forever. He shall bring forth his great words that are called Christ Jesus,

54 As Christ Jesus being the true eternal life, that is called God forever. And in doing so, that our true God may forever, be seen as being:

55 The tabernacle of God is with men, and he will dwell with them of the earth, forever. And these in Christ, they shall be his people, forever.

56 And our true and kind one, who is called God forever. He shall always be seen in the earth, as he is God in Christ Jesus, forever.

57 And our true kind eternal God, he shall with the coming of his Son who is called Jesus Christ, forever. God shall then, wipe away all tears from our true eyes, forever. And true eternal seen death, it shall be no more.

58 And, moreover, crying and pain. Those things, they shall never be found, in that great and ever lasting true day, forever.

59 And the desire to faithfully sin forever. That true desire, it shall not even come to mind, as for it to be obtained by the redeemed, forever.

60 What a blessed true day, it is, and shall be in me (God) forever, as saith thy eternal true one, who is called Jesus Christ in me (God), forever.

61 For truly, Christ shall come and sit physically upon my throne in Jerusalem, that thou shalt make for me now in Israel, forever. And this eternal life, that is called Jesus Christ. He (Christ Jesus) shall sit on my (God) true throne, forever.

62 And I (God), truly do make all things new forever, as saith thy eternal kind God, forever. And those things, they are faithful and just, true sayings,

63 That are found, given by me (God), as being eternally forever and ever seen and true. And they are, most certainly, truly forever and ever true.

64 And in that eternal true day, all that are found faithful in Jesus Christ, forever. They shall, most surely, as being eternally forever,

65 They shall forever, eternally inherit all that I (God) Am, as I (God) Am found in Jesus the Son, forever.

66 And those that chose Satan and Satan's true ways of bestiality. They shall not be found with me forever, in that great true day that is called God forever.

67 And truly, the city that is called Jesus Christ (Christianity), it shall not ever need the comfort of the sun, nor the moon, and nor the comfort of the stars, forever,

68 For I Am God and I shall comfort those in my true Son, who (Jesus Christ) is called Jesus Christ, forever. And that true comfort, it is without true end,

69 As that eternal, true comfort, is me forever. And I Am eternal seen true life, forever. As saith, thy eternal seen true God, as I Am eternally seen, as being the Son, who is called Jesus Christ, forever.

70 And I Am seen, as being, eternal true truth, forever. And I shall never end, as forever true, as saith, he that formeth man and maketh man to live forever,

71 In Christ Jesus, forever. As this eternal seen true Christ Jesus, is found in my eternal seen true spirit, that is called life, forever.

Part 9 w / 37 verses   Prophet Judge

1 Roger, a servant and apostle of Jesus Christ: I (Roger Dale Wallace) Am called of God the Father and called of His eternal true Son, as a servant in Christ.

2   And through Christ Jesus, I (Roger) have been found faithful unto God, in Christ forever. And in Christ, I (Roger) have been commanded and have obtained through Christ, unto the Father. As a eternal judge in Christ the Son, forever.

3   And, as I Roger, Am called unto that calling, that is found in Christ unto the Father, forever certain. It is given of the True Father, unto them of the earth, forever sure and true. And is seen as a ordained and true, end time, eternal, true prophet judge.

4   That calling, it is heavenly and is found in all that Christ is commanded of God, to be unto creation forever sure. And that calling, it is found in true faith, and is most surely, heavenly forever true of God,

5   And is given through Christ, unto the body of Christ, as eternally forever and ever true, of the Father, as heavenly forever true.

6   And is, most surely, given of God the Father, forever true. And is seen through Christ, as eternally forever true, of "Our Eternal True Father," as heavenly forever true, of God forever.

7   Therefore, I (Roger Dale Wallace) Am sent of Christ and of the true Father, as a "End of the days," true prophet judge, who is sent unto Israel and unto the world, as eternally forever and

forever true, in (in means the word through) Christ forever certain.

8   Those things, they are so. For in the scriptures, those things were recorded by me (God), to occur. And they are now occurring in the earth, as forever true by me (God), heavenly forever true.

9   And those eternal true things, they are found recorded by me (God), in Isaiah 1:26-27.

10   And, as it is written, so shall it forever, saith God, eternally forever and ever lastingly, forever true of me (God), as forever said by me (God), forever true.

11   Isaiah 1:26:

12   "And I will restore thy judges as at the first, and thy counselors as at the beginning: afterward thou shalt be called, The city of righteousness, the faithful city."

13   Isaiah 1:27:

14   "Zion shall be redeemed with judgment, and her converts with righteousness."

15   In Isaiah 1:26, it can be said, like this:

16   And I (God) will restore in these days of the earth, and is forever true of me (God) forever,

thy prophet judges and thy prophetess judges, and they are most certainly, eternally forever true, as now restored unto Israel and unto the world, eternally forever true of me (God), forever.

17 Some of those past true judges, that were seen of me (God), in the nation of Israel at one time in thy past. Some of them that were seen, they were: Samuel, Isaiah, Ezekiel, and many other true ones as well.

18 And starting in 1948 AD and forever, I will and I do now, restore unto the nation of Israel, thy prophet and prophetess counselors, as found given of me,

19 Unto you through the Body of Christ, as eternally forever true, saith God eternally forever sure of myself (God), heavenly and ever lastingly, eternally forever true.

20 These counselors come from afar, as Christians unto you forever, and they are sent unto you with the message of the gospel, that thou mayest inherit my (God) righteousness in Christ forever,

21 That all of the Israeli people, mayest truly be found through repentance unto me forever true, through Christ Jesus, as a people that are called "A city of righteousness."

22 yea a faithful city of righteousness, in Jesus Christ thy savior forever, and who is called God forever, saith God eternally forever and ever true, of myself (God) forever.

23 Therefore, come ye forth unto me in Christ the Son, and be thou unto me forever true, as Christ is true unto me in my (God) righteousness forever,

24 And in doing so, that the Israeli people, mayest truly be a people unto me (God), that is a people that is called Zion unto me (God), that is forever true of thyself forever

25 As a found, true, Israeli true nation of people. Who are truly seen, as a redeemed Israeli true people, and as true city (Israeli citizens are seen as a city), that is truly and surely, seen unto me (God) forever true, as thy self in Christ, forever true and forever seen.

26 Be thou unto me (God), forever true. As Christly converts unto me (God), in Christ the Son, forever true. And with all my (God) true righteousness, that is called God forever.

27 And that righteousness, it is my (God) true righteousness. That is found, given of myself, (God) in Christ the Son called Jesus. And is given as eternally forever and ever true, forever.

28 In this book, what I (RDW), Roger Dale Wallace, have written. It is, that this heavenly inspired and most true inspiration. It has been given unto me (RDW), to be written, through Christ, who is our Lord, and Savior, as forever true.

29 And this inspiration, found of Jesus Christ, the Son of God. It is, seen, by the righteous and holy command, given and found of God our Father,

30 And, it is, truly given of Christ, the Son. Who is Jesus Christ, who is, the eternal and most true Son, and, who is, the Son of God, forever.

31 I Roger Dale Wallace, I (RDW) Am of the brethren, who holds the testimony of Jesus Christ, which is, the spirit of prophecy.

32 Therefore, Let no man, alter nor change, the voice of this book, least the Son be angry, and thou perish in thy sinfulness, before God, as being forever seen.

33 And "Christ Jesus" and God "The Father." They are, most surely coming quickly, in this generation, to receive the dead and the living of our true earth,

34 As being forever seen. And that great event, it is, forth coming, and, it is, of our true God,

and, of His own, true Son, who is called, Jesus Christ,

35 And they (THE FATHER and the Son), shall reward all men, according to the deeds done, in one's own body, and in one's own soul, forever.

36 And I (Roger Dale Wallace) do say, humbly to thee, O Lord:

37 Come quickly, now, O Lord Jesus Christ, and receive us, of the earth, forever, as into the arms of our true God, forever. That we, may truly, be found forever, in the arms of our true God, for all of true eternity, and, forever.

Praise God For His Love And Mercy

Dear reader, I will tell you now, if you are not in right standing with God, and are still living in your sins, don't put it off any longer; Get right with God now. He knows all about you anyhow, and the price for your redemption from your sins has already been paid.

If we (you and I) ***confess our sins, He is faithful and just to forgive us our sins,*** (all of them) ***and to cleanse us from all unrighteousness. 1 John 1:9***

You are not reading this by accident... Somebody is concerned about your soul. Just accept by faith the shed blood of Jesus Christ for payment of your sins.

But he was wounded for our transgressions, he was bruised for our iniquities: the chastisement of our peace was upon him; and with his stripes we are healed. All we like sheep have gone astray; we have turned every one to his own way; and the Lord hath laid on him the iniquity of us all. Isaiah 53:5-6

Who His own self bare our sins in His own body on the tree, that we, being dead to sins, should live unto righteousness: by whose stripes ye were healed. 1 Peter 2:24

Forasmuch as ye know that ye were not redeemed with corruptible things, as silver and gold, from your vain conversation received by tradition from your fathers; but with the precious blood of Christ, as of a lamb without blemish and without spot. 1 Peter 1:18-19

You have nothing to lose but your old sinful life, pride, hate, guilt, fear, unbelief, loneliness and all other sins… Pray to Jesus……. Ask Him to save your soul.

The words of this song
Will tell you how to come to Him

Just as I am, without one plea,
But that Thy blood was shed for me,
And that Thou bidd'st me come to Thee,
O Lamb of God, I come! I come!

Just as I am, and waiting not,
To rid my soul of one dark blot,
To Thee whose blood can cleanse each spot,
O Lamb of God, I come! I come!

Just as I am, though tossed about,
With many a conflict, many a doubt,
Fightings within, and fears without,
O Lamb of God, I come! I come!

Just as I am, poor, wretched, blind;
Sight, riches, healing of the mind,
Yea, all I need, in Thee to find,

O Lamb of God, I come! I come!

Just as I am, Thou wilt receive,
Wilt welcome, pardon, cleanse, relieve;
Because Thy promise I believe,
O Lamb of God, I come, I come.

Just as I am, Thy love unknown,
Hath broken every barrier down;
Now, to be Thine, yea, Thine alone,
O Lamb of God, I come! I come!

Charlotte Elliott (1789-1871)

Having therefore these promises, dearly beloved, let us cleanse ourselves from all filthiness of the flesh and spirit, perfecting holiness in the fear of God. 2 Corinthians 7:1

Let the wicked forsake his way, and the unrighteous man his thoughts: and let him return unto the Lord, and he will have mercy upon him; and to our God, for he will abundantly pardon. Isaiah 55:7

There are hindrances in this life. They are called: unclean spirits, evil spirits or devils. They affect us all.

If you in your deep heart want to respond... But there is a hindrance, pray this prayer:

Lord Jesus, I ask you to help me come to you. I ask you to rebuke the unclean spirits, evil spirits or devils that are hindering me right now. I ask you to bind them up with the three cords of your shed Blood that can not be broken. I ask you to cast them into the fire of the pit forever, never to return. Now Lord Jesus... Come into my heart and Save me now... Thank You Lord Jesus. I now receive you as my Lord and Savior. I ask you to authorize your Holy Ghost to fill me with His Power and Love. AMEN!

If you have received Jesus Christ as your Savior... Write and allow us to share your Joy!

Name: _____

Address: _____

City: _____ State: __ Zip: _____

You can email us at either address below:

INeedMoreInfoAboutJesus@
TheVillageCarpenter.info

Or

YesIAcceptJesus@
TheVillageCarpenter.info

Comments or Prayer Request:

ABOUT THE AUTHOR

Roger Dale Wallace is called of God to minister the Word of truth in an unprecedented way, to minister end time prophesying interpretations that have and do come only from God Himself through Jesus our Lord and Savior. Roger has been given unsealed and unclosed prophecy's that are now in our day, forever truly opened from the BIBLE and His vision is because of the openness of God's true Word. Roger has spent much time in the preparation of these testifying prophesying Bible writings that are found open in today's world. And as being a true servant of God-Roger has from sunrise to sunset or even in the darkness of night, given of himself to God-to write these true truths of God's open true Word, forever. Roger is a father and grandfather.

He has seen life as many have, and yet God speaks to him to always help all to understand the love of Christ-forever.

Author's Other Books Coming Soon

"THE SUN BE DARKENED AND THE MOON SHALL NOT GIVE HER LIGHT"
(A Short Study)

"THE SEVEN THUNDERS ARE NOW SOUNDING FOREVER"

"LITTLE BOOK OPENED" (Short Version)

"VISION OF THE IMAGE OF THE EARTH WITHOUT LIFE"

"THE ARK (Short Version)"

"THE ARK OF THE TESTAMENT"
(Main Book)

"GOD'S PRECIOUS TRUE WORDS"

"I AM FOUND OF ISRAEL"

"END TIME JUDGMENTS"

"O' ISRAEL"

"THE IMAGE OF THE BEAST"

"LIVING DEATH"

"MY MOST HOLY TRUE NAME"

"THEY THAT WORSHIP THE BEAST"

"PLEADING WITH THE HEATHEN"

"THE TWO WITTNESSES"

"A LAST DAY STUDY FOR
END TIME PROPHECY"

For information, please see

TheVillageCarpenter.info

Additional copies may be obtained from

THE VILLAGE CARPENTER
WORLD WIDE MINISTRIES

Email

RogerWallace@TheVillageCarpenter.info

The Village Carpenter Publishing House
PO Box 133
Lakeview, Ohio 43331 USA

Some Other Books We Published

Study notes:
_____
_____
_____
_____
_____
_____
_____

Study notes:

Study notes:
___

Study notes:

Study notes:

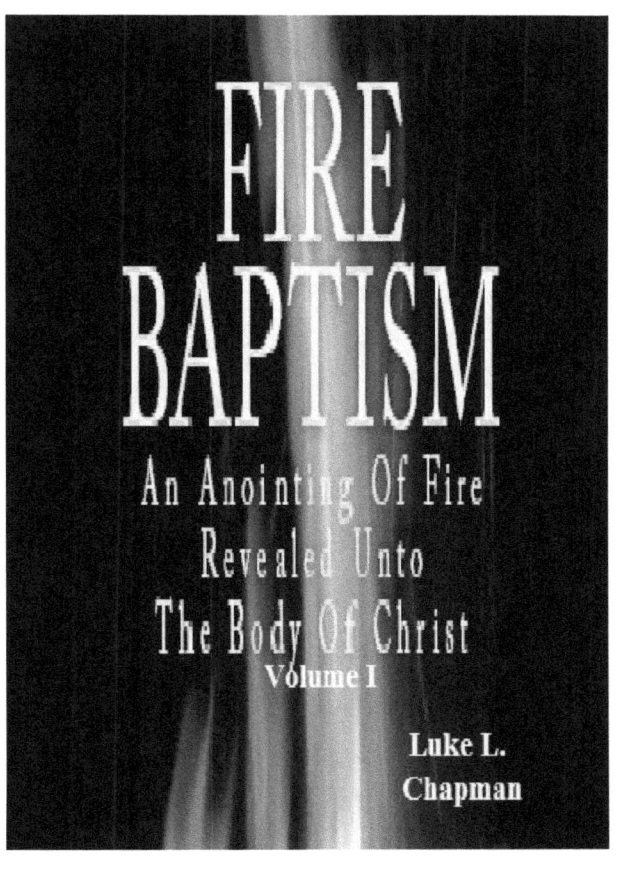

Study notes:

Study notes:
_____
_____
_____
_____
_____
_____
_____

Study notes:

Study notes:
_____
_____
_____
_____
_____
_____
_____
_____

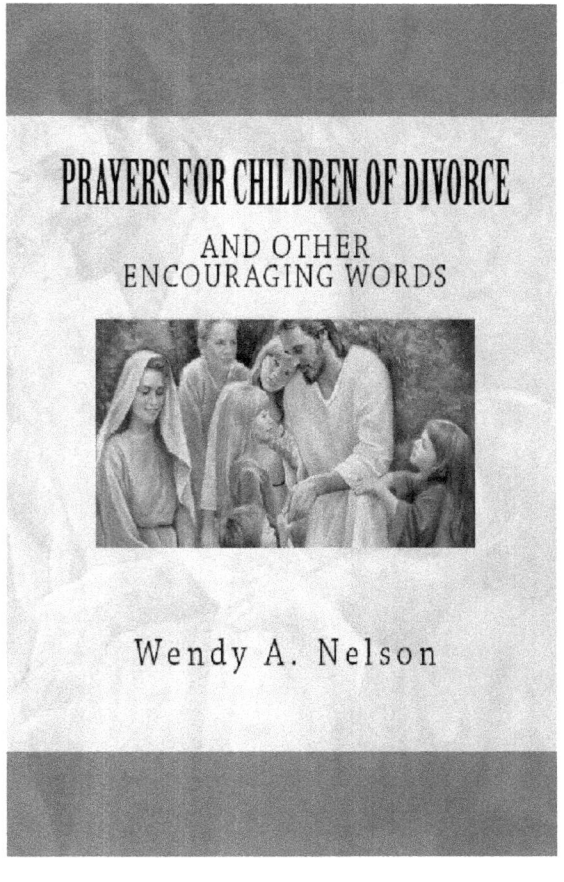

Study notes:

Study notes:

Study notes:
_____
_____
_____
_____
_____
_____
_____
_____

Study notes:

Study notes:
___
___
___
___
___
___
___

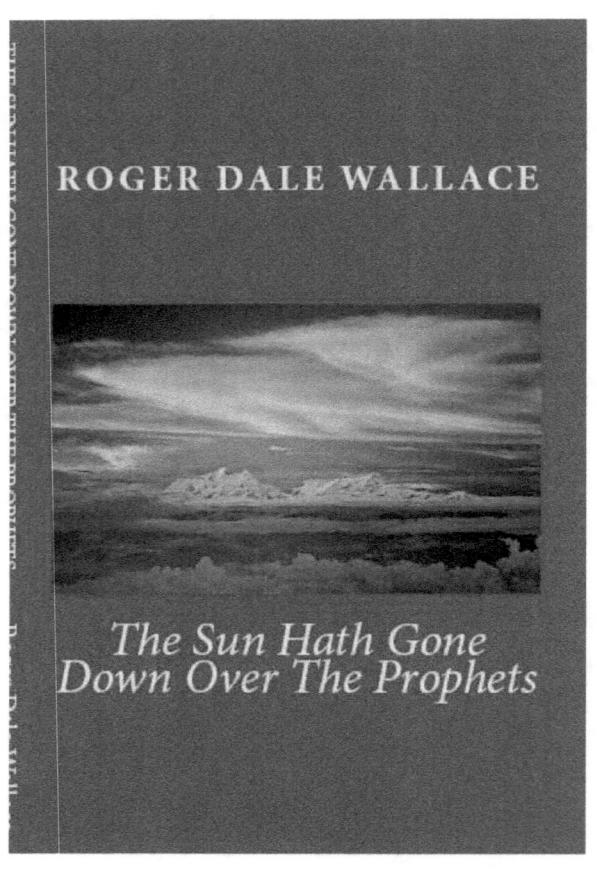

Study notes:
_____
_____
_____
_____
_____
_____
_____

Study notes:

Study notes:

Study notes:
_____
_____
_____
_____
_____
_____
_____

Study notes:

_____
_____
_____
_____
_____
_____
_____

Study notes:
_____
_____
_____
_____
_____
_____
_____
_____

Study notes:
_____
_____
_____
_____
_____
_____
_____

Study notes:

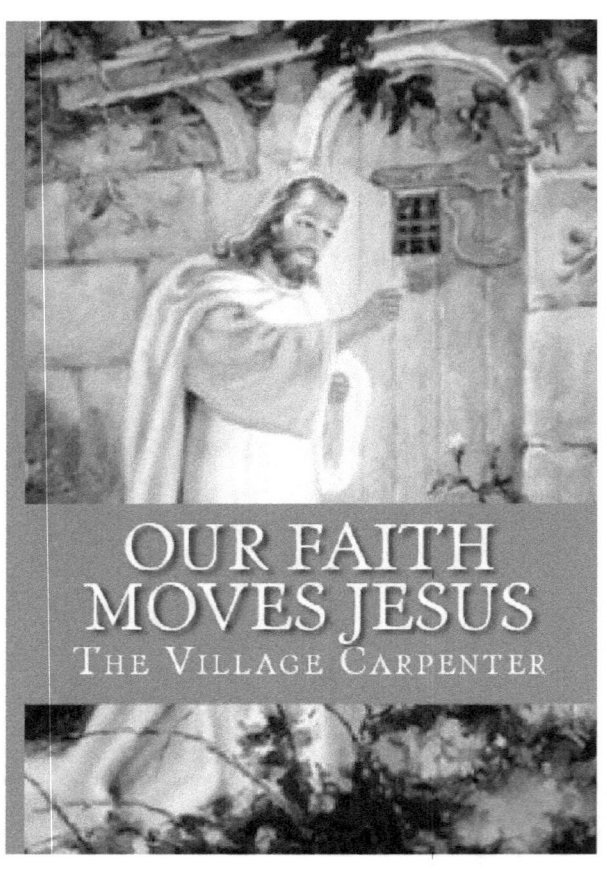

Study notes:
_____
_____
_____
_____
_____
_____
_____

All books are available in Braille, Giant Print, Kindle… Auto-delivered wirelessly and for corporate training, premiums, or special promotions.

Your Book Could Be Next!

For details contact: Charles Lee Emerson, Proprietary Markets, The Village Carpenter Publishing House, PO Box 133, Lakeview, Ohio 43331 USA.

www.ingramcontent.com/pod-product-compliance
Lightning Source LLC
Chambersburg PA
CBHW070157240426
43671CB00007B/471